Христос Воскресе
Воштину воскресе

BASIC RUSSIAN

BOOK ONE

MISCHA H. FAYER

National Textbook Company
a division of *NTC Publishing Group* • Lincolnwood, Illinois USA

Mischa H. Fayer coauthored *Simplified Russian Grammar* and was formerly Head of the Russian Department and Director of the Russian School and the Institute of Soviet Studies at Middlebury College, Vermont. He was also Chairperson of the Department of Oriental and Slavic Languages at the University of Kentucky.

1993 Printing

Published by National Textbook Company, a division of NTC Publishing Group.
©1985, 1977 by NTC Publishing Group, 4255 West Touhy Avenue,
Lincolnwood (Chicago), Illinois 60646-1975 U.S.A.
Manufactured in the United States of America.

2 3 4 5 6 7 8 9 BC 9 8 7 6

PREFACE

Knowledge of Russian opens up a fascinating world of art, history, music, literature, science, and industry. *Basic Russian: Book One* offers beginning students an invitation to share and experience these events and contributions by presenting the essentials of the Russian language as simply, clearly, and effectively as possible.

Russian is an Indo-European language and shares many common roots with Latin, Spanish, French, German, and English. It has similar sentence structure and inflection patterns, and has borrowed many words from these languages. Russian is, however, a highly inflected language, requiring students to be familiar with the declensions of nouns, adjectives, and pronouns before translating or conversing.

Basic Russian combines the audiolingual approach with a traditional approach, so that an understanding of grammatical principles accompanies intensive oral practice. Stress is placed on aural comprehension, reading, and self-expression. Yet, the material has been organized to provide maximum flexibility and to meet the individual needs of the students.

Each unit contains a reading selection with accompanying vocabulary, a conversational section with vocabulary, rules of pronunciation and phonetic drills, grammar rules, exercises for written or oral work, translation exercises from English to Russian, and questions designed to augment oral drill and function as a review and summary of material studied. In addition, supplementary material, including everyday expressions, short reading selections, proverbs, riddles, Russian songs, pronunciation charts, tables of declensions and conjugations, and comprehensive Russian-English, English-Russian vocabularies, are presented in the Appendix.

Basic Russian: Book One provides beginning students with the basic tools for constructing a firm and solid foundation of the Russian language. Each page is a key that will open doors of excitement, satisfaction, and knowledge.

INTRODUCTION TO THE TEACHER

Objectives

The main objective of this text is to reduce all difficulties to the barest minimum and to present essentials simply, clearly, and as effectively as possible for the learning process. There is no intention, however, to avoid those principles of grammar or the idiomatic constructions which are indispensable for a solid foundation in the language. Further simplification of the grammar could only be achieved by the omission of important elements of grammar without which the student cannot hope to learn the language properly.

The stress is on aural comprehension, reading, and self-expression. No attempt is made, however, to impose a specific method on the teacher. The author believes that the best method is the one that the individual teacher considers most effective for the objective he has set for himself and his students.

For that reason, the material has been organized to provide maximum flexibility from the standpoint of teaching procedures. The teacher who prefers the oral approach can reduce written work to a minimum and allow more time for the new audio-lingual exercises included in this revised edition. Those who believe in written work will find a great abundance and variety of drills and exercises. Teachers who believe in the fourfold process for successful mastery of a foreign language will be able to combine aural drill, reading, and conversation with writing.

The pace is also left to the discretion of the teacher, but it is assumed that, under normal conditions, it will be possible to cover the text in one year or less, depending upon the level of instruction—high school or college.

Organization of the Material

The text contains twenty-eight units organized into five major sections. Each of these sections usually consists of six units, the last of which is a review of the material covered within the section as a whole. In two of the sections, there are five rather than six units, but in both these cases one of the units is expected to require twice the amount of time given to the others. Thus, each major section contains the equivalent of six units.

Supplementary material, including everyday expressions, short reading selections (with vocabulary), proverbs, and riddles are given in the Appendix for use in those classes in which an accelerated pace seems possible or desirable. In addition, the Appendix includes Russian songs, pronunciation charts, tables of declensions and conjugations, and comprehensive Russian-English and English-Russian vocabularies.

With respect to the plan of the individual units themselves, a few words are in order. Unit 1 is primarily intended to introduce the Russian alphabet, both as it is written and printed. Thereafter, each unit follows a standard pattern, with only slight modification in a few instances. This pattern is as follows:

1. The Basic Text—a connected reading selection with accompanying vocabulary.
2. A Разговóр (Conversation) or a second installment of the basic text, with vocabulary.
3. Произношéние—rules of pronunciation and phonetic drills (in the first ten lessons).
4. Граммáтика—rules of grammar.
5. Упражнéния—exercises for written or oral work.
6. Перевóд—translation exercises from English to Russian.
7. Вопрóсы—questions.

In effect, each unit contains seven parts through Unit 10, and six parts thereafter. It is easy, therefore, to assign one part of the unit, and in some cases two, for each daily assignment and thus cover one unit a week.

A brief description of the nature of the parts included in each unit will indicate how the book as a whole is organized.

Basic Text. The first part of the unit offers *connected* reading material, almost from the outset. Such material is more readily remembered than disconnected sentences given merely to introduce some point of grammar. It is also more helpful and interesting for the purposes of drill and conversation.

With respect to the presentation of vocabulary in conjunction with the basic text, Units 2–7 introduce a maximum of fifteen new words, of which four or five are cognates. This reduces the number of completely unfamiliar words to only about ten for each assignment. Beginning with Unit 8, a maximum of twenty new words is introduced. Vocabulary building is gradual, and new words and expressions are introduced on the basis of their frequency value or the immediate needs of classroom and other everyday situations. Occasionally, a word is introduced regardless of its frequency value because it makes the material more humorous or interesting. This is necessary, especially in the beginning, in order to present stimulating and connected narratives despite an extremely limited vocabulary. In addition, a number of proper names are given with the purpose of further enlivening the text. These are not considered essential to the students' functional vocabulary and thus need not receive the same attention.

Разгово́р or Second Reading Installment. The second part of the unit reviews the new words given in the basic text and introduces some additional vocabulary. In Units 2–7, a maximum of seven simple new words are presented. Thereafter, between ten and fifteen new words are introduced, several of which are cognates.

Произноше́ние. The rules of pronunciation are presented with numerous illustrations and phonetic drills, and should be studied in conjunction with the reading selections for the most effective results. By distributing the material on pronunciation over the first ten units, it is possible to introduce the basic elements of pronunciation gradually. New words are introduced, not only with a view to their frequency value, but also to the new phonetic elements they involve. In the Appendix, complete pronunciation charts are offered, with cross references to the specific discussions in the text.

Грамма́тика. The fourth part of the unit explains the new grammatical principles involved in the reading selections. The explanations are accompanied by examples, tables, and illustrations, and are sufficiently detailed to require only a minimum of class time, leaving the teacher more time for dictation, conversation, and blackboard work. In the advanced lessons, the grammar is presented in two installments, each of which is coordinated with one of the two reading selections. Thus it is possible to work on the first portion of the grammar in connection with the first reading selection, and separately on the second portion in connection with the other selection. Tables in the Appendix completely summarize the declensions and conjugations studied in the course of the text.

Упражне́ния and Перево́д. The Упражне́ния are exercises for written or oral work, which aim to fix the new material in the student's memory and make it functional. In a sense, they constitute a preparation for the Перево́д, the English-to-Russian translation exercises that follow; for they are simpler and easier than the latter.

Вопро́сы. The questions given in Russian at the end of each unit are intended as an oral drill, summary, and review of the material covered in the unit. This part should not be attempted before the students have mastered all the preceding parts of the unit. The questions, whether used for written assignments or oral work in class, should always be answered by the students with complete sentences so that they may obtain more practice in the language.

The five *Review Units* that appear at the end of each major section review the vocabulary and grammar covered in the preceding units by means of a variety of exercises. These are occasionally accompanied by tables that summarize and bring together the more important grammatical rules and inflection patterns.

In the *Appendix*, complete Russian-English and English-Russian vocabularies are given. In the case of the former, the perfective and imperfective forms of the verbs studied both appear, as well as irregular forms of nouns in the genitive singular, the nominative plural, and the genitive plural. In addition, cross references appear in these vocabularies, which enable the student to turn immediately to detailed explanations in the text.

This, then, describes the basic organization of the book. Its main virtue is that it comprehends all of the basic elements of good language instruction but at the same time allows the individual instructor great flexibility in his choice of approach. The teacher who wishes to stress the oral method of instruction may skip the presentation of the alphabet and the writing drills given in Unit 1 and begin with Units 2 and 3, which provide materials for oral practice. In addition, he can make use of the section on everyday expressions which appears in the Appendix. Because of the abundance of exercises and drills, teachers may omit some of them or assign them on an oral rather than a written basis. On the other hand, teachers who conduct their classes at a faster than average pace can draw on the supplementary materials in the Appendix and thus present a full year's work without recourse to another book.

In presenting the grammatical material and in selecting the vocabulary, idioms, and phrases, the author has relied on authoritative works of Russian scholars. He hopes that the gradual, systematic, and graphic presentation of grammar, the simple everyday vocabulary (largely based on Harry H. Josselson's *The Russian*

Word Count, 1953) and the connected and interesting reading matter will make the study of Russian an enjoyable experience for the student. The author feels that, with the aid of a carefully graded and organized text, the study of Russian will prove as easy and enjoyable as that of the other foreign languages taught in our schools.

CONTENTS

CONTENTS

CONTENTS

CONTENTS

UNIT 1

THE RUSSIAN ALPHABET

The Russian alphabet is called the *Cyrillic* alphabet after the monk St. Cyril, who lived in the ninth century and is reputed to have devised it. It contains many letters identical with or resembling Greek and Latin characters, and is therefore much easier to master than is generally assumed by beginners.

The alphabet consists of 31 letters (or 33 if the ё and й are counted as separate letters). The fact that there are more letters in Russian than in English actually makes spelling easier, because Russian sounds, with few exceptions, can thus be represented by individual letters instead of by various combinations of letters as, for example, in the English words *rough* or *beauty*.

The Written Alphabet

The written and printed alphabets closely resemble each other. Mastery of one will facilitate learning the other, regardless of which is learned first. If you wish to learn the *printed* alphabet before the *written* alphabet, turn to page 10.

The written alphabet is given first because (1) Russians ordinarily do not print, and (2) writing is faster and will save time. You can learn to write Russian in a short time with facility and speed if you form the proper writing habits. Observe these simple rules:

1. Make the capital letters larger than the small letters.
2. Keep the small letters equal in size.
3. Add no strokes, curves, or loops of your own to the letters. This only leads to confusion.

1

4. All strokes and loops should go as far below the solid line and as high above the dotted line as is indicated on the charts.

5. When forming each stroke, proceed in the direction of the arrow, as indicated in the charts. Do each stroke in numerical order.

Memorize the letters in groups of five using their Russian names, and remember their alphabetical order. To avoid confusion, never refer to them by their English equivalents.

Group I

a. How to pronounce *А а* through *Д д*

Written	Russian Name	Approximate English Sound	Examples
1. *А а*	ah	*a* in *car*	*Áнна*
2. *Б б*	beh	*b* in *book*	*Бáба*
3. *В в*	veh	*v* in *visit*	*Бáза*
4. *Г г*	gheh	*g* in *glad*	*Газóн*
5. *Д д*	deh	*d* in *do*	*Дáма*

b. How to write *А а* through *Д д*.

Аа Бб Вв Гг Дд

Drill 1. Pronounce each letter aloud several times by its Russian name. Then write each capital and small letter several times. After you have learned to write them accurately, write the following combinations. (Do not link the letters in these exercises.)

Combinations:

Ба, Ва, Га, Da; Аа, Аda, Бáda, Бáга,
Гáda; Dва, Daб, Габ, Баг, Бáга; Аda,
Бáda, Dáга, Бáба, Баб

Group II

a. How to pronounce *Е е* through *К к.*

Written	Russian Name	Approximate English Sound	Examples
6. *Е е*	yeh	ye in yes	*Éва*
7. *Ж ж*	zheh	s in treasure	*Жáда*
8. *З з*	zeh	z in zone	*Зóна*
9. *И и*	ee	ee in see	*Úда*
10. *К к*	kah	k in king	*Кот*

b. How to write *Е е* through *К к.*

Е е Ж ж З з И и К к

Drill 2. Practice writing and pronouncing the following syllables and words. Do not attempt to learn the meanings of the words; they are given only for purposes of practice.

Syllables:

Еж, Ез, Ек; Иж, Из, Ик; Аж, Аз, Ак; Ке, Ки, Киз; Кеж, Кез, Кед; Зек, Зик, Заг, Гаж, Дак, Вик; Ика.

Words:

Как, Кабáк, Казáк; Кинó, Кабáн, Вид; Úда, Зóна, Кабúна; Жáда, Бáза, Éва; Жáжда, Избá, Вáнна.

Group III

a. How to pronounce *Л л* through *П п*.

Written	Russian Name	Approximate English Sound	Examples
11. *Л л*	ell	*ll* in we*ll*	*Лóндон*
12. *М м*	em	*m* in ja*m*	*Máма*
13. *Н н*	en	*n* in *n*arrow	*Нóта*
14. *О о*	aw	*o* in sport	*Вóлга*
15. *П п*	peh	*p* in *p*ark	*Пáпа*

b. How to write *Л л* through *П п*.

Drill 3. Practice writing and pronouncing these syllables and words.

Syllables:

Ла, Ле, Ли, Ло; Мо, Ми, Ме, Ма; На, Не, Ни, Но; По, Пи, Пе, Па; Бал, Мел, Гин, Дон; Доп, Пон; Мик, Зим, Жак.

Words:

Дом, Пол, Кол, Пóлка, Пáлка; Вóлга, Вон, Лом; Зимá, Лéна, Заказáл, Дáма, Жáлко, Жáло, Жáлоба.

Group IV

a. How to pronounce *Р р* through *Ф ф*.

Written	Russian Name	Approximate English Sound	Examples
16. *Р р*	err	*r* in rose	*Радио*
17. *С с*	ess	*s* in stop	*Стол*
18. *Т т*	teh	*t* in tip	*Тон*
19. *У у*	oo	*oo* in booty	*Утро*
20. *Ф ф*	eff	*f* in fact	*Факт*

b. How to write *Р р* through *Ф ф*.

Рр Сс Тт Уу Фф

Drill 4. Practice writing and pronouncing these syllables and words.

Syllables:

*Ру, Су, Ту, Фу; Фа, Фе, Фи, Фо; Со, Си, Са;
То, Ти, Та; Фур, Тур, Сот, Сор; Фом,
Жеф, Тим, Жук, Стоп.*

Words:

*Устал, Тормоз, Кусок, Урок; Доступ,
Ворон, Вагон, Фабрика; Варвара,
Город, Сторож; Дума, Двор, Фронт.*

Group V

a. How to pronounce $\mathcal{X}$ x through $\mathcal{W}_{\!\!f}$ $\mathit{w_{\!\!f}}$.

	Written	Russian Name	Approximate English Sound		Examples
21.	$\mathcal{X}$ x	*hah*	*h*	in *h*and (strongly aspirated)	$\mathcal{X}op$
22.	$\mathcal{U}_{\!\!f}$ $\mathit{u_{\!\!f}}$	*tseh*	*ts*	in fla*ts*	$\mathcal{U}_{\!\!f}bem$
23.	$\mathcal{U}$ u	*cheh*	*ch*	in *ch*eck	$\mathcal{U}ac$
24.	$\mathcal{W}$ w	*shah*	*sh*	in *sh*ort	$\mathcal{W}\kappa\acute{o}\lambda a$
25.	$\mathcal{W}_{\!\!f}$ $\mathit{w_{\!\!f}}$	*shchah*	*shch* in fre*sh cheese*		$\mathcal{W}_{\!\!f}\mathit{u}$

b. How to write $\mathcal{X}$ x through $\mathcal{W}_{\!\!f}$ $\mathit{w_{\!\!f}}$.

Drill 5. Practice writing and pronouncing these syllables and words.

Syllables:

Ха, Хе, Хи, Хо, Ху; Цу, Цо, Ци, Це, Ца; Чу, Чо, Чи, Че, Ча; Шо, Ши, Ше, Шу, Ша; Ще, Щи, Щу, Що, Ща; Хуф, Щос, Шер, Час; Цап, Шоп, Щук, Хат.

Words:

Шапка, Папка, Хата, Мост; Хор, Сахар, Вахта, Бухта; Шкаф, Рука, Кузнец, Работница; Маша, Машина, Учебник; Щепка, Щит, Щука.

Group VI

a. How to pronounce *ъ* through *Я я*.

Written	Russian Name	Approximate English Sound	Examples
*26. *ъ*	(hard sign)	(has no sound)	*Отъезд*
*27. *ы*	yerih	*y* in syllable	*Рыба*
*28. *ь*	(soft sign)†	(has no sound)	*Пальто*
29. *Э э*	eh	*e* in egg	*Этаж*
30. *Ю ю*	you	*u* in use	*Юмор*
31. *Я я*	ya	*ya* in yard	*Ялта*

* These letters are never used at the beginning of a word; hence they have no written capitals.

† Indicates that the preceding consonant is pronounced soft.

b. How to write *ъ* through *Я я*.

Drill 6. Practice writing and pronouncing these syllables and words.

Syllables:

Бы, Бэ, Бе, Бя; Вэ, Ве, Вю, Вя;
Ха, Шэ, Тю, Сэ, Мы, Яр.

Words:

Это, Яма, Сын, Шляпа; Няня, Индюк,
Быстро, Юноша; Экзамен, Гармония,
Тыква; Рынок, Фрукты, Улица;
Соль, Боль, Мать, Спать, Читать,
Конь, Лошадь.

Group VII

a. How to pronounce *Ё ё* and *Й й*.

Note: The two dots (called a *diaeresis*) over the *е* (*ё*) change the sound from *ye* to *yo* (as in *yolk*). The sign ⌣ over the *и* (*й*) shortens the sound from *ee* to *y* (as in bo*y*).

Written	Russian Name	Approximate English Sound	Examples
Ё ё	*yaw*	*yo* in *yolk*	*Ёлка*
Й й	short **и**	*y* in boy	*Чай*

Drill 7. Practice writing and pronouncing these syllables and words.

Syllables:

Аи, Ай; Ии, Ий; Ои, Ой; Уи, Уй; ыи, ый;
Юи, Юй; Эи, Эй; Еи, Ей; Ёи, Ёй; Яи, Яй.

Words:

Мой, Твой, Тройка; Умей, Чайка,
Яйца, Быстрей, Крайний.

Linking the Letters

Russian letters must be properly joined to avoid confusion and illegibility. Apply the following suggestions whenever you write in Russian.

a. Avoid any overlapping of letters.

right: *гражданин*

wrong: *гражданин* —because the hook of

the *а* and the hook of the *ж* overlap. It is impossible to tell

where the *а* ends and the *ж* begins. Also note that in the last

two letters, the hook of the *и* fuses with the first stroke of the *н*,

which should be a straight line *н* .

b. Set off *л*, *м*, and '*я* from preceding letters.

right: *тётя*;   right: *время*;

wrong: *тётя*;   wrong: *время*;

c. Make a break after *б* and *д* : *берег*; *дама*.

d. Make a break after *о* when it is followed by *л*, *м*, or *я* :

пол; *потом*; *твоя* .

e. Do not confuse *и* with *ч*, or *ш* with the English *w* :

год; *что*; *шум*.

Note: The first word below is illegible because:

н is not set off from *А* ;

Compare: { *Анилия* }   *и* is not set off from *л* ;

{ *Англия* }   *л* lacks a loop at the bottom ;

и and *я* overlap.

The Printed Alphabet

Memorize the letters in groups of five using their Russian names, and remember their alphabetical order.   To avoid confusion, never refer to them by their English equivalents.

Russians ordinarily do not print.   In the beginning, however, print the individual letters and words to remember them better. Later, use the Russian script exclusively.

Print uses mostly plain lines, whereas script uses curved lines and hooks.   Straighten the curves, remove the hooks wherever possible, and note how little difference there really is between the written and printed letters.

Compare the script with the print and note the similarities.

SCRIPT	PRINT		SCRIPT	PRINT
1. *A a* = *A* =	А а	17. *C c* =	С с
2. *Б б* = *Б* =	Б б	18. *Тт*	Т т
3. *B b* = *B* =	В в	19. *У у* =	У у
4. *Г г* = *Г* =	Г г	20. *Ф ф* =	Ф ф
5. *Д д*	Д д	21. *X x* =	Х х
6. *E e* =	Е е	22. *Ц ц* = *Ц* =	Ц ц
7. *Ж ж* =	Ж ж	23. *Ч ч* = *Ч* =	Ч ч
8. *З з* =	З з	24. *Ш ш* = *Ш* =	Ш ш
9. *И и* = *И* =	И и	25. *Щ щ* = *Щ* =	Щ щ
10. *K к* = *K* =	К к	26. *ъ* =	ъ
11. *Л л* =	Л л	27. *ы* =	ы
12. *М м* = *М* =	М м	28. *ь* =	ь
13. *H н* = *H* =	Н н	29. *Э э* =	Э э
14. *O o* =	О о	30. *Ю ю* = *Ю* =	Ю ю
15. *П п* = *П* =	П п	31. *Я я* = *Я* =	Я я
16. *P р* = *P* =	Р р		

Group I

Printed	Russian Name	Approximate English Sound	Examples
1. **А а**	*ah*	*a* in c*a*r	Áнна
2. **Б б**	*beh*	*b* in *b*ook	Бáба
3. **В в**	*veh*	*v* in *v*isit	Вáза
4. **Г г**	*gheh*	*g* in *g*lad	Газóн
5. **Д д**	*deh*	*d* in *d*o	Дáма

Drill 1. Pronounce each letter aloud several times by its Russian name. Then print the following combinations several times.

Combinations : Ба, Ва, Га, Да; Аа, Áда, Вáда, Бáга, Гáда; Два, Даб, Гав, Баг, Вáга; Áба, Бáба, Дáга, Вáва, Бав.

Group II

Printed	Russian Name	Approximate English Sound	Examples
6. **Е е**	*yeh*	*ye* in *ye*s	Éва
7. **Ж ж**	*zheh*	*s* in trea*s*ure	Жáба
8. **З з**	*zeh*	*z* in *z*one	Зóна
9. **И и**	*ee*	*ee* in s*ee*	Йда
10. **К к**	*kah*	*k* in *k*ing	Кот

Drill 2. Practice printing and pronouncing the following syllables and words. Do not attempt to learn the meanings of the words; they are given only for purposes of practice.

Syllables : Еж, Ез, Ек; Иж, Из, Ик; Аж, Аз, Ак; Ке, Ки, Киз; Кеж, Кез, Кед; Зек, Зик, Заг; Гаж, Дак, Вик; Йка.

Words :   Как, Кабáк, Казáк; Кинó, Кабáн, Вид; Йда, Зóна, Кабúна; Жáба, Бáза, Éва, Жáжда, Избá, Вáнна.

Group III

Printed	Russian Name	Approximate English Sound	Examples
11. Л л	*ell*	*ll* in we*ll*	Ло́ндон
12. М м	*em*	*m* in ja*m*	Ма́ма
13. Н н	*en*	*n* in *n*arrow	Но́та
14. О о	*aw*	*o* in sp*o*rt	Во́лга
15. П п	*peh*	*p* in *p*ark	Па́па

Drill 3. Practice printing and pronouncing these syllables and words.

Syllables: Ла, Ле, Ли, Ло; Мо, Ми, Ме, Ма; На, Не, Ни, Но; По, Пи, Пе, Па; Бал, Мел, Гин; Дон; Доп, Пон, Мик, Зим, Жак.

Words: Дом, Пол, Кол, По́лка, Па́лка; Во́лга, Вон, Лом; Зима́, Ле́на, Заказа́л; До́ма, Жа́лко, Жа́ло, Жа́лоба.

Group IV

Printed	Russian Name	Approximate English Sound	Examples
16. Р р	*err*	*r* in *r*ose	Ра́дио
17. С с	*ess*	*s* in *s*top	Стол
18. Т т	*teh*	*t* in *t*ip	Тон
19. У у	*oo*	*oo* in b*oo*ty	У́тро
20. Ф ф	*eff*	*f* in *f*act	Факт

Drill 4. Practice printing and pronouncing these syllables and words.

Syllables: Ру, Су, Ту, Фу; Фа, Фе, Фи, Фо; Со, Си, Са; То, Ти, Та; Фур, Тур, Сот, Сор; Фом, Жеф, Гим, Жук, Стоп.

Words: Уста́л, То́рмоз, Кусо́к, Уро́к; До́ступ, Во́рон, Ваго́н, Фа́брика; Варва́ра, Го́род, Сто́рож; Ду́ма, Двор, Фронт.

Group V

Printed	Russian Name	Approximate English Sound	Examples
21. **Х** х	*hah*	*h* in *h*ard (strongly aspirated)	<u>Х</u>ор
22. **Ц** ц	*tseh*	*ts* in fla*ts*	<u>Ц</u>вет
23. **Ч** ч	*cheh*	*ch* in *ch*eck	<u>Ч</u>ас
24. **Ш** ш	*shah*	*sh* in *sh*ort	<u>Ш</u>ко́ла
25. **Щ** щ	*shchah*	*shch* in fre*sh ch*eese	<u>Щ</u>и

Drill 5. Practice printing and pronouncing these syllables and words.

Syllables: Ха, Хе, Хи, Хо, Ху; Цу, Цо, Ци, Це, Ца; Чу, Чо, Чи, Че, Ча; Шо, Ши, Ше, Шу, Ша; Ще, Щи, Щу, Що, Ща; Хуф, Щос, Шер, Час; Цап, Шоп, Шум, Хат.

Words: Ша́пка, Па́пка, Ха́та, Мост; Хор, Са́хар, Ва́хта, Бу́хта; Шкаф, Рука́, Кузне́ц, Рабо́тница; Ма́ша, Маши́на, Уче́бник; Ще́пка, Щит, Щу́ка.

Group VI

Printed	Russian Name	Approximate English Sound	Examples
26. **Ъ** ъ	(hard sign)	(has no sound)	Отъе́зд
27. **Ы** ы	*yerih*	*y* in s*y*llable	Ры́ба
28. **Ь** ь	(soft sign)*	(has no sound)	Пальто́
29. **Э** э	*eh*	*e* in *e*gg	Эта́ж
30. **Ю** ю	*you*	*u* in *u*se	Ю́мор
31. **Я** я	*ya*	*ya* in *y*ard	Я́лта

* Indicates that the preceding consonant is pronounced soft.

Drill 6. Practice printing and pronouncing these syllables and words.

Syllables: Бы, Бэ, Бе, Бя; Вэ, Ве, Вю, Вя; Ха, Шэ, Тю, Сэ, Мы, Яр.

Words: Это, Яма, Сын, Шляпа; Няня, Индюк, Быстро, Юноша; Экзамен, Гармония, Тыква; Рынок, Фрукты, Улица; Соль, Боль, Мать, Спать, Читать, Конь, Лошадь.

Group VII

Note: The two dots (called a diaeresis) over the **e** (**ё**) change the sound from *ye* to *yo* (as in *yo*lk). The sign ‿ over the **и** (**й**) shortens the sound from *ee* to *y* (as in bo*y*).

Printed	Russian Name	Approximate English Sound	Examples
Е ё	*yaw*	*yo* in *yo*lk	Ёлка
Й й	short **и**	*y* in bo*y*	Чай

Drill 7. Practice printing and pronouncing these syllables and words.

Syllables: Аи, Ай; Ии, Ий; Ои, Ой; Уи, Уй, Ыи, Ый, Юи, Юй; Эи, Эй; Еи, Ей; Ёи, Ёй; Яи, Яй.

Words: Мой, Твой, Тройка; Умей, Чайка, Яйца, Быстрей, Крайний.

Произношéние (Pronunciation)

1-A. Hard and Soft Vowels

a. Russian vowels are divided into two groups: five *hard* and five corresponding *soft* vowels. Learn them in pairs, as this will help your pronunciation and your understanding of important grammatical principles.

hard: **а э о у ы**
soft: **я е ё ю и**

b. The first four *soft* vowels represent a combination of the *y* sound in *yes* and the corresponding *hard* vowels, thus:

$$y + \mathbf{a} = \mathbf{я}$$
$$y + \mathbf{э} = \mathbf{e}$$
$$y + \mathbf{o} = \mathbf{ё}$$
$$y + \mathbf{y} = \mathbf{ю}$$

c. When the hard vowels are pronounced, the tongue does not touch the roof of the mouth (the *palate*).

d. If the tongue is raised against the *palate* when **а, э, о,** or **у** is pronounced, the sound becomes softened or *palatalized.* **Я** is thus a palatalized **а**; **е,** a palatalized **э**; **ё,** a palatalized **о**; and **ю,** a palatalized **у**.

U N I T 2

КТО Э́ТО?

— Кто э́то? — Э́то я.*

— Кто э́то? — Э́то ты.

— Кто э́то? — Э́то он.   Э́то она́.

— Я профе́ссор.   Ты студе́нт.   Он то́же студе́нт.

— Кто э́то? — Э́то Ива́н.   Ива́н студе́нт.

— Кто э́то? — Э́то Ве́ра.   Ве́ра студе́нтка.

— Кто ты? — Я студе́нт.

— Кто он? — Он то́же студе́нт.

— Кто она́? — Она́ студе́нтка.

— Кто э́то? — Э́то А́нна.   Она́ то́же студе́нтка.

Слова́рь (Vocabulary)

кто who
э́то this
кто э́то? who (is) this?
я I
ты you (*fam. pron.*†)
он he
она́ she (pronounce the **o** like the *o* in *come*)

профе́ссор professor ‡ (*m.*) (*used for man or woman*)
студе́нт student ‡ (*m.*)
то́же also
Ива́н Ivan
Ве́ра Vera
студе́нтка student (*f.*)
А́нна Anne

* Dashes are used to distinguish the remarks of one speaker from those of another.

† All abbreviations are explained on p. 252.

‡ **Студе́нт** means *student of an institution of higher learning* and **профе́ссор** means *teacher* at such an institution.   The Russian words for *pupil* and *teacher* are harder to remember and pronounce, and will therefore be introduced at a later time.

16

Разгово́р (Conversation)

— Э́то студе́нт? — Да, э́то студе́нт.

— Э́то студе́нтка? — Да, э́то студе́нтка.

— Э́то профе́ссор? — Да, э́то профе́ссор.

— Э́то то́же профе́ссор? — Нет, э́то студе́нт.

— Ива́н профе́ссор? — О нет! Ива́н не профе́ссор. Он студе́нт.

— Ве́ра профе́ссор? — Нет, Ве́ра не профе́ссор. Она́ студе́нтка. Ива́н и Ве́ра студе́нты.

— Э́то Ве́ра? — Нет, э́то не Ве́ра. Э́то Анна.

— Э́то студе́нт и́ли студе́нтка? — Э́то студе́нт.

— Э́то Анна и́ли Ве́ра? — Э́то Ве́ра.

— Э́то профе́ссор и́ли студе́нт? — Э́то профе́ссор.

Слова́рь (Vocabulary)

да yes
нет no
не not
О oh

О нет! oh no!
и and
студе́нты (*pl.*) students
и́ли or

Произноше́ние (Pronunciation)

Study the following rules, then practice the phonetic drill at the end of this unit.

2-A. Stressed and Unstressed "a"

a. When the Russian **a** is stressed, it is pronounced like the English *a* in c*a*r. For example: Ива́н, она́.

b. When the **a** is unstressed, it is pronounced like the English *a* in cig*a*rette. For example: Ве́р**a**, студе́нтк**a**.

2-B. Syllabification

a. A *syllable* consists of one or more letters and constitutes one unit of sound. There are as many syllables in a word as there are vowels. For example:

да (one vowel—one syllable)
Ве́-ра (two vowels—two syllables)

b. Syllabification means dividing words into syllables according to established rules. Correct syllabification is important both for pronunciation and for dividing a word at the end of a line.

c. Rules of syllabification.

1. Two consecutive vowels form two separate syllables:

ду-э́т, а́р-ми-я, э-го-и́ст

2. The semivowel **й** cannot be pronounced by itself and must always be used in combination with another vowel. It cannot, therefore, form a syllable by itself. For example:

ай, у-ме́й, ге-ро́й

3. A single consonant between two vowels forms a syllable with the following vowel. For example:

И-ва́н, Ве́-ра, о-на́

4. When several consonants come between two vowels, the last one usually goes with the following vowel. For example:

жур-на́л, сту-де́нт-ка

5. Only syllables can be "carried" from the end of one line to the beginning of the next.

Study Hints. To master new words with greater facility, pronounce the long ones by syllables at first, paying careful attention to the stress. Then pronounce the word as a unit until you can remember it.

Грамма́тика (Grammar)

2-1. Present Tense of "to be"

In modern Russian, the *present tense* of the verb *to be* is usually understood, but not stated.

Э́то студе́нт.   This (*is*) a student.

Ива́н не профе́ссор.   Ivan (*is*) not a professor.

2-2. Articles in Russian

There is no definite or indefinite article in Russian. Therefore, when a Russian sentence is being translated into English, the definite article *the* or the indefinite article *a* must be supplied according to the sense of the sentence.

Она́ студе́нтка.   She is *a* student.

2-3. The Pronoun "you"

Like other languages, Russian possesses two forms of the pronoun *you*. **Ты** (in French, *tu*; in German, *du*; in English, *thou*) is the *familiar singular* form of the pronoun *you*, and is used in addressing a close friend, a member of one's family, a child, or an animal. **Вы** (in French, *vous*; in German, *Sie*) is the *polite* form of *you*, and is used in all other circumstances. One would say "**Ты** студéнт" (you are a student) to a friend, but "**Вы** профéссор" (you are a professor) to his teacher.

2-4. The Nominative Case

The *nominative case* is used to express:

a. The subject of a sentence.

> **Я** профéссор.   *I* am a professor.

b. The predicate noun.

> Вéра **студéнтка**.   Vera is a *student*.

2-5. Intonation in Questions

A rise in *intonation* (that is, in the pitch of the voice) at the end of a sentence indicates a question.

> Это студéнт (*with a falling intonation*).   This is a student.
> Это студéнт (*with a rising intonation*)?   Is this a student?

2-6. The Use of **нет** and **не**

Do not confuse the words **нет** and **не**. **Нет** means *no* and **не** means *is not*. **Не** always stands before the word negated.

> **Нет**, это **не** Вéра.   *No*, this *is not* Vera.

Упражнéния (Exercises)

Replace the English words in parentheses with the appropriate Russian words.

1. Он (student). 2. Онá (student). 3. Он и онá (students). 4. Я (also) студéнт. 5. Ты (professor)? 6. (No), я (not) профéссор. 7. (You) и я (students).

Перево́д (Translation)

Translate the following sentences into Russian, but omit words in parentheses.

1. Who (is) this?   2. (Is) this you?   (Use the familiar **ты.**)
3. Yes, it (is) I.   4. (Is) this Ivan or Vera?   5. Yes, it (is) Ivan and Vera.   6. (Is) Ivan (a) student (*m.*)?   7. Yes, Ivan (is a) student (*m.*).   8. (Is) Vera also (a man) student?   9. No, Vera (is) not (a man) student.   She (is a woman) student.   10. Vera and Ivan (are) students.   11. (Is) Anne (the) professor?   12. No, Anne (is) not (the) professor.

Вопро́сы (Questions)

Answer the following questions in Russian, using complete sentences.

1. Кто э́то?   2. Э́то студе́нт?   3. Э́то студе́нтка?   4. Он и она́ студе́нты?   5. Он студе́нт и́ли профе́ссор?   6. Она́ студе́нтка и́ли профе́ссор?   7. Э́то А́нна и́ли Ве́ра?   8. Э́то он и́ли она́?   9. Ты профе́ссор и́ли студе́нт?   10. Э́то Ве́ра и́ли А́нна?

Phonetic Drill

Listen to the teacher (or the tape) and repeat aloud several times the following words.

каранда́ш, кабине́т, салфе́тка, буты́лка, магази́н, фи́зика, а́тлас, газе́та, ка́рта, дра́ма, Во́лга.

Pattern Drills

Listen to the teacher (or the tape) and repeat the following questions and answers.

1. **Кто ты?**
   Я Ива́н.
   Я студе́нт.
   Я студе́нтка.
   Я профе́ссор.
   Я Ве́ра.
   Я А́нна.

2. **Кто он?**
   Он студе́нт.
   Он профе́ссор.

3. **Кто она́?**
   Она́ студе́нтка.

4. **Кто э́то?**
   Это я.   Это студе́нт.
   Это ты.   Это она́.
   Это он.   Это А́нна.
   Это Ива́н.   Это студе́нтка.

5. **Это Ива́н?**   **Да, э́то Ива́н.**
   _____ студе́нт?   Да, _____.
   _____ студе́нты?   Да, _____.
   _____ профе́ссор?   Да, _____.
   _____ Ве́ра?   Да, _____.
   _____ А́нна?   Да, _____.

6. **Это он?**   **Нет, э́то она́.**
   _____ Ива́н?   Нет, _____ Ве́ра.
   _____ профе́ссор?   Нет, _____ студе́нт.

7. **Это она́?**   **Нет, э́то он.**
   _____ Ве́ра?   Нет, _____ Ива́н.
   _____ студе́нтка?   Нет, _____ профе́ссор.

U N I T 3

ЧТО Э́ТО?

— Что э́то? — Э́то стол.

— Что э́то? — Э́то стул. Э́то стол и стул.

— Что э́то? — Э́то ка́рта, а э́то карти́на.

— Где стол? — Стол тут.

— А где стул? — Стул там.

— Что на столе́? — На столе́ ка́рта.

— Что на сту́ле ? — На сту́ле карти́на.

— А где журна́л? Он то́же на сту́ле?

— Нет, он не на сту́ле. Он на столе́.

— Кни́га то́же на столе́? — Да, она́ то́же на столе́.

— Что на ка́рте?

— На ка́рте—*СССР. Тут Москва́, а там Волгогра́д.

* The dash here means that the word *is* is understood, and that any other possible meaning is excluded.

Слова́рь (Vocabulary)

что (*pr.* **што**) what
стол table
стул chair
ка́рта map
а and
карти́на picture
где where
тут here
там there

на on, upon
на столе́ on the table (pronounce the **o** like the *o* in *come*)
журна́л magazine
кни́га book
СССР U.S.S.R. (*pr.* **Эс Эс Эс Эр**)
Москва́ Moscow
Волгогра́д Volgograd

22 Россиа - Russia

Разгово́р (Conversation)

— Э́то стол? — Да, э́то стол.

— Э́то то́же стол? — Нет, э́то не стол, а стул.

— Где кни́га? — Кни́га на сту́ле.

— Э́то карти́на? — Да, э́то карти́на.

— Э́то то́же карти́на? — Нет, э́то не карти́на, а ка́рта.

— Где на ка́рте Москва́ и где Волгогра́д?

— Москва́ тут, а Волгогра́д там.

— Где студе́нты? Они́ в кла́ссе?

— Да, они́ в кла́ссе.

— А где Ива́н и Ве́ра? — Они́ то́же тут.

— Ива́н и Ве́ра, где вы? — Мы тут, в кла́ссе.

— А́нна, вы в кла́ссе? — Да, я в кла́ссе.

— Я профе́ссор? — Да, вы профе́ссор.

— Кто в кла́ссе? — Профе́ссор и студе́нты в кла́ссе.

Слова́рь (Vocabulary)

a but (**a** means *and*; after a negative, it means *but*)
Нет, э́то не стол, а стул No, this is not a table, *but* a chair
они́ they
класс class
в in (when used with the *prepositional*, **в** indicates *location* of an object; see
¶ **3-3**)
вы you
мы we

Произноше́ние (Pronunciation)

Study the following rules, then practice the phonetic drill at the end of this unit.

3-A. Stressed and Unstressed "o"

a. The stressed **o** is pronounced like the English *o* in sport. For example: то́же, стол.

b. The pronunciation of the unstressed **o** depends upon its position in the word with respect to the stressed syllable.

1. When the **o** is *pre-tonic* (that is, when it immediately precedes a stressed syllable), it is pronounced like the *o* in *come*. For example: она́, Москва́.

2. When the **o** is *post-tonic* (that is, when it follows the stressed syllable) or when it appears in any other position, it has the indistinct sound of the *o* in *lemon*. For example: э́то, профе́ссор.

3-B. The Final "д"

Pronounce a final **д** like **т**. Pronounce Волгоград as if it were written Волгограт.

3-C. В классе

Pronounce **в классе** as if it were spelled **фклассе**. That is, pronounce the **в** like **ф**, and say the phrase as if it were all one word.

3-D. Accent Marks

Since Russian vowels have different sounds, depending on whether they are stressed or unstressed, it is extremely important for good pronunciation to stress each word correctly.

Accent marks are not part of Russian spelling but are given throughout the book. No accent mark appears on one-syllable words.

Грамматика (Grammar)

3-1. Conjunctions: и and а

a. **и** is a *joining* conjunction:

Иван **и** Вера студенты.   Ivan *and* Vera are students.

b. **а** is a *separating* conjunction:

Анна тут, **а** Вера там.   Anne is here, *and* Vera is there.

c. **а** is also used to express *difference* or *contrast*:

Он не профессор, **а** студент.   He is not a professor, *but* a student.

Note: After a negative, **а** means *but*.

3-2. Genders

There are three genders in Russian—masculine (*m.*), feminine (*f.*), and neuter (*n.*).

a. A *consonant* is the common ending for the *masculine*. For example:

стол, студент, Волгоград.

b. **-а** is the common ending for the *feminine*. For example:

карта, студентка, Москва.

c. **-o** is the common ending for the *neuter.* For example:

перо́ (pen), окно́ (window).

3-3. The Prepositional Case

a. This case is called the *prepositional case* because it is used only with a preposition, such as **на** or **в**. It is also referred to as the *locative case* because it is frequently used to indicate the *location* of an object.

Где карти́на? Карти́на **на столе́.** The picture is *on the table.*
Где студе́нты? Они́ **в кла́ссе.** They are *in class.*

Note: In the examples above, the prepositional is used to answer the question **где?** (where?).

b. To form the prepositional for a masculine noun, *add* the letter **-e** to the nominative singular form of the word. To form the prepositional for a feminine noun, *replace* the nominative ending of **-a** with **-e**. For neuter nouns, *replace* the nominative ending of **-o** with **-e**. As the following table shows, the characteristic ending for the prepositional case is **-e.**

Case	Masculine	Feminine	Neuter
Nominative	стул стол	ка́рта Москва́	перо́ окно́
Prepositional	сту́ле столе́*	ка́рте Москве́	пере́ окне́

* Note the shift of stress.

3-4. Personal Pronouns

The personal pronouns, which have already been presented separately before, are given all together in the table below so as to distinguish between the first, second, and third persons in both the singular and plural. Memorize them.

	SINGULAR		PLURAL	
1st person:	**я**	I	**мы**	we
2nd person:	**ты**	you (*fam.*)	**вы**	you (*pl.,* or *pol. sing.*)
3rd person:	**он** **она́** **оно́**	he she it	**они́**	they

Упражнéния (Exercises)

In place of the blanks, use suitable words to form a meaningful sentence:

1. Э́то не журнáл, а _____. 2. Э́то не стол, а _____. 3. Он не профéссор, а _____. 4. Онá не студéнт, а _____. 5. Студéнты в _____. 6. Волгогрáд тут, а Москвá _____. 7. Э́то картúна, и э́то _____ картúна. 8. Кáрта в _____. 9. Картúна на _____. 10. Москвá в _____.

Перевóд (Translation)

Omit the words in parentheses and include the words in brackets. Henceforth the present of the verb *to be* will not be enclosed in parentheses to indicate its omission in Russian.

1. The table is here, and the chair is there. 2. On the table (there is) a map, a picture, and a book. 3. On the chair (there is) a magazine. 4. Moscow is here, and Volgograd is there. 5. We are students and they are students. 6. Is this Vera or Anne? This is Vera. Anne is in class. 7. Is Vera a professor? Oh no, she is not a professor, but a student. 8. Where is Volgograd? Volgograd is in the U.S.S.R. [в СССР]. 9. Is Moscow also in the U.S.S.R.? Yes, Moscow is also in the U.S.S.R. 10. The students are not in Moscow, but in Volgograd.

Вопрóсы (Questions)

1. Что на столé? 2. Что на стýле? 3. Что на кáрте? 4. Москвá в СССР? 5. Волгогрáд тóже в СССР? 6. Кто в клáссе? 7. Профéссор тóже в клáссе? 8. А где Ивáн и Вéра?

Phonetic Drill

Listen to the teacher (or the tape) and repeat aloud several times the following words or phrases.

он, онá, кто, профéссор, стол, на столé, Москвá, окнó, пальтó, дровá, нóвый, óстрый, опя́ть, поня́ть.

сад, рад, град, назáд, парáд, Волгогрáд, в клáссе.

Pattern Drills

Listen to the teacher (or the tape) and repeat the sentences in the following substitution drills.   Then read each sentence in the ''Student'' column making the appropriate substitution according to the model sentence.

1. See ¶3-1b before drilling.

Teacher	*Student*
Журна́л тут, а кни́га там.	**Он тут, а она́ там.**
Студе́нтка тут, а студе́нт там.	Она́ _____, а он _____.
Ива́н _____, а Ве́ра _____.	Он _____, а он _____.
Москва́ ____, а Волгогра́д _____.	Она́ _____, а он _____.

2. See ¶3-1c before drilling.

Э́то не кни́га, а журна́л.	**Э́то не журна́л, а кни́га.**
Э́то не ка́рта, а карти́на.	Э́то не карти́на, а _____.
Э́то не стол, а стул.	Э́то не стул, а _____.
Э́то не Москва́, а Волгогра́д.	Э́то не Волгогра́д, а _____.
Он не профе́ссор, а студе́нт.	Он не студе́нт, а _____.

3. See ¶3-2 and 3-3 before drilling.

Карти́на на столе́.	**Где карти́на?**	**Она́ на столе́.**
Ка́рта на сту́ле.	Где ка́рта?	____ на _____.
Студе́нт в кла́ссе.	Где студе́нт?	____ в _____.
Студе́нты в кла́ссе.	Где студе́нты?	____ в _____.
Ве́ра в Москве́.	Где Ве́ра?	____ в _____.
А́нна в Волгогра́де.	Где А́нна?	____ в _____.

U N I T 4

ШКÓЛА

Вот шкóла. В шкóле класс. В клáссе профéссор и студéнты.

Вот стенá. На стенé доскá и кáрта. Тут стол и стул. На
столé журнáл, кнúга и газéта. На столé перó и карандáш.

Профéссор Петрóв читáет кнúгу, а Ивáн читáет газéту.
Вéра читáет журнáл.

Áнна сегóдня дóма. Онá нездорóва. Пётр сегóдня тóже
дóма, но он здорóв.

Словáрь (Vocabulary)

шкóла school
вот here is, here are
стенá wall (see ¶4-A)
доскá blackboard
газéта newspaper
перó pen
карандáш pencil
Петрóв Petrov (*surname*) (see ¶4-B)
читáет reads

кнúгу *acc. of* кнúга (see ¶4-3)
сегóдня (*pr.* севóдня) today
дóма (*adv.*) at home
здорóва (*adj., f.*) well, healthy
не здорóва not well, sick
Пётр Peter
но but (see ¶4-4)
здорóв (*adj., m.*) well, healthy (see ¶4-B)

Разговóр (Conversation)

— Э́то шкóла? — Да, э́то шкóла.

— Э́то тóже шкóла? — Нет, э́то не шкóла, а класс.

— Кто в клáссе? — Профéссор Петрóв и студéнты в клáссе.

— Где стол? — Стол в клáссе.

— Что на столé? — На столé журнáл, кнúга и газéта.

— Что ещё на столé? — На столé перó и карандáш.

28

— Что на стене́? — На стене́ доска́ и ка́рта.

— Что чита́ет господи́н Петро́в? — Господи́н Петро́в чита́ет кни́гу.

— А что чита́ют студе́нты? — Они́ чита́ют газе́ту.

— А́нна то́же чита́ет газе́ту? — Нет, она́ чита́ет журна́л.

— Пётр, что ты чита́ешь до́ма? — До́ма я чита́ю газе́ту и́ли журна́л.

— Ве́ра и Ива́н, что вы чита́ете до́ма?

— До́ма мы чита́ем газе́ту и́ли журна́л.

— Вы мно́го чита́ете? — Да, мы мно́го чита́ем.

— Это о́чень хорошо́!

Слова́рь (Vocabulary)

ещё (*adv.*) more
что ещё? what else ?
господи́н * Mr., gentleman
они́ чита́ют they read, they are reading
ты чита́ешь you (*fam. sing.*) read, you are reading
вы чита́ете you (*pl. or pol. sing.*) read, you are reading
мы чита́ем we read, we are reading
мно́го much (*colloq.* a lot)
о́чень very
хорошо́ well, good
э́то о́чень хорошо́! that (this) is very good!

* The word **господи́н** is now used only by Russians living abroad or by Soviet citizens in addressing foreigners. In addressing each other, Soviet citizens use the words **граждани́н** and **гражда́нка** (*citizen, m. & f.*) or **това́рищ** (*comrade*).

Произноше́ние (Pronunciation)

Study the following rules, then practice the phonetic drill at the end of this unit.

4-A. Stressed and Unstressed " e "

a. A stressed **e** at the beginning of a word or after a vowel is pronounced like *ye* in *yes*. For example:

Е́ва, е́сли, уе́хал, пое́л.

b. An unstressed **e** in the pre-tonic position is pronounced like *e* in *e*vent. For example:

стена́, перо́, Петро́в.

c. After **ж**, **ш**, or **ц**, the unstressed **e** is pronounced like *i* in b*i*t. For example:

то́же, пи́шет, цена́.

4-B. The Final " в "

At the end of a word, **в** is pronounced like **ф**. For example:
здоро́в (*pr.* здоро́ф), Петро́в (*pr.* Петро́ф).

Грамма́тика (Grammar)

4-1. Э́то, вот, тут, and там

Note the difference in the meanings of **э́то**, **вот**, **тут**, and **там**.

a. **Э́то** means *this is* or *it is*. It is used to describe or define something. For example:

Э́то шко́ла.   This is a school.

b. **Вот** usually means *there is* or *here is* when pointing out something or calling attention to something (in French, *voilà* and *voici*). For example:

Вот шко́ла.   Here is the (or a) school.
Вот пальто́.   Here is the overcoat.

c. **Тут** means *here*, and **там** *there*; these words are used only to indicate the location of objects.

4-2. The First Conjugation. Infinitive: чита́ть (to read)

a. Most Russian verbs have the ending **-ть** in the infinitive, and are conjugated in the present tense like **чита́ть** (*to read*).

b. To form the *present tense* of **чита́ть**, drop the ending **-ть** from the infinitive and add the personal endings to **чита-** (i.e., to the stem of the infinitive).

	SINGULAR
я чита́**ю**	I read, I am reading
ты чита́**ешь**	you read, you are reading
он чита́**ет**	he reads, he is reading
она́ чита́**ет**	she reads, she is reading
оно́ чита́**ет**	it reads, it is reading

	PLURAL
мы чита́**ем**	we read, we are reading
вы чита́**ете**	you read, you are reading
они́ чита́**ют**	they read, they are reading

Note: The *stem* is that part of an inflected word which remains unchanged throughout a given inflection. This applies to verbs, adjectives, nouns, and pronouns.

c. Memorize the present tense of **читáть** as well as the personal endings.

	SINGULAR		PLURAL
я	**-ю**	мы	**-ем**
ты	**-ешь**	вы	**-ете**
он онá онó	**-ет**	они́	**-ют**

d. There are two basic *conjugations* (i.e., patterns of endings) for Russian verbs.   To determine which conjugation a verb belongs to, examine the ending of the second person singular.   If the second person singular ending is **-ешь** (e.g., ты читá**ешь**), the verb belongs to the First Conjugation.   The distinctive ending which characterizes the Second Conjugation will be discussed in **¶7-1**. Henceforth in the vocabulary, we shall designate all verbs of the First Conjugation by the Roman numeral I.

4-3. The Accusative Case

a. The accusative case in Russian is used to express the *direct object* of a transitive verb.   For example:

Вéра читáет **журнáл**.   Vera is reading a *magazine*.
Петрóв читáет **кни́гу**.   Petrov is reading a *book*.

b. Masculine and neuter nouns denoting *inanimate objects* are alike in the nominative and accusative singular.*   For example:

nom.	журнáл	стул	Сталингрáд	перó
acc.	журнáл	стул	Сталингрáд	перó

c. Feminine nouns, *animate and inanimate*, change the ending **-a** to **-y** in the accusative singular.

nom.	кни́га	Вéра	Москвá
acc.	кни́гу	Вéру	Москву́

* For the accusative of masculine nouns denoting *animate objects*, see **¶10-3**.

4-4. The Conjunction: но

Но, meaning *but,* states a fact contrary to the one logically expected.   Whereas **а** in the sense of *but* stresses difference or contrast, **но** shows contradiction.

Пётр до́ма, **но** он здоро́в.   Peter is home, *but* he is well.

Normally a schoolboy who is well would be in school, not at home.   Here the opposite is a fact.

In the sentence, "He is old but vigorous," the word *but* should be rendered by **но** in Russian, because vigor is not ordinarily associated with old age—quite the contrary.

Упражне́ния (Exercises)

Supply the proper endings of **чита́ть** in the present tense, and replace the English words in parentheses with Russian ones in the proper cases.

1. Что на (the table), (a pen) и́ли (a pencil)?   2. Что ещё на (the table), (a map) и́ли (a picture)?   3. (The map) на (the wall), а (the picture) на (the table).   4. Я чита́____ (a book).   5. Áнна чита́____ (a magazine).   6. Студе́нты мно́го чита́____.   7. Что ты чита́____ в (class)?   8. Они́ чита́____ (the newspaper) до́ма.   9. Что вы чита́____ сего́дня?   Я сего́дня чита́____ (a newspaper).   10. Петро́в чита́____ о́чень хорошо́.

Перево́д (Translation)

1. Here is the professor, and here are the students.   2. Here is a blackboard, and there is a map.   3. The map is on the wall.   4. This is not a pencil, but a pen.   5. This is not a book, but a magazine.   6. I am home today.   I am not well.   7. Ivan is also home today, but he is well.   8. Is Anne well?   No, she is not well.   9. Where is Anne, at home or in school?   10. She is in school, but she is not well.   11. What is Mr. Petrov reading?   He is reading a newspaper.   12. What else is he reading?   He is reading a magazine.   13. What are the students reading today?   14. Peter, Vera, and Ivan are reading a book.   15. They are reading much, and that is very good.

Вопро́сы (Questions)

1. Где шко́ла? 2. Кто в шко́ле? 3. Что на стене́? 4. Где стол и стул? 5. Что на столе́? 6. Что ещё на столе́? 7. Что чита́ет господи́н Петро́в? 8. Он хорошо́ чита́ет? 9. Вы то́же хорошо́ чита́ете? 10. Где А́нна сего́дня? 11. Пётр то́же до́ма? 12. Кто здоро́в и кто не здоро́в? 13. Вы мно́го чита́ете до́ма? 14. Вы чита́ете хорошо́? 15. Кто о́чень хорошо́ чита́ет, Ива́н и́ли Ве́ра?

Phonetic Drill

Study ¶4-A and 4-B.   Listen to the teacher (or the tape) and repeat aloud several times the following words.

Е́сли, Е́ва, есть, е́хать, е́здить, дела́, стена́, несла́, река́, сестра́, перо́, вы́ше, ни́же, ре́же, то́же, полоте́нце, здоро́в, Петро́в, Ле́рмонто́в, Гончаро́в, Турге́нев, Че́хов.

Pattern Drills

A. Study ¶4-1.   Listen to the teacher (or the tape) and repeat the same nouns in the following repetition drills, substituting **вот** for **э́то** and **там** for **тут**.

Teacher	*Student*
1. **Э́то шко́ла.**	**Вот шко́ла.**
Э́то стена́.	Вот _____.
Э́то доска́.	Вот _____.
Э́то перо́.	Вот _____.
Э́то каранда́ш.	Вот _____.

2. **Стена́ тут,   а доска́ там.**
   Газе́та _____, а кни́га _____.
   Перо́ _____, а каранда́ш _____.
   Журна́л _____, а газе́та _____.
   Ка́рта _____, а карти́на _____.

B. Study ¶4-3.   Listen to the teacher (or the tape) and repeat the first clause in the following substitution drill.   Then read the second clause supplying the appropriate form of **чита́ть** in the present tense.

Teacher	*Student*
Я читáю кнúгу,	**а ты читáешь журнáл.**
Ты читáешь газéту,	а я _____ кнúгу.
Он читáет журнáл,	а онá _____ газéту.
Мы читáем кнúгу,	а вы _____ журнáл.
Вы читáете газéту,	а мы _____ кнúгу.
Онú читáют журнáл,	а он _____ газéту.

C. Study ¶4-4. Listen to the teacher (or the tape) and repeat the following completion drills supplying the appropriate forms of **здорóв, здорóва, нездорóва, здорóвы,** and **нездорóвы.**

1. **Я сегóдня дóма, но я здорóв.**
   Ты _____, но ты _____.
   Он _____, но он _____.

2. **Онá сегóдня дóма, но онá здорóва.**
   Студéнтка_____, но онá _____.
   Вéра _____, но онá _____.
   Áнна _____, но _____.

3. **Мы сегóдня дóма, но мы здорóвы.**
   Вы _____, но вы_____.
   Онú _____, но онú _____.

4. **Я сегóдня в клáссе, но я нездорóв.**
   Ты _____, но ты _____.
   Он _____, но он _____.
   Онá _____, но онá нездорóва.
   Студéнтка _____, но онá _____.
   Вéра_____, но онá _____.
   Áнна _____, но онá _____.

5. **Студéнт и студéнтка в клáссе, но онú нездорóвы.**
   Áнна и Вéра_____, но онú _____.
   Ивáн и Пётр _____, но онú _____.
   Студéнты _____, но онú _____.
   Профéссор и студéнты _____, но онú _____.

U N I T 5

МОЯ КÓМНАТА

Вот кóмната. Э́то моя́ кóмната. Онá óчень краси́вая. Тут
окнó, а там дверь.

В кóмнате нóвый стол. Э́то мой стол. На столé лáмпа,
бумáга, перó и карандáш. Мел тóже на столé, но я пишý
мéлом тóлько на доскé в клáссе. Дóма я пишý карандашóм и́ли
перóм. Моё нóвое перó всегдá на столé. Я читáю по-рýсски
хорошó, но пишý óчень плóхо.

Словáрь (Vocabulary)

моя́ (*f.*) my	**я пишý** I write (see ¶ 5-4)
кóмната room	**мéлом** with chalk (see ¶ 5-5)
краси́вая (*f.*) beautiful	**тóлько** only
окнó window	**моё** (*n.*) my
дверь (*f.*) door	**нóвое** (*n.*) new
нóвый (*m.*) new	**всегдá** (*pr.* фсегдá) always
мой (*m.*) my	**по-рýсски** (*adv.*) Russian, in Rus-
лáмпа lamp	sian (see ¶ 5-6)
бумáга paper	**плóхо** (*adv.*) badly, poorly
мел chalk	

Memorize the nominative forms of the following words in their
three genders:

	m.	*f.*	*n.*	
adj. & pron.	мой	моя́	моё	my, mine
adj.	краси́вый	краси́вая	краси́вое	beautiful
adj.	нóвый	нóвая	нóвое	new

35

Разгово́р (**Conversation**)

— Э́то ко́мната? — Да, э́то ко́мната.

— Э́то ва́ша ко́мната? — Да, э́то моя́ ко́мната.

— Где окно́ и где дверь в ко́мнате? — Окно́ тут, а дверь там.

— Э́то ваш стол? — Да, э́то мой но́вый стол.

— Что на столе́? — На столе́ ла́мпа, бума́га, перо́ и каранда́ш.

— Ва́ша ла́мпа то́же но́вая? — Да, она́ но́вая и о́чень краси́вая.

— Чем вы пи́шете на доске́? — На доске́ я пишу́ ме́лом.

— А чем вы пи́шете на бума́ге? — На бума́ге я пишу́ перо́м и́ли карандашо́м.

— Как пи́шет ва́ше но́вое перо́ — хорошо́ и́ли пло́хо?

— Моё но́вое перо́ всегда́ пи́шет о́чень хорошо́.

— Вы уже́ чита́ете по-ру́сски?

— Да, я уже́ чита́ю по-ру́сски, но о́чень ме́дленно.

— А как вы пи́шете по-ру́сски?

— Я пишу́ по-ру́сски пло́хо и о́чень, о́чень ме́дленно, но по-англи́йски я пишу́ бы́стро и хорошо́.

Слова́рь (**Vocabulary**)

ваш, ва́ша, ва́ше (*adj. & pron.*; *pl. & pol. sing.*) your, yours
чем with what
как how
уже́ already
ме́дленно (*adv.*) slowly
по-англи́йски (*adv.*) English, in English (see ¶ 5-6)
бы́стро rapidly, fast

Произноше́ние (**Pronunciation**)

5-A. The Sibilants : ж, ч, ш, and щ

a. When **ж**, **ч**, **ш**, or **щ** is pronounced, a hissing sound is produced. That is why these letters are called *sibilants*, from the Latin *sibilare* meaning *to hiss*.

b. **ю** can never be written after the sibilants **ж**, **ч**, **ш**, **щ**, and must be replaced by the corresponding hard vowel **y** (see ¶ 1-A). This explains why, in **пишу́** (*I write*), the personal ending following the **ш** is **-у**, instead of the regular **-ю**, and in **пи́шут** (*they write*), **-ут** instead of **-ют**.

Грамма́тика (Grammar)

5-1. Agreement of Adjectives

a. An adjective agrees with the noun it modifies in gender, case, and number.

m.	мой стол	my table
	ваш стол	your table
f.	моя́ ла́мпа	my lamp
	ва́ша ла́мпа	your lamp
n.	моё окно́	my window
	ва́ше окно́	your window
m.	но́вый, краси́вый стол	a new, beautiful table
f.	но́вая, краси́вая ла́мпа	a new, beautiful lamp
n.	но́вое, краси́вое окно́	a new, beautiful window

5-2. Position of Adjectives

a. Attributive adjectives precede the noun they modify. For example:

но́вый стол	a *new* table
но́вая ла́мпа	a *new* lamp
но́вое окно́	a *new* window

b. Predicative adjectives follow the noun. The present tense of *to be* is then understood. For example:

стол **но́вый**	the table *is new*
ла́мпа **но́вая**	the lamp *is new*
окно́ **но́вое**	the window *is new*

c. When an adjective follows a noun, it can also be translated by adding the word *one* to its English equivalent. For example:

Стол но́вый.   The table is new   *or*   The table is a new *one.*

Ко́мната но́вая.   The room is new   *or*   The room is a new *one.*

5-3. Agreement of Personal Pronouns

Personal pronouns must agree in gender and in number with the nouns to which they refer. For example:

Где стол?   **Он** в ко́мнате.   Where is the table?   *It* is in the room.

Где Ива́н?   **Он** в шко́ле.   Where is Ivan?   *He* is in school.

Где бума́га?   **Она́** на столе́.   Where is the paper?   *It* is on the table.

Где А́нна?   **Она́** до́ма.   Where is Anne?   *She* is home.

Ва́ше перо́ но́вое? Да, оно́ но́вое. Is your pen new (a new one)? Yes, *it* is new (a new one).

Note: **он** and **она́** often mean *it* in English, depending on the gender of the word to which they refer.

★ 5-4. Infinitive: писа́ть (I) *to write*

a. Present tense:

я пишу́	I write	мы пи́шем	we write
ты пи́шешь	you write	вы пи́шете	you write
он пи́шет	he writes	они́ пи́шут	they write
она́ пи́шет	she writes		
оно́ пи́шет	it writes		

b. **пиш-** is the *present stem* of **писа́ть**. It is obtained by dropping the personal ending **-ешь** from the second person singular **ты пи́шешь**.

c. Many verbs form the present tense from the *present stem*, *not* from the *infinitive stem.*
Compare:

$$\textbf{чита́ -ть} \begin{cases} \text{я } \textbf{чита́ } \text{-ю} \\ \text{ты } \textbf{чита́ } \text{-ешь} \end{cases}$$

$$\textbf{писа́ -ть} \begin{cases} \text{я } \textbf{пиш } \text{-у́} \\ \text{ты } \textbf{пи́ш } \text{-ешь} \end{cases}$$

It is therefore important to memorize the *infinitive* as well as the *first* and *second person* singular of the present tense for every new verb.

5-5. The Instrumental Case

a. The instrumental case is used with or without a preposition, depending on the idea to be conveyed.

1. When used *without* a preposition, the instrumental indicates the *instrument* or *means* by which an action is performed, or the *agent* by whom it is performed. Thus it answers the question **чем**? (*with what?*) or **кем**? (*by whom?*). For example:
Профе́ссор пи́шет перо́м. The professor is writing *with* (*by means of*) a pen. (**Чем** он пи́шет? *With what* is he writing?)

In the sentence "The book was written *by the professor*," the last three words are rendered in Russian by only one—**профе́ссором**.

In the question *"By whom* was the book written?" the first two words are rendered by **кем**.

2. For the use of the instrumental *with* a preposition, see **¶8-2**.

b. Masculine nouns ending in a consonant in the nominative singular add **-ом** to form the instrumental.*

nom.	мел	карандаш
instr.	мéл**ом**	карандаш**óм**

c. Neuter nouns in **-о** add **-м**.*

nom.	перó	окнó
instr.	пер**óм**	окн**óм**

d. Feminine nouns in **-а** change the ending to **-ой** or **-ою**.*

nom.	кáрта	Москвá
instr.	{ кáрт**ой**	{ Москв**óй**
	{ кáрт**ою**	{ Москв**óю**

5-6. По-рýсски and по-англи́йски

По-рýсски and по-англи́йски are adverbs, but are rendered in English as nouns. For example:

Я читáю по-рýсски.	I read Russian.
Он пи́шет по-англи́йски.	He writes English.

Упражнéния (Exercises)

A. Supply the appropriate personal pronoun for the following words. For example: студéнтка **онá**.

1. мел _____. 2. лáмпа _____. 3. дверь _____.
4. окнó _____. 5. кóмната _____. 6. класс _____. 7. здорóв _____. 8. здорóва _____.
9. Пётр _____. 10. Вéра _____. 11. стенá _____.
12. Москвá _____. 13. Сталингрáд _____. 14. карти́на _____. 15. перó _____.

● B. Supply an appropriate noun to agree with the following adjectives. For example: нóвая **кни́га**.

1. мой _____. 2. ваш _____. 3. моя́ _____. 4. вáша _____. 5. моё _____.
6. вáше _____. 7. краси́вый _____. 8. нóвый _____. 9. нóвая _____. 10. краси́вое

* For exceptions, see **¶25-3b**.

_____.   11. нóвое _____.   12. краси́вая
_____. 13. _____ здорóва.

* C. Supply the proper personal ending for the verbs and the appropriate case ending for the nouns. For example: Я пишý перóм.

1. Я сегóдня чита́____ кни́г____. 2. Кни́г____ тут. 3. Он чита́____ журнáл. 4. Онá пи́ш____ мéл____ на доск____.
5. Чем вы пи́ш____ дóма? 6. Дóма мы пи́ш____ карандáш____ и́ли пер____. 7. Вы пи́ш____ и чита́____ по-рýсски хорошó?
8. Да, я чита́____ и пи́ш____ хорошó, но óчень мéдленно.
9. Как студéнты пи́ш____ и чита́____ по-англи́йски? 10. Они́ пи́ш____ и чита́____ óчень бы́стро.

Перевóд (Translation)

Translate, omitting the words in parentheses.
1. Is this your room? 2. Yes, this is my room. 3. Is your room new? 4. Yes, it is new (a new one) and beautiful. 5. Where is the window? 6. The window is here, and the door is there.
7. What do you write with on paper? 8. On paper I write with a pen, and on the blackboard I write with chalk. 9. Do you already read Russian? 10. Yes, I read Russian, but very slowly. 11. English I read fast (rapidly). 12. Do you write Russian well or poorly? 13. I write Russian poorly and slowly. 14. And how do you read Russian? 15. I read Russian very fast.

Вопрóсы (Questions)

1. Э́то вáша кóмната? 2. Где окнó и где дверь? 3. Ваш стол в кóмнате? 4. Что на столé? 5. Как вы чита́ете по-рýсски? 6. Как вы пи́шете по-англи́йски? 7. Чем вы пи́шете на бумáге? 8. Чем вы пи́шете на доскé? 9. Чем профéссор Петрóв всегдá пи́шет в клáссе? 10. Студéнты чита́ют по-англи́йски бы́стро и́ли мéдленно? 11. Вы чита́ете по-рýсски тóлько в шкóле? 12. Дóма вы всегдá чита́ете по-англи́йски?

Pattern Drills

A. Study ¶5-1 and 5-2. Listen to the teacher (or the tape) and repeat the phrases in the following transformation drills. Then

read the phrases changing the position of the *attributive* adjectives
to make them *predicative*.

Teacher	*Student*
1. **мой стол**	**стол мой**
my table	the table is mine
мой стул	стул _____
мой журна́л	журна́л _____
мой каранда́ш	каранда́ш _____
мой мел	мел_____
2. **моя́ ка́рта**	**ка́рта моя́**
моя́ карти́на	карти́на _____
моя́ кни́га	кни́га _____
моя́ газе́та	газе́та_____
моя́ ко́мната	ко́мната _____
моя́ ла́мпа	ла́мпа_____
3. **моё перо́**	**перо́ моё**
моё окно́	окно́ моё

B. Repeat the above phrases inserting the adjective **но́вый**,
но́вая, or **но́вое** according to the following model phrases.

1. мой **но́вый** стол   мой стол **но́вый**
2. моя́ **но́вая** ка́рта   моя́ ка́рта **но́вая**
3. моё **но́вое** перо́   моё перо́ **но́вое**

C. Repeat the phrases in A and B replacing **мой** with **ваш**,
моя́ with **ва́ша**, and **моё** with **ва́ше**.

D. Study ¶**5-4** and **5-5**. Listen to the teacher (or the tape) and
repeat the following sentences. Then read each sentence replacing
перо́ with **каранда́ш** and with **мел**.

Teacher	*Student*
Я пишу́ перо́м.	**Я пишу́ карандашо́м, я пишу́ ме́лом.**
Ты пи́шешь _____.	Ты _____, ты _____.
Он пи́шет _____.	Он _____, он _____.
Она́ пи́шет _____.	Она́ _____, она́ _____.
Мы пи́шем _____.	Мы _____, мы _____.
Вы пи́шете _____.	Вы _____, вы _____.
Они́ пи́шут _____.	Они́ _____, они́ _____.

E. Listen to the teacher (or the tape) and repeat the following drill.

Я пишу́ ме́лом на доске́.
Ты пи́шешь _____.
Он пи́шет _____.
Мы пи́шем _____.
Вы пи́шете _____.
Они́ пи́шут _____.

F. Practice the following substitution drill.

Teacher	*Student*
Стол но́вый?	**Да, он но́вый.**
Ла́мпа но́вая?	Да, она́ но́вая.
Окно́ краси́вое?	Да, оно́ краси́вое.
Карти́на краси́вая?	Да, _____.
Перо́ но́вое?	Да, _____.
Ко́мната краси́вая?	Да, _____.

U N I T 6

Грамма́тика (Grammar)

6-1. Nouns: Table of Case Endings

Memorize the following table.

	MASCULINE	FEMININE	NEUTER
nom.	стул	ка́рта	перо́
	стол	Москва́	окно́
acc.	стул	ка́рту	перо́
	стол	Москву́	окно́
instr.	сту́лом	ка́рт**ой, -ою**	пер**о́м**
	стол**о́м**	Москв**о́й, -о́ю**	окн**о́м**
prep.	сту́л**е**	ка́рт**е**	пер**е́**
	стол**е́**	Москв**е́**	окн**е́**

Alphabet Review

A. Write the Russian script in alphabetical order; then check with the book for errors or omissions. Rewrite the alphabet until no errors occur.

B. Do the same with the printed alphabet.

Vocabulary Review

A. Write the Russian equivalent for each of the following words and indicate where the stress falls with an accent mark. If you are

43

not sure of the Russian word or its spelling, look it up in the English-Russian vocabulary.

1. who	13. at home
2. also	14. today
3. where	15. slowly
4. here	16. rapidly
5. there	17. Russian (in Russian)
6. more	18. English (in English)
7. very	19. already
8. much	20. only
9. well, good	21. always
10. well (healthy) (*m.*)	22. in
11. well (healthy) (*f.*)	23. on
12. or	24. how

B. Write the Russian equivalent for each of the following nouns, insert accent marks, and indicate the gender of each. Underline the ending which shows the gender. For example:

window—окно́ (*n.*)

paper—бума́га (*f.*)

1. professor	8. map	15. wall
2. student (girl)	9. picture	16. school
3. class	10. Moscow	17. newspaper
4. magazine	11. Stalingrad	18. room
5. book	12. pencil	19. paper
6. table	13. pen	20. lamp
7. chair	14. blackboard	21. door

C. Use one of the following adjectives in the proper gender with each of the above nouns.

1. мой, моя́, моё
2. краси́вый, краси́вая, краси́вое
3. ваш, ва́ша, ва́ше
4. но́вый, но́вая, но́вое

D. Use the vocabularies of Exercises A, B, and C in a spelling match.

Reading and Comprehension Drill

Read each of the following affirmative sentences aloud; then re-read them, changing your intonation to form questions (see ¶2-5).

Next, answer the questions both in the affirmative and the negative, using complete sentences.   For example:

Вѐра краси́вая студѐнтка.   (affirmative)

Change to: Вѐра краси́вая студѐнтка?   (interrogative)

Possible answers:

Да, она́ краси́вая студѐнтка.
О да! Она́ о́чень краси́вая.
Нет, она́ не краси́вая студѐнтка.
О нет! Она́ не краси́вая.

For another example:

На стенѐ карти́на.   (affirmative)

Change to: На стенѐ карти́на?   (interrogative)

Possible answers:

Да, на стенѐ карти́на.
Нет, на стенѐ не карти́на, а ка́рта.

1. Э́то студѐнт.
2. Ива́н профѐссор.
3. Пётр и А́нна студѐнты.
4. Вѐра то́же студѐнтка.
5. Ка́рта на столѐ.
6. На стенѐ доска́.
7. Пётр в Москвѐ.
8. Петро́в сего́дня до́ма.
9. Студѐнты в шко́ле.
10. А́нна чита́ет кни́гу.
11. Студѐнтка здоро́ва.
12. Они́ чита́ют журна́л.
13. Господи́н Петро́в пи́шет карандашо́м.
14. Ла́мпа но́вая и краси́вая.
15. Ва́ше перо́ всегда́ на столѐ.
16. Вы хорошо́ чита́ете по-англи́йски.
17. Они́ пло́хо пи́шут по-ру́сски.
18. Ты уже́ бы́стро чита́ешь.

Grammar Review

Supply the proper forms for the words in parentheses.   For example:

Э́то (ваш) (room)—Э́то ва́ша ко́мната.

Петро́в (писа́ть) (with a pen)—Петро́в пи́шет перо́м.

1. Ваш стол в (room) (new).
2. До́ма вы всегда́ (чита́ть) (Russian).
3. На (paper) я (писа́ть) (with a pen).
4. Э́то (my) ко́мната.
5. Они́ сего́дня (чита́ть) (a book).
6. Петро́в в (class).

7. (Нóвый) (краси́вый) лáмпа.
8. (Your) окнó (нóвый).
9. Они́ (читáть) (a magazine).
10. Он здорóв, а онá (sick).

Перевóд (Translation)

1. Who is this? 2. Yes or no? 3. Who is she? 4. Who are they? 5. What else? 6. This is my room. 7. I am not well (*m.*). 8. Here is a school. 9. The school is in Moscow. 10. The students are in class. 11. She is also a student. 12. That (this) is very good. 13. This is not a map, but a picture. 14. Vera is not a student, but a professor. 15. This is a table, and this is a chair. 16. The book is on the table. 17. The newspaper is on the chair. 18. Where is the magazine? 19. What is on the map? 20. Moscow is here and Stalingrad is there. 21. A blackboard and a map are on the wall. 22. A pen and a pencil are on the table. 23. With what are you writing—with a pen or a pencil? 24. What is she reading—a newspaper or a magazine? 25. Anne is home today, but she is well. 26. We write Russian poorly and slowly. 27. You read English well and fast (rapidly). 28. My window is very beautiful. 29. On the table is a beautiful new lamp. 30. I write with chalk on the blackboard.

U N I T 7

МОЙ УЧИ́ТЕЛЬ

Я учени́к. Я уже́ чита́ю и пишу́ по-ру́сски. Я та́кже понима́ю по-ру́сски, но ещё не говорю́. Я хоро́ший учени́к.

Мой учи́тель — господи́н Петро́в. Он ру́сский. Он пло́хо говори́т по-англи́йски, потому́ что он то́лько оди́н год в Аме́рике. Но он о́чень хоро́ший учи́тель.

В кла́ссе господи́н Петро́в всегда́ стои́т. Он стои́т о́коло ка́рты, о́коло доски́ и́ли о́коло стола́. Тепе́рь он стои́т о́коло окна́.

Слова́рь (Vocabulary)

учи́тель (*m.*) teacher (man)
учени́к pupil (boy)
та́кже also, in addition
понима́ю I understand
понима́ть (I); понима́ю, -ешь, -ют to understand
ещё не говорю́ I do not yet speak
говори́ть (II); говорю́, -и́шь, -я́т to speak, to talk, to say
хоро́ший, хоро́шая, хоро́шее good
ру́сский (*noun & adj., m.*) Russian
потому́ что because
оди́н one
год year
Аме́рика America (*colloq.* the U.S.A.)
он то́лько оди́н год в Аме́рике he has been only one year in the U.S.A.
стои́т he stands
стоя́ть (II); стою́, -и́шь, -я́т to stand
о́коло (*requires gen. case*) near
тепе́рь now

УЧЕНИ́К И УЧЕНИ́ЦА (Разгово́р)

— Вы учени́ца? — Да, я учени́ца.

— Ива́н то́же учени́ца? — Нет, Ива́н не учени́ца, он учени́к.

— Вы хоро́шая учени́ца? — Да, я о́чень хоро́шая учени́ца, потому́ что я мно́го рабо́таю.

— Ива́н то́же хоро́ший учени́к? — О нет! Он о́чень плохо́й учени́к.

— Почему́ он плохо́й учени́к? — Потому́ что он ма́ло рабо́тает. В кла́ссе он ничего́ не чита́ет и ничего́ не пи́шет. Он то́лько говори́т и говори́т.

— Ва́ша учи́тельница, госпожа́ Ивано́ва, зна́ет, что он не рабо́тает и то́лько говори́т в кла́ссе? — Да, она́ о́чень хорошо́ э́то зна́ет.

Слова́рь (Vocabulary)

учени́ца pupil (girl)
хоро́шая (*f.*) good
рабо́таю I work
рабо́тать (I); рабо́таю, -ешь, -ют to work
плохо́й, плоха́я, плохо́е bad, poor
почему́ why
ма́ло little (not much)
ничего́ (*pr.* **ничево́**) nothing
ничего́ не чита́ет he reads nothing, he does not read anything
то́лько говори́т и говори́т he only talks and talks
учи́тельница teacher (woman)
госпожа́ Miss, Mrs.
Ивано́ва Ivanova
зна́ет knows
знать (I); зна́ю, -ешь, -ют to know

Sing this song in rounds to the tune of *Frère Jacques:*

Я не зна́ю,
Я не зна́ю,
　　Ничего́!
　　Ничего́!
Ничего́ не зна́ю,
Ничего́ не зна́ю,
　　Хорошо́!
　　Хорошо́!

Произношéние (Pronunciation)

7-A. Change of "ы" to "и" after Sibilants

The letter **ы** can never be written after the sibilants **ж, ч, ш,** or **щ** and must be replaced by the corresponding soft vowel **и** (see ¶ 1-A). Hence the ending **-ий** in хорóший, instead of **-ый** as in нóвый.

7-B. The Gutturals: г, к, and x

a. Pronounce the letters **г, к,** and **x,** and note that they are pronounced in the throat. They are therefore called *gutturals,* from the Latin *guttur* meaning *throat.*

b. The letter **ы** can never be written after the gutturals **г, к,** or **x** (or after the sibilants **ж, ч, ш,** or **щ**), and must be replaced by **и**. For example:

nom.	кáрта	кнúга	доскá	госпожá
gen.	кáрты *but* кнúги		доскú	госпожú (see ¶ 7-3)

Граммáтика (Grammar)

7-1. The Second Conjugation. Infinitive: говорúть (to speak)

a. To form the present tense of **говорúть**, add the personal endings to the present stem, that is, to **говор-**.

SINGULAR

я говорю́	I speak, I am speaking
ты говорúшь	you speak, you are speaking
он говорúт	he speaks, he is speaking
онá говорúт	she speaks, she is speaking
онó говорúт	it speaks, it is speaking

PLURAL

мы говорúм	we speak, we are speaking
вы говорúте	you speak, you are speaking
онú говоря́т	they speak, they are speaking

b. Memorize the present of **говорúть** as well as the personal endings.

	SINGULAR		PLURAL
я	**-ю**	мы	**-им**
ты	**-ишь**	вы	**-ите**
он			
онá	**-ит**	онú	**-ят**
онó			

Compare these personal endings with those of the First Conjugation (see ¶4-2) and commit them to memory.

c. The distinguishing mark of the Second Conjugation is the vowel **и** in the second person singular ending **-ишь** (ты говорúшь). This may be compared with the distinguishing mark of the First Conjugation, namely, the vowel **е** in second person singular ending **-ешь** (ты читáешь). Henceforth in the vocabulary, verbs of the Second Conjugation will be designated by the Roman numeral II, just as verbs of the First Conjugation are designated by the Roman numeral I. Verbs which do not fit either of these conjugations will be marked *irr.* (irregular).

7-2. The Verb in the Negative

a. The verb in the negative is formed by placing **не** before the affirmative. **Стоя́ть** (*to stand*) is conjugated both in the affirmative and the negative to illustrate this point.

AFFIRMATIVE	NEGATIVE	
я стою́	я **не** стою́	I do not stand, I am not standing
ты стои́шь	ты **не** стои́шь	you do not stand, you are not standing
он стои́т	он **не** стои́т	he does not stand, he is not standing
онá стои́т	онá **не** стои́т	she does not stand, she is not standing
онó стои́т	онó **не** стои́т	it does not stand, it is not standing
мы стои́м	мы **не** стои́м	we do not stand, we are not standing
вы стои́те	вы **не** стои́те	you do not stand, you are not standing
онú стоя́т	онú **не** стоя́т	they do not stand, they are not standing

b. To negate an action, **не** must precede the verb regardless of the presence of other negative words in the sentence. For example:

> Он **ничего́ не** зна́ет. He knows nothing.
> (*Literally:* He *nothing not* knows.)

7-3. The Genitive Case

a. The genitive denotes possession and corresponds to the *possessive* in English. For example:

> стена́ шко́л**ы**   the wall *of* the school
> кни́га студе́нт**а**   the student'*s* book

The case ending in Russian performs the same function as the preposition **of** or the **'s** in English.

b. The genitive is also used with certain prepositions, such as **о́коло.** For example:

> о́коло стол**а́**   near the table
> о́коло ка́рт**ы**   near the map
> о́коло окн**а́**   near the window

c. Formation of the genitive singular.

1. *Masculine* nouns ending in a *consonant* add **-a** to form the genitive:

nom.	студе́нт	учени́к	стул	стол
gen.	студе́нт**а**	ученик**а́**	сту́л**а**	стол**а́**

2. *Feminine* nouns ending in **-a** change **-a** to **-ы**:

nom.	Ве́р**а**	ка́рт**а**	стен**а́**
gen.	Ве́р**ы**	ка́рт**ы**	стен**ы́**

Exceptions: Nouns whose stems end in **г, к,** or **х** (the gutturals), or in **ж, ч, ш,** or **щ** (the sibilants) take **-и** instead of **-ы**:*

nom.	кни́г**а**	доск**а́**	госпож**а́**
gen.	кни́г**и**	доск**и́**	госпож**и́**

3. *Neuter* nouns ending in **-o** change **-o** to **-a**:

nom.	пер**о́**	окн**о́**
gen.	пер**а́**	окн**а́**

* See ¶**7-A** and **7-B.**

7-4. Subordinating Conjunctions: что and потому́ что

When **что** or **потому́ что** introduces a subordinate clause, it is separated by a comma from the main clause:

Она́ зна́ет, **что** он не рабо́тает.   She knows that he does not work.
Он ма́ло зна́ет, **потому́ что** он плохо́й учени́к.

He knows little because he is a bad pupil.

Упражне́ния (Exercises)

A. Supply the proper endings, accents, and meanings.   (Master
¶7-1 before doing this exercise.)

1. они́ пиш____	8. он говор____
2. вы работа____	9. они́ сто____
3. мы говор____	10. я понима____
4. он зна____	11. они чита____
5. она́ понима____	12. мы зна____
6. мы сто____	13. мы работа____
7. я чита____	14. вы пиш____

B. Give the genitive form for the following nouns, and supply the accents for both the nominative and the genitive.   (Master
¶7-3 before doing this exercise.)

1. студент	11. стена
2. студентка	12. окно
3. ученик	13. журнал
4. ученица	14. стул
5. господин	15. лампа
6. госпожа	16. бумага
7. профессор	17. доска
8. Анна	18. мел
9. Вера	19. карандаш
10. комната	20. перо

C. Supply the proper endings in the blanks, and replace the English words in parentheses with the Russian equivalent in the correct gender and case:

1. Она́ учени____. 2. Она́ понима́____ (English). 3. Мы ещё не говор____ (Russian). 4. (My) учи́тельница (Mrs.) Ивано́ва. 5. Она́ ру́сск*ая*____. 6. Она́ о́чень (good) учи́тельница.   7. Она́ сто____ о́коло (table) и́ли о́коло (blackboard).

Перево́д (Translation)

Omit the words in parentheses and include the words in brackets.

Who Knows Why?

1. My teacher (*f.*) is Mrs. Ivanova.   2. She is Russian.   3. She is a very good teacher.   4. She says [**говори́т**] that I am a good pupil (*f.*).   5. I do not know why she is saying this [**э́то**], because I always work very little.   6. I read and write Russian only in class. 7. At home I read nothing and write nothing.   8. My teacher has been in America only one year, and she does not yet speak English very well.   9. She understands English, but in class we speak only Russian.   10. Mr. Petrov is also a teacher, and he is also Russian. 11. Mr. Petrov and Mrs. Ivanova are now in school.   12. They speak Russian very fast and I understand nothing.   13. Why do I understand nothing—because I am not a Russian, or because I am a bad pupil?   14. Who knows why?

Вопро́сы (Questions)

1. Кто вы?   2. Вы Ива́н и́ли Пётр?   3. Вы уже́ чита́ете по-ру́сски?   4. Как вы чита́ете по-ру́сски, бы́стро и́ли ме́дленно? 5. Вы та́кже говори́те по-ру́сски?   6. Как вы говори́те по-ру́сски, хорошо́ и́ли пло́хо?   7. Кто ва́ша учи́тельница? 8. Она́ ру́сская?   9. Она́ хоро́шая и́ли плоха́я учи́тельница? 10. Как она́ говори́т по-англи́йски?   11. Она́ в Аме́рике то́лько оди́н год?   12. Господи́н Петро́в то́же ру́сский учи́тель?   13. Он учи́тель Ива́на и Ве́ры?   14. Почему́ Ива́н ничего́ не зна́ет?   15. Господи́н Петро́в зна́ет, что Ива́н ма́ло рабо́тает?

Pattern Drills

Conjugations are best learned through repetition.   Listen to the teacher (or the tape) and repeat the following repetition drills. Then read aloud the sentences in the "Student" column.   Repeat each drill at least ten times.

A. Study ¶7-1, the Second Conjugation affirmative.

Teacher	*Student*
Я говорю́ по-ру́сски.	**Я говорю́ по-англи́йски.**
Ты говори́шь _____.	Ты _____.
Он говори́т _____.	Он _____.
Она́ говори́т _____.	Она́ _____.
Мы говори́м _____.	Мы _____.
Вы говори́те _____.	Вы _____.
Они́ говоря́т _____.	Они́_____.

B. Study ¶7-2, the Second Conjugation negative.

Я не говорю́ по-англи́йски.
etc.

Я не говорю́ по-ру́сски.
etc.

C. The adverbs **хорошо́** and **пло́хо.**

**Я хорошо́ говорю́ и
понима́ю по-англи́йски.**
etc.

**Я пло́хо говорю́ и
понима́ю по-ру́сски.**
etc.

D. Study ¶7-2 and 7-3. Listen to the teacher (or the tape) and repeat the following sentences. Then read each sentence substituting different nouns in the genitive according to the model.

Я стою́ о́коло студе́нта.
Ты стои́шь о́коло Ива́на.
Он стои́т о́коло ученика́.
Она́ стои́т о́коло ка́рты.
Мы стои́м о́коло окна́.
Вы стои́те о́коло учи́тельницы.
Они́ стоя́т о́коло стены́.

Я стою́ о́коло студе́нтки.
Ты _____ Ве́ры.
Он _____ учени́цы.
Она́ _____ карти́ны.
Мы _____ доски́.
Вы _____ профе́ссора.
Они́ _____ стола́.

E. Double negatives (see ¶7-2b).

Я ничего́ не зна́ю.
Ты ничего́ не зна́ешь.
Он ничего́ не зна́ет.
Мы ничего́ не зна́ем.
Вы ничего́ не зна́ете.
Они́ ничего́ не зна́ют.

Я ничего́ не говорю́.
Ты_____.
Он _____.
Мы _____.
Вы _____.
Они́ _____.

F. Conjugate the following, as in E.

> Я ничего́ не чита́ю.
> Я ничего́ не пишу́.
> Я ничего́ не понима́ю.

G. Conjugate the following, as in E.

> Я ещё не чита́ю по-ру́сски.
> Я ещё не говорю́ по-ру́сски.
> Я ещё не пишу́ по-англи́йски.

U N I T 8

НА́ША СЕМЬЯ́

Сего́дня вся семья́ до́ма. Вот оте́ц. Он чита́ет газе́ту. Мать сиди́т на дива́не и чита́ет журна́л.

Мой оте́ц до́ктор. Он рабо́тает весь день, а ве́чером отдыха́ет. Мать учи́тельница, но она́ рабо́тает то́лько у́тром. А я ничего́ не де́лаю, потому́ что я не люблю́ рабо́тать.

Бори́с, мой ма́ленький брат, игра́ет с соба́кой. Ма́ша, моя́ сестра́, даёт соба́ке шокола́д. Оте́ц говори́т, что э́то не хорошо́, но на́ша соба́ка о́чень лю́бит шокола́д.

Слова́рь (Vocabulary)

на́ша (*f.*) our
семья́ (*f.*) family (see ¶ 10-B)
весь, вся, всё (*pr.* **фся, фсё**; see ¶ 8-D) entire, whole
оте́ц father
мать (*f.*) mother
сиде́ть (**II**); **сижу́, сиди́шь, сидя́т** to sit
дива́н divan — Sofa
до́ктор doctor
день (*m.*) day
весь день the whole day, all day
ве́чером in the evening
отдыха́ть (**I**); **отдыха́ю, -ешь, -ют** to rest
у́тром in the morning
де́лать (**I**); **де́лаю, -ешь, -ют** to do
я не люблю́ рабо́тать I do not like to work
люби́ть (**II**); **люблю́, лю́бишь, лю́бят** to love, to like
Бори́с Boris
ма́ленький, -ая, -ое (see ¶ 7-B) little, small
брат brother
игра́ть (**I**); **игра́ю, -ешь, -ют** to play

с (*with instr.*) with
соба́ка dog
с соба́кой with the dog
Ма́ша Masha
сестра́ sister
дава́ть (I); **даю́, даёшь, даю́т** to give
соба́ке (*dat.*) to the dog
наш, на́ша, на́ше our
шокола́д (*pr.* **шокола́т**; see ¶3-B) chocolate

СЕМЬЯ́ ЖИВЁТ В ДЕРЕ́ВНЕ (Разгово́р)

— Где вы рабо́таете? — Я рабо́таю в го́роде.

— А где вы живёте? — Я живу́ в дере́вне.

— Вы рабо́таете в го́роде, но живёте в дере́вне. Почему́ вы не живёте в го́роде?

— Потому́ что я о́чень люблю́ дере́вню. Там всегда́ ти́хо и я хорошо́ отдыха́ю по́сле рабо́ты.

— Ва́ша семья́ то́же живёт в дере́вне?

— Да, вся на́ша семья́ живёт в дере́вне.

— Что де́лает ва́ша мать? Она́ то́же рабо́тает?

— Да, она́ рабо́тает в магази́не, когда́ она́ здоро́ва.

— А где рабо́тает ва́ша сестра́?

— Она́ нигде́ не рабо́тает.

— Она́ то́лько тепе́рь не рабо́тает?

— О нет! Она́ никогда́ не рабо́тает и всегда́ сиди́т до́ма.

— Что же она́ де́лает до́ма?

— Она́ игра́ет с соба́кой, и́ли сиди́т на дива́не и ничего́ не де́лает.

Слова́рь (Vocabulary)

жить (I); **живу́, живёшь, живу́т** to live, to dwell
дере́вня (*f.*) (*acc.* **дере́вню**) village, country
го́род (*pr.* **го́рот**) town
ти́хо quiet
по́сле (*with gen.*) after
рабо́та work
магази́н store
когда́ when
нигде́ nowhere
она́ нигде́ не рабо́тает she works nowhere, she does not work anywhere
никогда́ never
сиде́ть до́ма to stay home
же (*emphatic*) then, but
что же what then

Произношéние (Pronunciation)

Study the following rules, then practice the phonetic drill at the end of this unit.

8-A. Prepositions

Prepositions consisting of a single consonant, such as **в** (*in*) and **с** (*with*), are pronounced as part of the following word. For example:

в‿кóмнате	*fkómnate*	(in the room)
с‿собáкой	*ssobákoy*	(with the dog)

8-B. Hard and Soft Consonants

a. Pronounce the English words *do* and *dew*, or *pooh* and *pew*, and note the differences. The *d* in *do* or the *p* in *pooh* are hard, whereas in *dew* and *pew* they are soft.

b. A hard vowel (**а, э, о, у,** or **ы**) indicates that the preceding consonant is to be pronounced *hard*. For example:

нáша	(*n*asha)
шкóла	(sh*k*o*l*a)

c. The **ь** (the soft sign) or a soft vowel (**я, е, ё, ю,** or **и**) indicates that the preceding consonant is to be pronounced *soft*. For example:

сегóдня	(sevod*n͡ia*)—no **y** sound. **н** softened
студéнт	(stud*i͡e*nt)—no **y** sound. **д** softened
день	(dye*n*') (*cf.* **н** with *n* in *onion*)
читáть	(cheeta*t*')

Note: **Я** is pronounced **ya** and **e** is pronounced **ye** only at the beginning of a word or at the beginning of a syllable (see ¶**4-A** and **10-A**). Here the *î* is used only as a symbol to indicate the softness of the preceding consonant. Therefore do not insert any **y** sound in pronouncing soft consonants.

8-C. Hard Consonants: ж, ш, and ц

a. The consonants **ж, ш,** and **ц** are always hard. Therefore, they can never be followed by a soft vowel sound.

b. When a soft vowel follows a hard consonant, it is pronounced like its corresponding hard sound. For example:

жить	is pronounced	жыть
центр	is pronounced	цэнтр
машúна	is pronounced	машы́на

8-D. The Diaeresis

A stressed **e** often becomes **ё**. In such cases, the *diaeresis* (the two dots over the **e**) indicates the stress, and the accent mark is not used.

Грамма́тика (Grammar)

8-1. Typical Irregularities in the Present Tense

The following verbs contain some typical irregularities in the present tense. Memorize them carefully, noting the exceptions.

a. Infinitive: **сиде́ть** (II) *to sit*

я сижу́	мы сиди́м
ты сиди́шь	вы сиди́те
он сиди́т	они́ сидя́т

Note: **д** changes to **ж** in the first person singular. Remember that the *second person singular* regularly determines the inflection pattern of the present tense.

b. Infinitive: **люби́ть** (II) *to love, to like*

я люблю́	мы лю́бим
ты лю́бишь	вы лю́бите
он лю́бит	они́ лю́бят

Note: **л** is inserted in the first person singular, and the stress falls on the ending; in all other persons, the stress falls on the stem vowel.

c. Infinitive: **дава́ть** (I) *to give*

я даю́	мы даём
ты даёшь	вы даёте
он даёт	они́ даю́т

Note: In the present stem, the syllable **ва** of the infinitive disappears. The **e** in the personal endings changes to **ё** and is stressed.

d. Infinitive: **жить** (I) *to live*

я живу́	мы живём
ты живёшь	вы живёте
он живёт	они́ живу́т

Note: The letter **в** is inserted after the infinitive stem, and **e** changes to **ё** in the personal endings.

8-2. The Instrumental Case with the Preposition c *

a. When used with the preposition **c**, the instrumental case often indicates association or mutual participation, and means *with, together with, along with.* For example:

Я живу́ с сестро́й в дере́вне.   I live with my sister in the country.
Я говорю́ по-ру́сски с бра́том.   I speak Russian with my brother.

b. With whom? is translated **c кем?**

С кем вы живёте?   With whom do you live?

8-3. The Dative Case

a. The dative in Russian expresses the *indirect object.*   It answers the question **кому́** (*to whom*) or **чему́** (*to what*).

b. The case ending performs the same function as does the preposition *to* in English.   For example:

Ма́ша даёт бра́ту кни́гу.   Masha is giving a book *to* her brother.
Кому́ она́ даёт кни́гу?   *To* whom is she giving a book?

c. Formation of the dative singular.

1. *Masculine* nouns ending in a *consonant* add **y** to form the dative:

nom.	стул	стол	брат
dat.	сту́лу	столу́	бра́ту

2. *Neuter* nouns ending in **-o** change **-o** to **-y**:

nom.	перо́	окно́
dat.	перу́	окну́

3. *Feminine* nouns ending in **-a** change **-a** to **-e**:

nom.	ка́рта	Москва́
dat.	ка́рте	Москве́

Упражне́ния (Exercises)

A. Put the English words in the *dative* and the Russian words in parentheses in the *accusative.*

1. Я даю́ *brother* (кни́га).   2. Ты даёшь *Mr.* Петро́ву (ла́мпа).
3. Он даёт *sister* (ка́рта).   4. Мы даём *dog* (шокола́д).   5. Вы даёте *pupil* (стул).   6. Они́ даю́т *doctor* (карти́на).

* See also ¶ 5-5.

B. Supply the proper equivalents for the words in parentheses.

1. Я живу́ (at home). 2. Ты живёшь в (town). 3. На́ша семья́ (lives) в (the country). 4. Мы (do not live) тут. 5. Вы всегда́ (live) с (sister). 6. Господи́н Петро́в и госпожа́ Петро́ва (live) в (Stalingrad).

C. Supply the personal verb endings and give the proper case endings to the words in parentheses. Indicate accents.

1. Я никогда́ не сиж_____ на (стул). 2. Ты говор_____ с (брат) и с (сестра). 3. Они́ сто_____ о́коло (диван). 4. Вы никогда́ не отдыха_____ по́сле (работа). 5. В (деревня) о́чень ти́хо. 6. Что ва́ша мать дела_____ весь день? 7. Он зна_____, что госпожа́ Ивано́ва сид_____ до́ма ве́чером? 8. Почему́ Ма́ша да_____ (собака) шокола́д? 9. Моя́ ма́ленькая сестра́ нигде́ не работа_____. 10. Когда́ я в (город), я работа_____ в (магазин).

Перево́д (Translation)

Omit the words in parentheses and include those in brackets.

1. I work in a store. 2. The store is in town, but I live in the country. 3. My whole [вся моя́] family lives in the country. 4. After work I do nothing. 5. I stay home and rest. 6. I never read anything [I never nothing not read] when I am home. 7. I only play with the dog. 8. My sister Vera does not work anywhere. 9. She does not like to work. 10. But she likes to read, and reads all day. 11. My father is a doctor and works in the morning. 12. In the evening he is always reading or writing. 13. Mother likes to sit on the divan when she is resting. 14. The dog is always near the divan when mother is in the room. 15. Mother likes the dog, and the dog knows it.

Вопро́сы (Questions)

1. С кем сестра́ игра́ет? 2. Что ещё она́ де́лает? 3. Почему́ брат ничего́ не де́лает? 4. Где мать рабо́тает? 5. Когда́ она́ не рабо́тает? 6. Где живёт ва́ша семья́? 7. Почему́ она́ живёт в дере́вне, а не в го́роде? 8. Что де́лает ваш ма́ленький брат Бори́с? 9. Что вы де́лаете ве́чером по́сле рабо́ты? 10. Почему́ соба́ка стои́т о́коло дива́на, когда́ мать сиди́т на дива́не? 11. Кому́ Бори́с даёт шокола́д? 12. Вы живёте с ссстро́й и́ли с бра́том? 13. Почему́ ва́ша сестра́ Ма́ша ещё не

говори́т по-ру́сски?   14. Вы всегда́ рабо́таете, когда́ же вы отдыха́ете?   15. До́ктор зна́ет, что вы не отдыха́ете?   16. Что же он говори́т?

Phonetic Drill

Listen to the teacher (or the tape) and repeat several times the following syllables, words, and phrases.

1. Study ¶3-C and 8-A.

   a. В кни́ге, в журна́ле, в газе́те, в ко́мнате, в кла́ссе, в магази́не, в дере́вне, в го́роде, в Москве́, в Волгогра́де.

   b. С соба́кой, с отцо́м, с сестро́й, с учи́телем, с профе́ссором, с Ива́ном, с Ве́рой, с А́нной, с ученико́м, с ма́мой.

2. Study ¶8-B and 8-D.

   a. Syllables:

   ва-вя; во-вё; да-дя; ла-ля; ло-лё; лу-лю; ма-мя; мо-мё; му-мю; но-нё; на-ня; вэ-ве; дэ-де; лэ-ле; мэ-ме; тэ-те; ту-тю; та-тя.

   b. Words:

   лес, нет, газе́та, Ве́ра, мел, ме́дленно, дверь, мать, дива́н, чита́ть, писа́ть, игра́ть, тепе́рь, стоя́ть, де́лать, люблю́, ма́ленький, большо́й, день, тень.

3. Study ¶8-C.

   цирк, ци́фра, центр, офице́р, инжене́р, на́ция, револю́ция.

Pattern Drills

A. Study ¶8-1, 8-2, and 8-3. The following pattern drills combine the use of the *dative* and the *instrumental* case with four basic verbs.

   1. Listen to the teacher (or the tape) and repeat the following sentences. Then read each sentence substituting **брат** for **сестра́**.

Teacher	*Student*
Я сижу́ с сестро́й на дива́не.	Я сижу́ с бра́том на дива́не.
Ты сиди́шь ⸻.	Ты ⸻.
Он сиди́т ⸻.	Он ⸻.

Мы сиди́м _____.   Мы _____.
Вы сиди́те _____.   Вы _____.
Они́ сидя́т _____.   Они́ _____.

 2. Note the second meaning of **сиде́ть**, *to stay*.

Teacher   *Student*

Я всегда́ сижу́ до́ма.   Я никогда́ не сижу́ до́ма.
Ты всегда́ сиди́шь до́ма.   Ты _____.
Он всегда́ сиди́т до́ма.   Он _____.
Мы всегда́ сиди́м до́ма.   Мы _____.
Вы всегда́ сиди́те до́ма.   Вы _____.
Они́ всегда́ сидя́т до́ма.   Они́ _____.

Teacher   *Student*

Я люблю́ жить в дере́вне.   Я не люблю́ жить в го́роде.
Ты лю́бишь_____.   Ты _____.
Он лю́бит _____.   Он _____.
Мы лю́бим _____.   Мы _____.
Вы лю́бите _____.   Вы _____.
Они́ лю́бят _____.   Они́ _____.

Я живу́ с Ве́рой в Москве́.   Я живу́ с Бори́сом в Волгогра́де.
Ты живёшь _____.   Ты _____.
Он живёт _____.   Он _____.
Мы живём _____.   Мы _____.
Вы живёте _____.   Вы _____.
Они́ живу́т _____.   Они́ _____.

Я даю́ бра́ту шокола́д.   Я даю́ сестре́ шокола́д.
Ты даёшь _____ кни́гу.   Ты _____ кни́гу.
Он даёт _____ журна́л.   Он _____ журна́л.
Мы даём _____ карти́ну.   Мы _____ карти́ну.
Вы даёте _____ газе́ту.   Вы _____ газе́ту.
Они́ даю́т _____ бума́гу.   Они́ _____ бума́гу.

B. Drill on the following pattern sentences.

 1. Я не живу́ с Ве́рой, а живу́ с А́нной.
 2. Я не живу́ с Бори́сом, а живу́ с Ива́ном.
 3. Я не рабо́таю до́ма, а рабо́таю в магази́не.

C. Drill on the use and position of *negative adverbs* with verbs
in the *negative*.

Teacher	*Student*
1. Я никогда́ не рабо́таю.	Я нигде́ не рабо́таю.
Ты _____ рабо́таешь.	Ты _____.
Он _____ рабо́тает.	Он _____.
Мы _____ рабо́таем.	Мы _____.
Вы _____ рабо́таете.	Вы _____.
Они́ _____ рабо́тают.	Они́ _____.
2. Я никогда́ не отдыха́ю.	Я нигде́ не отдыха́ю.

UNIT 9

I

Я ПРЕДПОЧИТА́Ю ЖИТЬ В ГО́РОДЕ

Я живу́ и рабо́таю в го́роде. У меня́ там ма́ленькая, некраси́-
вая ко́мната. Пол в ко́мнате но́вый, но потоло́к о́чень ста́рый.

В ко́мнате у меня́ то́лько оди́н большо́й стол, два кре́сла и три
сту́ла. Больша́я ла́мпа стои́т на полу́ о́коло окна́. О́чень
ма́ленькая, ста́рая и некраси́вая ла́мпа стои́т на столе́. Тепе́рь
у меня́ есть но́вый дива́н, и я всегда́ предпочита́ю сиде́ть на
дива́не. Мой оте́ц не понима́ет, почему́ я хочу́ жить в го́роде.

Слова́рь (Vocabulary)

предпочита́ть (I); предпочита́ю, -ешь, -ют to prefer
у (*with gen.*) by, at
у меня́ I have (*lit.* by me)
у меня́ есть I have, I do have (*lit.* by me there is)
некраси́вый, -ая, -ое unattractive, ugly
пол floor
потоло́кᴧ ★ (*gen.* **потолка́**) ceiling (see ¶ 9-5)
ста́рый, -ая, -ое old
большо́й, больша́я, большо́е big
два (*m. & n.*) two
кре́сло armchair
три (*m., f., & n.*) three
на полу́ (*irr. prep. of* **пол**) on the floor
хоте́ть (*irr.*); **хочу́, хо́чешь, хотя́т** to want, wish (see ¶ 9-4)

★ The symbol ᴧ after a word in the Vocabulary indicates that the last **e** or **o**
of the stem is dropped when the noun is declined.

II

Я ПРЕДПОЧИТА́Ю ЖИТЬ В ГО́РОДЕ (Continued)

У отца́ о́чень большо́й дом в дере́вне. В до́ме отца́ у меня́ больша́я и краси́вая ко́мната. Но я там никогда́ не могу́ рабо́тать, и́ли отдыха́ть.

У отца́ в до́ме живу́т: моя́ сестра́ Ка́тя и её муж Пе́тя, мой брат Фе́дя и его́ жена́ На́дя, дя́дя Ва́ня и тётя Та́ня. Де́душка и ба́бушка то́же живу́т у нас. Все говоря́т о́чень гро́мко и я никогда́ не могу́ чита́ть, рабо́тать и́ли отдыха́ть. Но оте́ц не понима́ет, почему́ я не хочу́ жить у него́ в дере́вне.

Слова́рь (Vocabulary)

оте́ц[fl] (*gen.* **отца́**) father (see **¶9-5**)
у отца́ father has
дом house
мочь (I); могу́, мо́жешь, мо́гут to be able to, to be in a position to
Ка́тя (*f.*) Katya
её her
муж (*pr.* **муш**) husband (see **¶9-A**)
Пе́тя (*m.*) Petya
Фе́дя (*m.*) Fedya
его́ (*pr.* **ево́**) his
жена́ wife
На́дя (*f.*) Nadya
дя́дя (*m.*) uncle
Ва́ня (*m.*) Vanya
тётя (*f.*) aunt
Та́ня (*f.*) Tanya
де́душка (*m.*) grandfather
ба́бушка grandmother
у нас at our house
все all, everybody
гро́мко loudly
у него́ (*pr.* **у нево́**) **в дере́вне** at his home in the village

Произноше́ние (Pronunciation)

Study the following rules, then practice the phonetic drill at the end of this unit.

9-A. Voiced and Voiceless Consonants

a. Pronounce the sound **ш**; then without changing the position of your tongue or lips, pronounce the sound **ж**. You will note that when you pronounce the **ж**, something vibrates in your throat. It is the vocal cords which produce the voice. Hence the **ж** is a *voiced consonant.* When you pronounce **ш**, the vocal cords remain inactive; that is, the **ш** is uttered by means of the breath, without participation of the voice. The **ш** is therefore a *voiceless consonant.*

b. For the sake of accurate pronunciation and spelling, it is important to remember the following *voiced* and *voiceless* consonants in pairs:

Voiced:	**б**	**в**	**г**	**д**	**ж**	**з**
Voiceless:	**п**	**ф**	**к**	**т**	**ш**	**с**

c. Under certain circumstances, voiced consonants are pronounced like the corresponding voiceless ones:

1. At the end of a word. For example:

клу**б**	(*club*)	is pronounced клу**п**
здоро́**в**	(*well*)	is pronounced здоро́**ф**
дру**г**	(*friend*)	is pronounced дру**к**
го**д**	(*year*)	is pronounced го**т**
му**ж**	(*husband*)	is pronounced му**ш**
гла**з**	(*eye*)	is pronounced гла**с**

2. When a voiced consonant precedes a voiceless one. For example:

всегда́	(*always*)	is pronounced **ф**сегда́
второ́й	(*second*)	is pronounced **ф**торо́й
во́**д**ка	(*vodka*)	is pronounced во́**т**ка
ска́**з**ка	(*tale*)	is pronounced ска́**с**ка
ло́**ж**ка	(*spoon*)	is pronounced ло́**ш**ка
тру́**б**ка	(*pipe*)	is pronounced тру́**п**ка

Грамма́тика (Grammar)

Part I

9-1. Personal Pronouns in the Genitive and Accusative

The personal pronouns in their various cases are used to form important idiomatic expressions. Therefore, learn the following inflections:

SINGULAR

nom.	я	ты	он	она́	оно́
gen.	меня́	тебя́	его́	её	его́
acc.	меня́	тебя́	его́	её	его́

PLURAL

nom.	мы	вы	они́
gen.	нас	вас	их
acc.	нас	вас	их

9-2. Possessive Phrases

a. **у**+*pronoun* or *noun* in the *genitive.*

1. The verb *to have* is most frequently rendered in Russian by the preposition **у**+*pronoun* or *noun* in the *genitive*:

у меня́	I have	у нас	we have
у тебя́	you have	у вас	you have
у него́★	he has	у них★	they have
у неё★	she has		

у отца́	father has
у сестры́	sister has
у О́льги	Olga has

2. *At the home of* is also rendered by the preposition **у** + *pronoun* or *noun* in the *genitive*:

Дéдушка живёт **у меня́**.	Grandfather is living at my home (house).
Дя́дя живёт **у тебя́**.	Uncle is living at your home (house).
Мы живём **у них**.	We live at their home.
Мой муж **у вас**?	Is my husband at your house?
Нет, он **у сестры́**.	No, he is at his sister's house.

3. The above construction is also used in place of possessives like **мой, ваш**, etc.:

У меня́ в ко́мнате большо́й стол.	In *my* room there is a big table.
у отца́ в до́ме	in *father's* house

4. **У кого́?** means *who has?* or *at whose house?*:

У кого́ моё перо́?	*Who has* my pen?
У кого́ живёт учи́тель?	*At whose house* does the teacher live?

★ Pronouns of the third person take the prefix **н-** when they are governed by a preposition.

b. **y** + *pronoun* or *noun* in the *genitive* + **есть.**

1. To emphasize possession in the sense of right to make use of an object, **есть** (third person singular of **быть**, *to be*, in the present) is added.   Compare:

У когó дéньги?	Who has *the* money? (In whose safekeeping is it? The banker may have it, but he cannot spend it.)
У когó **есть** дéньги?	Who has some money (to spend)?
У когó автомобúль?	Who has *the* automobile? (In whose care is it at present? The garageman may have it, but only to grease it or fix it.)
У когó **есть** автомобúль?	Who has *an* automobile? (*I.e.,* to drive. Right to use the car is here implied.)

2. **Есть** is also used in questions and answers:

У вас **есть** кóмната?	Have you a room?
Да, **есть.**	Yes, I have.

9-3. The Genitive with два, три, and четы́ре

After **два, три,** and **четы́ре** (four), the noun is in the genitive singular, not in the nominative plural.   **Два** is the form for the masculine and neuter, and **две** for the feminine.

два стýла	two chairs (*lit.* two of a chair)
два крéсла	two armchairs
две кнúги	two books
три столá	three tables
четы́ре дéвушки	four girls

9-4. Infinitive: хотéть (*irr.*) *to want, to wish*

PRESENT TENSE

я хочý	мы хотúм
ты хóчешь	вы хотúте
он хóчет	онú хотя́т

Note: In the singular, the endings are those of Conjugation I; in the plural, those of Conjugation II.

Part II

9-5. Fleeting "o" or "e"

Many masculine nouns ending in **-ок, -ец,** or **-ень** drop the **o** or **e** when declined.   For example:

nom.	потоло́к	оте́ц	день
gen.	потолка́	отца́	дня
dat.	потолку́	отцу́	дню

9-6. Infinitive: мочь (I) *to be able (physically), to be in a position to*

PRESENT TENSE

я могу́	мы мо́жем
ты мо́жешь	вы мо́жете
он мо́жет	они́ мо́гут

9-7. Omission of the Possessive

When reference is to close members of the family, possessives like **мой, наш,** and **ваш** can be omitted.   For example:

Оте́ц не понима́ет, почему́ я не хочу́ жить у него́.
My father does not understand why I do not want to live at his house.

Упражне́ния (Exercises)

A. Translate.

1. I do not want to work.   2. You do not want to stay home. 3. He does not want to stand on the floor.   4. We do not want to read anything.   5. You do not want to live in town.   6. They do not want to live at his house; at her house; at their (somebody else's) house.

B. Translate the above sentences, substituting **мочь** for **хоте́ть.**

C. Replace the English words in parentheses with the appropriate expressions of possession, and supply the proper case endings for the Russian words in parentheses.   Include words in brackets.

1. (I have) в ко́мнате три (кре́сло).   2. (My sister has) в до́ме четы́ре (дива́н).   3. Мой дя́дя живёт (at our house). 4. Мы живём (at their house).   5. Её муж тепе́рь (at father's

house). 6. (Who has the) соба́ка? 7. (Who has a) [есть] соба́ка?
8. (Who has the) газе́та? 9. (Who has a) [есть] газе́та? 10. Две
(кни́га) у меня́ на столе́. 11. Кни́га (is on his table). 12. (Father
has a) дива́н. 13. Его́ жена́ (is at your house). 14. Её сестра́
(is at father's house).

D. Supply the proper form (in the present tense) of the verbs in
parentheses, and fill in the blanks with a suitable word.

1. Я (мочь) рабо́тать _____, но не (хоте́ть). 2. Ты
о́чень _____ (понима́ть) по-ру́сски, но не (хоте́ть)
говори́ть. 3. Он (мочь) говори́ть, но не (хоте́ть). 4. Все
студе́нты (писа́ть) по-англи́йски на _____. 5. Все
(дава́ть) соба́ке _____. 6. Дя́дя и тётя (говори́ть)
о́чень гро́мко в _____. 7. Мы (предпочита́ть) жить
в _____. 8. Моя́ жена́ (предпочита́ть) сиде́ть _____.
9. Больша́я ла́мпа (стоя́ть) на _____. 10. Мать всегда́
(сиде́ть) на _____, когда́ она́ чита́ет.

Перево́д (Translation)

Omit words in parentheses and include those in brackets.

1. Katya is at grandfather's. 2. Vanya is at (his) brother's.
3. My wife is at (her) sister's. 4. Only I am home. 5. Grandfather and grandmother, uncle Fedya and aunt Tanya are now in the
country. 6. When everybody [all] is home, they talk very loudly
and I cannot work. 7. When it is quiet in the house, I like to sit
on the divan and read. 8. My dog always sits on the floor near the
armchair. 9. The dog is very ugly, but I love her [её] and she
also loves me [меня́]. 10. I have a big room. 11. The ceiling in
the room is old and the floor is also old, but the room is very
beautiful. 12. There are two divans and three armchairs in my
room [by me in the room]. 13. Why do you not play with the dog?
14. I prefer to play with (my) brother and [with] sister. 15. (My)
mother does not understand why I prefer to live in town.

Вопро́сы (Questions)

1. Где вы живёте? 2. У вас там больша́я и́ли ма́ленькая
ко́мната? 3. Пол у вас но́вый и́ли ста́рый? 4. А потоло́к
то́же но́вый? 5. У вас в ко́мнате два и́ли три кре́сла? 6. Где
стои́т больша́я ла́мпа? 7. А где стои́т ма́ленькая ла́мпа?

8. Большáя лáмпа красúвая úли некрасúвая? 9. Где вы предпочитáете сидéть, когдá вы дóма? 10. Отéц понимáет, почемý вы не хотúте жить в гóроде? 11. Кто живёт у отцá? 12. Почемý вы не мóжете отдыхáть в дóме отцá?

Phonetic Drill

Study ¶9-A. Listen carefully to the teacher (or the tape) and repeat several times the following words.

хлеб, сад, рад, шоколáд, гарáж, этáж, раз, без, из, лóвко, блúзко, францýзский, зáвтра, зáвтрак, снег, всюду, Кúев, трýбка, прóбка, вдруг, скáзка, зуб, рукáв, встрéча, стóрож.

Pattern Drills

Note: The possessive phrases in ¶9-2 vary in meaning, depending upon the word order and other words in the sentence.

A. Study ¶9-2*a*.ɪ. Listen to the teacher (or the tape) and repeat several times the following possessive phrases.

Teacher		*Student*	
У меня	I have	У меня	I have
у тебя	you have	у тебя	you have
у негó	he has	у негó	he has
у неё	she has	у неё	she has
у нас	we have	у нас	we have
у вас	you have	у вас	you have
у них	they have	у них	they have

B. Study ¶9-2*b*.ɪ. Then do the following question-and-answer drills on possessive phrases meaning I *have a* . . . .

1. Listen to the teacher (or the tape) and repeat the following questions. Then answer each question according to the models in the "Student" column.

Teacher	*Student*
У когó **есть** кáрта?	У меня **есть** кáрта.
Who has *a* map?	I have *a* map.
У когó **есть** лáмпа?	У тебя **есть** лáмпа.
_____ крéсло?	У негó **есть** крéсло.
_____ журнáл?	У неё **есть** журнáл.
_____ карандáш?	У нас **есть** карандáш.

———————— картина?   У вас **есть** картина.
———————— бумага?   У них **есть** бумага.

2. Answer the above questions varying the possessive phrases in your answers.   For example, instead of **у меня есть** say **у него есть** or **у них есть**, etc.

C. Study **¶9-2b.1**.   Then do the following drills on possessive phrases meaning "I have *the . . . .*"

1. Follow the instructions in B.1 above and note the different meanings of **у меня есть** . . . ("I have *a . . .*") and **у меня** . . . ("I have *the . . .*") and the different word order in the answers.

Teacher	*Student*
У кого карта?	Карта у меня.
Who has *the* map?	I have *the* map.
У кого лампа?	Лампа у тебя.
Who has *the* lamp?	You have *the* lamp.
——— кресло?	Кресло у него.
——— журнал?	Журнал у неё.
——— карандаш?	Карандаш у нас.
——— картина?	Картина у вас.
——— бумага?	Бумага у них.

2. Answer the questions in C.1 above, varying the possessive phrases in the answers.   For example, instead of **карта у меня** say **карта у неё** or **карта у нас**, etc.

D. Study **¶9-2a.2**.   Then do the following question-and-answer drills on possessive phrases meaning "at the home of . . . ."

1. Listen to the teacher (or the tape) and repeat the following questions.   Then answer the questions according to the models in the "Student" column.

Teacher	*Student*
У кого живёт учитель?	Он живёт **у меня**.
At whose house does the teacher live?	He lives *at my house*.
У кого работает Вера?	Она работает **у тебя**.
У кого отдыхает дядя?	——————— **у него**.
У кого живёт дедушка?	——————— **у неё**.
У кого живут студенты?	Они——————— **у нас**.
У кого работают Вера и Иван?	——————— **у вас**.
У кого отдыхают муж и жена?	——————— **у них**.

2. Answer the questions in D.1 replacing pronouns with nouns designating persons, as in the following models.

Учи́тель живёт у отца́.
Ве́ра рабо́тает у де́душки.
——————— у бра́та.
——————— у сестры́.
——————— у профе́ссора.
——————— у А́нны.
——————— у ба́бушки.

E. Study ¶9-4. Listen to the teacher (or the tape) and repeat the following sentences. Then read each sentence in the negative.

Teacher	*Student*
Я хочу́ чита́ть.	Я не хочу́ чита́ть.
Ты хо́чешь писа́ть.	Ты не хо́чешь писа́ть.
Он хо́чет рабо́тать.	Он не ———————.
Мы хоти́м отдыха́ть.	Мы не ———————.
Вы хоти́те игра́ть.	Вы не ———————.
Они́ хотя́т сиде́ть.	Они́ не ———————.

F. Listen to the teacher (or the tape) and repeat the following sentences. Then read each sentence in the negative.

Teacher	*Student*
Я могу́ чита́ть.	Я не могу́ чита́ть.
Ты мо́жешь писа́ть.	Ты не мо́жешь писа́ть.
Он мо́жет рабо́тать.	Он не ———————.
Мы мо́жем отдыха́ть.	Мы не ———————.
Вы мо́жете игра́ть.	Вы не ———————.
Они́ мо́гут сиде́ть.	Они́ не ———————.

UNIT 10

I

УРÓК

У нас тепéрь рýсский урóк. Мы изучáем рýсский язы́к. Учи́тель спрáшивает, а мы отвечáем. Мы все сегóдня отвечáем хорошó, потомý что урóк óчень интерéсный.

Учи́тель спрáшивает Ивáна: — Ивáн, когдá говорят «дóброе ýтро»?

Ивáн отвечáет: — «Дóброе ýтро» говорят ýтром.

— А когдá говорят «дóбрый день»?

— Днём говорят «дóбрый день».

Потóм учи́тель спрáшивает Вéру: — Вéра, что говорят вéчером?

Вéра хорошó знáет урóк и онá отвечáет: — Вéчером говорят «дóбрый вéчер».

— А когдá говорят «здрáвствуйте»?

— «Здрáвствуйте» говорят и ýтром, и днём, и вéчером и нóчью.

Вчерá Вéра тóже знáла урóк. Онá всегдá знáет урóк.

Словáрь (Vocabulary)

урóк lesson
изучáть (I); изучáю, -ешь, -ют to study (see ¶ 10-1)
язы́к language
рýсский язы́к Russian (see ¶ 10-2)
спрáшивать (I); спрáшиваю, -ешь, -ют to ask (questions) (used with *acc.* of person asked)

75

отвеча́ть (I); **отвеча́ю, -ешь, -ют** to answer
интере́сный, -ая, -ое interesting
Ива́на *acc. of* **Ива́н**
говоря́т one says, people say
до́брый, -ая, -ое good, kind
у́тро morning
до́брое у́тро good morning
днём in the daytime
пото́м then, afterwards
ве́чер evening
здра́вствуйте (*pr.* **здра́ствуйте**) how do you do?   hello!
и . . . и both . . . and
но́чью at night
вчера́ (*pr.* **фчера́**) yesterday
зна́ла (*f.*) knew

II

3 ques & answer

УРО́К (Continued)

Trans in English

Учи́тель пото́м спра́шивает Бори́са: — Бори́с, что вы гово-
ри́те хозя́йке до́ма, когда́ вы идёте домо́й?

Бори́с отвеча́ет: — Я говорю́ хозя́йке: «Я о́чень не хочу́
идти́ домо́й, но уже́ по́здно.»

— А что говори́т хозя́ин до́ма, е́сли вы до́лго сиди́те у них?

— Хозя́ин говори́т: «Вы мно́го рабо́тали сего́дня, и за́втра у
вас та́кже мно́го рабо́ты.» А я отвеча́ю хозя́ину: «Да, я
сего́дня мно́го рабо́тал, и за́втра у меня́ мно́го рабо́ты, но я
лу́чше рабо́таю, когда́ ма́ло сплю.»

Слова́рь (Vocabulary)

хозя́йка owner, mistress, hostess
хозя́йке до́ма to the hostess (to the owner of the house)
идти́ (I); **иду́, идёшь, иду́т** to go, to walk (see ¶ 10-7)
домо́й home, homeward (see ¶ 10-6)
о́чень не хочу́ идти́ домо́й I hate to go home
по́здно late
хозя́ин owner, master, host
е́сли if (**е́сли** never means *whether*)
до́лго (*adv.*) for a long time
вы рабо́тали you worked
за́втра tomorrow
мно́го рабо́ты much work (see ¶ 10-9)
лу́чше better
спать (II); **сплю, спишь, спят** to sleep

уже — already

Произношéние (Pronunciation)

Study the following rules, then practice the phonetic drill at the end of this unit.

10-A. Stressed and Unstressed "я"

a. Stressed **я** is pronounced like *ya* in *yard*, only shorter.

b. Unstressed **я** is pronounced very much like the Russian unstressed **е**. Thus, the **я** in **язы́к** sounds like the *ye* in *year*.

10-B. Separation Signs: "ь" and "ъ"

a. We have seen that a single consonant between two vowels is pronounced with the following vowel (see ¶ 2-B c-3). However, when **ь** or **ъ** is inserted between the consonant and the vowel, the latter becomes separated from the consonant and is pronounced as if it were the first letter in the following syllable; i.e., the presence of the sound **й** (as the English *y* in *yes*) is thus indicated, and

$$\text{ь} + \begin{cases} \text{е} \\ \text{ё} \\ \text{я} \\ \text{ю} \end{cases} \; or \; \text{ъ} + \begin{cases} \text{е} \\ \text{ё} \\ \text{я} \\ \text{ю} \end{cases} \; sound \; like \; \begin{cases} \text{йе} \\ \text{йё} \\ \text{йя} \\ \text{йу} \end{cases}$$

For example:

отъ - éзд	(ot-*yé*zt)
объ - яс - ня́ть	(ob-*yas*-niát')
семь - я́	(sem-*yá*)
ночь - ю	(nóch-*yu*)

b. The **ь** can indicate both softness of the preceding consonant and its separation from the following vowel. For example, the **м** in семь - я́ and the **т** in Тать - я́ - на are both soft and separated from the vowels that follow them.

Phonetic Drill. Pronounce the following words aloud:

Пять — пья́ница; се́мя — семья́; нюа́нс — о́сенью; тётя — статья́; Ко́ля — ко́лья; чей — чьей; отéц — отъéзд; сел — съел; обеща́ть — объéхать; идём — подъём.

Грамма́тика (Grammar)

Part I

10-1. Infinitive: изуча́ть (I) *to study*

The infinitive **изуча́ть** means *to study* something which requires a period of concentration. For example:

Она **изуча́ет** матема́тику.   She *is studying* mathematics.
Мы **изуча́ем** ру́сский язы́к.   We *are studying* Russian.

The object of study must *always* be stated with **изуча́ть**.

10-2. Ру́сский язы́к

The adjective **ру́сский** cannot be used by itself to mean *Russian language*. The noun **язы́к** must therefore be added.

10-3. Accusative of Masculine Animate and Inanimate Nouns

a. Masculine and neuter inanimate nouns have the same endings in the accusative as in the nominative.

nom.	стол	перо́
acc.	стол	перо́

b. Masculine animate nouns that end with a consonant in the nominative have the same ending in the accusative as in the genitive.

nom.	до́ктор	оте́ц	Ива́н
gen.	до́ктора	отца́	Ива́на
acc.	до́ктора	отца́	Ива́на

10-4. Accusative of Masculine Nouns Ending in -a

Masculine nouns that end in **-a** in the nominative change **-a** to **-y** in the accusative, just like regular feminine nouns.

nom.	де́душка
acc.	де́душку

10-5. Impersonal Expressions

The impersonal idea of *one, they, people* is conveyed by the third person plural of the verb in the present tense without the personal pronoun **они́**. For example:

> **говоря́т**   one says, they say, it is said

Part II

10-6. Adverbs: до́ма and домо́й

До́ма and **домо́й** are adverbs that can both be translated as *home*. Note, however, the following distinction.

a. **Дóма** is used with verbs of rest and means *at home*:

    Я сижý **дóма**.   I am staying *home* (at home).

b. **Домóй** is used with verbs of motion and means *home, homeward*:

    Я идý **домóй**.   I am going *home* (homewards).

10-7. Infinitive: идтú (I) *to go, to walk*

This verb denotes motion *on foot*, never in a conveyance.

PRESENT TENSE

я идý	мы идём
ты идёшь	вы идёте
он идёт	они идýт

10-8. The Past Tense

a. The past tense of most verbs is formed by dropping the ending **-ть** from the infinitive and adding to the stem:

-л   for the masculine ⎫
-ла for the feminine ⎬ of all three persons in the singular
-ло for the neuter   ⎭

and **-ли** for any gender of all three persons in the plural.

b. Past tense of **читáть**.

	Singular			Plural
	m.	*f.*	*n.*	*m., f., n.*
я	читáл	читáла		мы читáли
ты	читáл	читáла		вы читáли
он	читáл			
онá		читáла		они читáли
онó			читáло	

c. Past tense of **говорúть**.

я	говорúл	говорúла		мы говорúли
ты	говорúл	говорúла		вы говорúли
он	говорúл			
онá		говорúла		они говорúли
онó			говорúло	

10-9. The Genitive with Adverbs of Quantity

After adverbs of quantity, the genitive is used:

У меня́ мно́го **рабо́ты**.   I have much work.
У Ве́ры ма́ло **рабо́ты**.   Vera has little work.

Упражне́ния (Exercises)

A. Fill in the blanks with appropriate words.

1. Мы изуча́ем англи́йский _____. 2. Уро́к о́чень
_____. 3. У́тром говоря́т _____. 4. Днём
говоря́т _____. 5. Ве́чером говоря́т _____.
6. У нас сего́дня _____ рабо́ты. 7. У _____
есть соба́ка? 8. В ко́мнате у меня́ _____ дива́н,
_____ сту́ла, и _____ кре́сла. 9. Ла́мпа стои́т
на _____ о́коло _____. 10. Мы не хоти́м жить
в _____. 11. Мы тепе́рь идём _____. 12.
Вы всегда́ сиди́те в _____. 13. Де́душка и ба́бушка
говоря́т о́чень _____. 14. Вы _____ сиди́те у
хозя́ина.

B. Supply the proper forms of the words in parentheses.

1. Они́ (жить) _____ в (дере́вня) _____. 2. Ты
(идти́) _____ домо́й. 3. Вы всегда́ (сиде́ть) _____
до́ма. 4. Она́ хорошо́ (отвеча́ть) _____ в
(класс) _____. 5. Учи́тельница (спра́шивать) _____,
а учени́ца (отвеча́ть) _____. 6. Она́ (спра́шивать)
_____ (Ива́н) _____, а пото́м (Ве́ра) _____.
7. Вы (дава́ть) _____ (учени́ца) _____ шокола́д.
8. Мы ма́ло (спать) _____ но́чью.

C. Write the following verbs in the past tense, using this form:

	SINGULAR	PLURAL
m.	я, ты, он игра́л	мы
f.	я, ты, она́ игра́ла	вы } игра́ли
n.	оно́ игра́ло	они́

1. изуча́ть	5. дава́ть	9. сиде́ть
2. спра́шивать	6. хоте́ть	10. стоя́ть
3. отвеча́ть	7. де́лать	11. люби́ть
4. игра́ть	8. писа́ть	12. понима́ть

D. Supply the accusative of the following nouns.

1. уро́к	5. Ива́н	9. сестра́
2. хозя́ин	6. Бори́с	10. муж
3. у́тро	7. оте́ц	11. де́душка
4. хозя́йка	8. брат	12. соба́ка

Перево́д (Translation)

Omit the words in parentheses and include those in brackets.

1. They are studying English [the English language].   2. Our lesson is very interesting.   3. We work long (for a long time) in the daytime.   4. The teacher is asking Ivan.   5. Ivan answers well. 6. I say "good day" to the hostess and "hello" to the host.   7. It is already late, but I do not want to go home.   8. I work better if I sleep a lot [much], but I cannot sleep.   9. Are you still [ещё] sleeping? It is already very late.   10. Of course [коне́чно (*pr.* коне́шно)] it is late, but I want to sleep.

Вопро́сы (Questions)

1. У нас тепе́рь ру́сский и́ли англи́йский уро́к?   2. Что вы изуча́ете?   3. Кто спра́шивает и кто отвеча́ет?   4. Почему́ все хорошо́ отвеча́ют сего́дня?   5. Кого́ (whom) учи́тель спра́шивает?   6. Почему́ он спра́шивает Ива́на, а не Ве́ру? 7. Когда́ говоря́т "до́брое у́тро"?   8. Когда́ говоря́т "до́брый день"?   9. Когда́ говоря́т "до́брый ве́чер"?   10. Когда́ говоря́т "здра́вствуйте"?   11. Вы мно́го рабо́тали сего́дня? 12. Вы хорошо́ спи́те но́чью?

Phonetic Drill

Study ¶10-A and 10-B.   Listen to the teacher (or the tape) and repeat several times the following words.

Пять — пья́ница; се́мя — семья́; нюа́нс — о́сенью; тётя — статья́.

Ко́ля — ко́лья; чей — чьей; оте́ц — отъе́зд; сел — съел. обеща́ть — объе́хать; идём — подъём.

Pattern Drills

A. 1. Study ¶10-1 and 10-2.   Listen to the teacher (or the tape) and repeat the following sentences.   Then conjugate изуча́ть, substituting ру́сский for англи́йский.

Teacher	*Student*
Я изучаю английский язык.	Я изучаю русский язык.
Ты изучаешь английский язык.	Ты изучаешь русский язык.
Он изучает _____.	Он _____.
Мы изучаем _____.	Мы_____.
Вы изучаете _____.	Вы _____.
Они изучают _____.	Они_____.

2. Conjugate **изучать** with **новый язык, интересный язык,** and **красивый язык.**

B. Master the vocabulary in Part I of this unit. Listen to the teacher (or the tape) and repeat the sentences below. Then read the sentences substituting the following feminine nouns for the masculine ones according to the models in the ''Student'' column: **Вера, студентка, ученица, жена.**

Teacher	*Student*
Я спрашиваю брата.	Я спрашиваю сестру.
Ты спрашиваешь хозяина.	Ты спрашиваешь хозяйку.
Он спрашивает Бориса.	Он _____.
Мы спрашиваем студента.	Мы_____.
Вы спрашиваете ученика.	Вы _____.
Они спрашивают мужа.	Они_____.

C. 1. Study ¶10-6 and 10-7. Listen to the teacher (or the tape) and repeat the following sentences. Then conjugate **идти** with each of the nouns in the accusative given in the six sentences in the ''Student'' column.

Teacher	*Student*
Я иду домой.	Я иду в магазин. Я иду в класс.
I am going home.	Я иду в школу. Я иду в комнату.
Ты идёшь _____.	Я иду в город. Я иду в Москву.
Он идёт _____.	
Мы идём _____.	
Вы идёте _____.	
Они идут _____.	

2. Listen to the teacher (or the tape) and repeat the following sentences. Then drill on the sentences in the ''Student'' column using the teacher's sentence as a model.

Teacher	*Student*

Но́чью я сплю́ до́ма. Ут́ром я сижу́ до́ма.
  At night I sleep at home. Днём я рабо́таю до́ма.
Но́чью ты спи́шь до́ма. Ве́чером я чита́ю до́ма.
_____ он спит _____.
_____ мы спим ____.
_____ вы сии́те ____.
_____ они́ спят ____.

D. 1. Study ¶10-8. Listen to the teacher (or the tape) and repeat the following.

m.	*f.*	*n.*	*pl. (m., f., n.)*
я отвеча́л	я отвеча́ла		мы отвеча́ли
ты _____	ты _____		вы _____
он _____	она́ _____	оно́ отвеча́ло	они́ _____

Then conjugate the following verbs in the past tense: **игра́ть, де́лать, понима́ть, писа́ть, дава́ть.**

2. Listen to the teacher (or the tape) and repeat the following.

я люби́л	я люби́ла		мы люби́ли
ты ____	ты ____		вы _____
он ____	она́ ____	оно́ люби́ло	они́ _____

Then conjugate **говори́ть** in the past tense.

U N I T 11

КУДА́ ВЫ ИДЁТЕ?

1. **Па́вел**: Здра́вствуйте, Никола́й!
2. **Никола́й**: До́брое у́тро, Па́вел!
3. **П.**: Как вы пожива́ете?
4. **Н.**: О́чень хорошо́, спаси́бо.
5. **П.**: Куда́ вы идёте?
6. **Н.**: Я иду́ в парк.   А вы куда́ идёте?
7. **П.**: Я иду́ в шко́лу.
8. **Н.**: О́чень жаль, что вы идёте в шко́лу, а не в парк.
9. **П.**: Почему́ жаль?   Я о́чень люблю́ шко́лу.
10. **Н.**: Я то́же люблю́ шко́лу, но сего́дня о́чень хоро́ший день, и я не хочу́ сиде́ть в кла́ссе.   Я предпочита́ю гуля́ть.
11. **П.**: А я предпочита́ю шко́лу и всегда́ люблю́ сиде́ть в кла́ссе.
12. **Н.**: О́льга то́же бу́дет в па́рке.   Вы зна́ете О́льгу? Она́ о́чень краси́вая де́вушка.
13. **П.**: Коне́чно зна́ю.   Она́ краса́вица!   Я то́же иду́ в парк!
14. **Н.**: Нет!   Вы идёте в шко́лу.   До свида́ния.

Слова́рь (Vocabulary)

куда́ where to, whither
куда́ вы идёте? where are you going?
Никола́й Nicholas
Па́вел *fl* (*gen.* **Па́вла**) Paul

84

как вы поживаете? how are you?
поживать (I); **поживаю, -ешь, -ют** to get on
спасибо thanks, thank you
парк park
жаль it is a pity
очень жаль it is a great pity, it is too bad
день^Я (*m.*) (*gen.* **дня**) day
хороший день a beautiful day
гулять (I); **гуляю, -ешь, -ют** to walk (for pleasure), to take a walk
Ольга Olga
будет will be (see ¶ **11-2**)
девушка girl
конечно (*pr.* **конешно**) of course, certainly
красавица beauty, a beautiful girl
до свидания good-bye

II

УМНЫЙ ЧЕЛОВЕК

1. **Николай:** Алло!
2. **Павел:** Алло! Кто у телефона?
3. **Н:** Говорит Николай Смирнов. А! Это вы, Павел? Здравствуйте! Как поживаете?
4. **П.:** Спасибо, очень хорошо. А вы, Николай?
5. **Н.:** Я тоже хорошо. Где вы сейчас, Павел?
6. **П.:** Я сейчас в деревне у бабушки, но завтра буду в Нью-Йорке.
7. **Н.:** Ах, как жаль! Завтра я еду в Вашингтон.
8. **П.:** Как долго вы там будете?
9. **Н.:** Может быть два дня, а может быть и четыре.
10. **П.:** А что вы будете делать в Вашингтоне?
11. **Н.:** Пожалуйста не спрашивайте. Это пока ещё секрет.
12. **П.:** А! Я знаю! Ольга живёт в Вашингтоне! Она недавно была в Нью-Йорке, и вы с ней гуляли в парке.
13. **Н.:** Вы очень умный человек, но помните, пожалуйста, что всё это секрет.
14. **П.:** Хорошо. Буду помнить. До свидания.

Словарь (Vocabulary)

умный clever, smart
человек man, person
алло! hello!

телефóн telephone
кто у телефóна? who is on the phone?
Смирнóв Smirnov
сейчáс now, right now
бýду I shall be (see ¶ 11-2)
Нью-Йóрк New York
ах! oh!
éхать (**I**); **éду, éдешь, éдут** to go (by conveyance), to ride (see ¶ 11-4)
Вашингтóн Washington
как дóлго? how long?
мóжет быть perhaps
и *here:* even
что вы бýдете дéлать? what will you be doing?
пожáлуйста (*pr.* **пожáлуста**) please
не спрáшивайте do not ask
покá (*adv.*) for the time being
покá ещё as yet, still
секрéт secret
а! ah!
недáвно recently
былá was (*past tense of* **быть: был, былá, бы́ло, бы́ли**)
с ней (*instr. of* **онá**) with her
пóмнить (**II**); **пóмню, пóмнишь, пóмнят** to remember
всё э́то all this

Граммáтика (Grammar)

Part I

11-1. The Accusative with в and на

a. **в** or **на** + the accusative indicates motion toward a given object. For example:

Я идý **в шкóлу.**	I am going *to school.*
Я идý **на концéрт.**	I am going *to a concert.*

b. With verbs of motion, **в** means *into* and is used to indicate motion to the interior of an object (one having enclosed space):

1. Я идý **в шкóлу** means "I am going to school" (*and am also going inside it.*)

2. With **концéрт** or **урóк**, **на** must be used because these nouns designate occasions, not objects which one can enter (go inside).

c. Useful Hints: When the sentence answers the question **где?** (*where?*), use the *prepositional* with **в** or **на**; when it answers the question **кудá** (*where to? whither bound?*), use the *accusative.*

Part II

11-2. Future Tense of быть (*irr.*) *to be*

SINGULAR

я бу́ду	I shall be
ты бу́дешь	you will be
он бу́дет	he will be

PLURAL

мы бу́дем	we shall be
вы бу́дете	you will be
они́ бу́дут	they will be

Note: The present tense endings of the First Conjugation are added to the stem **буд-** to form the future of **быть**.

11-3. Compound Future Tense

a. This tense is formed by adding the infinitive to the future of **быть**:

я бу́ду чита́ть	I shall read, I shall be reading
ты бу́дешь чита́ть	you will read, you will be reading
он бу́дет чита́ть	he will read, he will be reading
мы бу́дем чита́ть	we shall read, we shall be reading
вы бу́дете чита́ть	you will read, you will be reading
они́ бу́дут чита́ть	they will read, they will be reading

b. Only verbs denoting incompleted or repeated action can be expressed . 1 the compound future tense. All verbs given thus far belong to this category.

11-4. Infinitive: éхать (I) *to go* (*by conveyance*)

This verb denotes motion by conveyance, never on foot.

PRESENT TENSE

я е́ду	мы е́дем
ты е́дешь	вы е́дете
он е́дет	они́ е́дут

11-5. The Imperative

The imperative is formed from the stem of the present tense (see ¶ 5-4).

a. If the stem ends in a consonant, add **-й** for the singular and **-йте** for the plural:

PRESENT	PRESENT STEM	IMPERATIVE
ты идёшь	ид-	иди́ go! (*fam. sing.*)
		иди́те go! (*pl.*, or *polite sing.*)
ты лю́бишь	люб-	люби́ love! (*fam. sing.*)
		люби́те love! (*pl.*, or *polite sing.*)

b. If the stem ends in a vowel, add **-й** and **-йте**:

PRESENT	PRESENT STEM	IMPERATIVE
ты чита́ешь	чита-	чита́й read! (*fam. sing.*)
		чита́йте read! (*pl.*, or *polite sing.*)

Упражнёния (Exercises)

A. Supply the verb endings and put the words in parentheses in the proper case. Indicate accents.

1. Куда́ вы ид_____? 2. Я идў____ в (шко́ла). 3. По-чему́ вы не еде́me__ в (го́род)? 4. Я предпочита_____ сиде́ть в (класс). 5. Вы зна_____ кто буд_____ в (парк)? 6. Нет, не зна_____. 7. Вы помн_____ (Ольга)? 8. Коне́чно помн_____. 9. Она́ неда́вно была́ в (Нью-Йорк). 10. Что вы бу́д_____ де́лать в (дере́вня)?

B. Give the familiar and polite forms of the imperative for the verbs in parentheses.

1. (Отвеча́ть) гро́мко. 2. (Писа́ть) ме́дленно. 3. (Жить) в дере́вне. 4. (Знать) уро́к. 5. (Рабо́тать) у́тром. 6. (Отды-ха́ть) ве́чером. 7. (Спать) но́чью. 8. (Говори́ть) по-ру́сски в кла́ссе. 9 (Изуча́ть) ру́сский язы́к. 10. (Сиде́ть) на полу́. 11. Это секре́т. Пожа́луйста не (спра́шивать). 12. Не (рабо́-тать) так мно́го.

C. Put the first ten sentences of Exercise B in the compound future, in different persons.

Перево́д (Translation)

Omit the words in parentheses and include the words in brackets.

1. Where are you going, Nicholas? 2. I am going to school. 3. It is too bad that you are not going to the park. 4. Olga will be walking (taking a walk) in the park. 5. She is a very beautiful girl.

6. They say that she is a beauty. 7. I am going to New York if you are also going. 8. Where shall we live and what shall we be doing there? 9. Please do not ask me [**меня**]. I do not as yet know. 10. What was your sister doing yesterday? 11. She stayed home and read all day. 12. How is she? 13. Thank you, she is well. 14. And how are (your) uncle and aunt? 15. They were recently in Washington; now they are in the country.

Вопро́сы (Questions)

1. Как вы пожива́ете сего́дня? 2. Как пожива́ет ваш де́душка? ва́ша ба́бушка? ваш дя́дя? ва́ша мать? 3. Что вы де́лали сего́дня? 4. Где вы за́втра бу́дете рабо́тать? 5. Где ва́ша сестра́ была́ вчера́? 6. А где была́ вся ва́ша семья́? 7. Где вы все бу́дете за́втра? 8. Вы предпочита́ете гуля́ть в па́рке и́ли сиде́ть до́ма? 9. О́льга краси́вая де́вушка? 10. Когда́ она́ была́ в Нью-Йо́рке? 11. Когда́ ваш оте́ц бу́дет до́ма? 12. Кто о́чень у́мный челове́к? 13. Почему́ он у́мный? 14. Где сейча́с Па́вел? 15. Как до́лго Никола́й бу́дет в Вашингто́не?

Pattern Drills

A. Study ¶11-1. Listen to the teacher (or the tape) and repeat the following questions and answers. Then answer the questions given in the "Student" column.

Teacher	Student
Я живу́ в го́роде.	
А где ты живёшь?	Я то́же живу́ в го́роде.
Ты гуля́ешь в па́рке.	
А где он гуля́ет?	Он то́же гуля́ет в па́рке.
Она́ рабо́тает в Вашингто́не.	
А где вы рабо́таете?	Мы рабо́таем в Нью-Йо́рке.
Мы идём на уро́к.	
А куда́ вы идёте?	Мы то́же идём на уро́к.
Вы идёте на рабо́ту.	
А куда́ они́ иду́т?	Они́ то́же иду́т на рабо́ту.
Они́ иду́т на конце́рт.	
А куда́ вы идёте?	Я то́же иду́ на конце́рт.

B. Study ¶11-1, 11-2, and **11-4.**   Listen to the teacher (or the tape) and repeat the following sentences.

Я éду на уро́к.	Я бу́ду на уро́ке всё у́тро.
Ты éдешь в парк.	Ты бу́дешь в па́рке весь день.
Он éдет на концéрт.	Он бу́дет на концéрте весь вéчер.
Мы éдем на рабо́ту.	Мы бу́дем на рабо́те всю ночь.
Вы éдете в шко́лу.	Вы бу́дете в шко́ле всё у́тро.
Они́ éдут в го́род.	Они́ бу́дут в го́роде весь день и всю ночь.

C. Study ¶11-3 and **9-3.**   Listen to the teacher (or the tape) and repeat the following sentences.   Then read each sentence again supplying the same noun in the required case according to the model in the ''Student'' column.

Teacher	*Student*
Сего́дня я éду в парк.	Я до́лго бу́ду гуля́ть в па́рке.
Сего́дня ты éдешь в го́род.	Ты бу́дешь рабо́тать в _____ оди́н день.
Вéчером мать éдет на концéрт.	Она́ бу́дет игра́ть на _____ весь вéчер.
Днём мы éдем в магази́н.	Мы бу́дем рабо́тать в _____ два дня.
У́тром вы éдете домо́й.	Вы бу́дете сидéть до́ма три дня.
Сего́дня ои́ éдут в Вашингто́н.	Они́ бу́дут отдыха́ть в _____ четы́ре дня.

D. Study ¶**11-5.**   Listen to the teacher (or the tape) and repeat the following sentences.   Then read each sentence supplying the imperative form of the verb in the plural.

Teacher	*Student*
Иди́ домо́й.	Иди́те домо́й.
Сиди́ до́ма.	_____ до́ма.
Люби́ отца́, бра́та и сестру́.	_____ отца́, бра́та и сестру́.
Рабо́тай днём, отдыха́й вéчером.	_____ днём, _____ вéчером.
Чита́й мно́го, говори́ ма́ло.	_____ мно́го, _____ ма́ло.
Спи всю ночь, рабо́тай весь день.	_____ всю ночь, _____ весь день.
Гуля́й в па́рке у́тром.	_____ в па́рке у́тром.
Отвеча́й гро́мко.	_____ гро́мко.

Пиши ме́дленно, но
говори́ бы́стро. _____ ме́дленно, но _____ бы́стро.
Живи́ в дере́вне, но _____ в дере́вне, но _____ в
рабо́тай в го́роде. го́роде.
Не сиди́ на полу́, а сиди́ Не _____ на полу́, а _____ на
на сту́ле. сту́ле.

E. The following dialogue is a reinforcement drill on greetings
and other social amenities.

Госпожа́ Ивано́ва

— Здра́вствуйте, господи́н
Петро́в!
— Как вы пожива́ете сего́дня?

— Я то́же хорошо́. А как
пожива́ет ва́ша сестра́?

— Он сего́дня нездоро́в.
— До свида́ния, господи́н
Петро́в!

Господи́н Петро́в

— Здра́вствуйте, госпожа́
Ивано́ва.
— О́чень хорошо́, спаси́бо. А
вы, госпожа́ Ивано́ва?
— Спаси́бо, она́ здоро́ва. И
моя́ жена́ тепе́рь то́же
здоро́ва. А как пожива́-
ет ваш муж?
— Ах, как жаль!
— До свида́ния, госпожа́
Ивано́ва.

F. See *Workbook for Basic Russian, Book One*, page 38. Note
that masculine as well as feminine names may end in **-a** or **-я.**
Then do the following repetition drill.

Girl

— До́брое у́тро, Ва́ня!
— Здра́вствуйте, Ми́ша!
— До́брый ве́чер, Пе́тя!
— До свида́ния, Фе́дя!
— Как пожива́ете, Гри́ша?

Boy

— Здра́вствуйте, Та́ня!
— До́брый день, Ве́ра!
— Здра́вствуйте, Ка́тя!
— До свида́ния, Ма́ша!
— Спаси́бо, О́льга. О́чень хорошо́.

U N I T **12**

REVIEW LESSON

Грамма́тика (**Grammar**)

12-1. Table of Regular Conjugations

The forms thus far covered of the two regular conjugations are given below. Review them thoroughly before doing the exercises.

CONJUGATION I   CONJUGATION II

INFINITIVE

чита́ть to read   **говори́ть** to speak

PRESENT TENSE

я чита́**ю**	я говор**ю́**
ты чита́**ешь**	ты говор**и́шь**
он чита́**ет**	он говор**и́т**
мы чита́**ем**	мы говор**и́м**
вы чита́**ете**	вы говор**и́те**
они́ чита́**ют**	они́ говор**я́т**

PAST TENSE

я, ты, он чита́**л**	я, ты, он говори́**л**
я, ты, она́ чита́**ла**	я, ты, она́ говори́**ла**
оно́ чита́**ло**	оно́ говори́**ло**
мы, вы, они́ чита́**ли**	мы, вы, они́ говори́**ли**

COMPOUND FUTURE TENSE

я бу́д**у**		я бу́д**у**	
ты бу́д**ешь**		ты бу́д**ешь**	
он бу́д**ет**	**}чита́ть**	он бу́д**ет**	**}говори́ть**
мы бу́д**ем**		мы бу́д**ем**	
вы бу́д**ете**		вы бу́д**ете**	
они́ бу́д**ут**		они́ бу́д**ут**	

IMPERATIVE

чита́**й**   говори́

чита́**йте**   говори́**те**

92

Verb Review

A. Conjugate the following regular verbs in all the forms given in ¶ 12-1 and indicate the stress throughout.   In case of doubt, refer to the vocabularies of individual lessons or the vocabulary section at the end of the book.

1. поживáть	5. гуля́ть	9. изучáть
2. пóмнить	6. спрáшивать	10. отвечáть
3. понимáть	7. дéлать	11. предпочитáть
4. знать	8. игрáть	12. рабóтать

B. The following verbs deviate from **читáть** or **говори́ть** in some respect.   Conjugate them in all forms as you did the regular verbs in Exercise A, and point out or underline the irregularities in the conjugations of these verbs.

Group I. The past tense is regular and has the stress on the stem in the three genders:

1. éхать	4. давáть
*2. сидéть	5. хотéть
3. люби́ть	6. писáть

Group II. The past tense is irregular or has the stress on **-á** in the feminine:

1. идти́   (*past:* шёл, шла, шло, шли)
2. мочь   (*past:* мог, моглá, моглó, могли́)
            (has no *future* and no *imperative*)
3. жить   (*past:* жил, жилá, жи́ло, жи́ли)
4. спать   (*past:* спал, спалá, спáло, спáли)

12-2. The Interrogative Pronoun: кто

a. The interrogative pronoun **кто** (*who*) refers to persons or animals, whereas **что** (*what*) refers to objects.

b. Memorize the declension of **кто** before doing the remaining exercises.

nom.	кто?	who?
gen.	когó?	of whom? whose?
dat.	комý?	to whom?
acc.	когó?	whom?
instr.	кем?	by whom?
prep.	о ком?	about whom?

Comprehension Drill

A. Translate the following sentences into idiomatic English.

1. Моя́ тётя неда́вно была́ у нас.   2. Её учи́тельница то́лько оди́н год в Аме́рике.   3. Все в до́ме говоря́т о́чень гро́мко.   4. Мы ещё не говори́м по-ру́сски.   5. Они́ сего́дня ничего́ не де́лают.   6. Ива́н никогда́ ничего́ не чита́ет.   7. О́чень жаль, что вы предпочита́ете ничего́ не де́лать.   8. Студе́нты изуча́ют ру́сский язы́к.   9. Говоря́т, что его́ сестра́ краса́вица.   10. Это пока́ ещё секре́т.

B. Translate the following questions into idiomatic English and answer them in Russian.

1. У кого́ мой каранда́ш?   2. У кого́ есть перо́?   3. У кого́ живёт ва́ша учени́ца?   4. Вы за́втра бу́дете рабо́тать весь день?   5. Кому́ (see ¶ 8-3) вы даёте карти́ну?   6. Вы сейча́с до́ма, и́ли в дере́вне?   7. Как пожива́ет ваш де́душка?   8. Как до́лго вы бу́дете в Вашингто́не?

Pronunciation Review

A. Pronounce the following words aloud, and explain why the bold-face vowels or consonants are pronounced as they are. Review preceding sections on pronunciation for correct answers.

1. оди́н   2. е́хать   3. бли́зко   4. да́же   5. пешко́м   6. му**ж** 7. д**о́**ма   8. домо́й   9. **я**зы́к   10. за́**в**тра   11. маши́на 12. **ж**ить   13. шокола́**д**   14. **н**е зна́ю   15. **с** бра́том

B. Pronounce the following accurately.

1. сего́дня   2. здра́вствуйте   3. ничего́   4. семья́   5. вся 6. всё   7. ма́ленький   8. большо́й   9. день   10. но́чью

Grammar Review

A. Change the following sentences into the past and the compound future.

1. Она́ изуча́ет ру́сский язы́к.
2. Учи́тельница спра́шивает.
3. Хозя́ин говори́т с хозя́йкой.
4. Вы понима́ете уро́к.
5. Мой брат и его́ жена́ живу́т у нас.

6. Ты даёшь газе́ту отцу́.

7. Они́ стоя́т о́коло па́рка.

B. Supply the proper case endings for the nouns or pronouns in parentheses.

1. Я живу́ с (оте́ц) и с (сестра́) в (дере́вня).

2. Кому́ вы даёте (кни́га), (учени́к) и́ли (учени́ца).

3. У (ты) в (ко́мната) три (кре́сло).

4. Учи́тель спра́шивает (Ива́н) и (Ве́ра).

5. Муж говори́т с (жена́).

Перево́д (Translation)

A. Translate orally at sight. Omit the words in parentheses and include the words in brackets.

1. I am a good pupil (*m.*). 2. She is a good teacher. 3. You have a poor [bad] pen. 4. The whole class is here today. 5. My mother worked all day today. 6. What will you be doing at home tomorrow? 7. Do not play with the dog! 8. Do not sit on the floor! 9. They have a very ugly room. 10. She loves (her) brother and (her) sister. 11. You are a very clever person. 12. When does one say "good evening"? 13. Her new armchair is at father's.

B. Write the following sentences.

1. We have been only one year in the U.S.A. 2. They do not as yet speak Russian. 3. We understand nothing when you speak fast. 4. My teacher (*m.*) is Russian, and of course speaks Russian very well. 5. I am going to the store after work. 6. We never work anywhere. 7. How long will you be in Moscow? 8. You stayed home very long.

U N I T 13*

I

У МЕНЯ НЕТ АВТОМОБИЛЯ

Мы живём далеко́ от го́рода, и я до́лжен ходи́ть в шко́лу пешко́м. Я о́чень не люблю́ ходи́ть, но у меня́ нет автомоби́ля. У отца́ есть автомоби́ль, но он до́лжен е́здить в конто́ру о́чень ра́но. Он рабо́тает в конто́ре ка́ждый день.

Моя́ сестра́ О́льга, коне́чно, то́же хо́дит в шко́лу пешко́м, но э́то ей нра́вится. Она́ да́же говори́т, что мы живём сли́шком бли́зко от шко́лы.

Слова́рь (Vocabulary)

у меня́ нет I do not have (see ¶ 13-1)
автомоби́ль (*m.*) (*gen.* **автомоби́ля**) automobile
у меня́ нет автомоби́ля I have no automobile (see ¶ 13-1)
далеко́ (*adv.*) far
от (*with gen.*) from
до́лжен, должна́, должно́ obliged to, have to, must
ходи́ть (**II**) *hab.*† ; **хожу́, хо́дишь, хо́дят** to walk (see ¶ 13-2 & 13-3)   *habitual*
пешко́м (*adv.*) on foot
ходи́ть пешко́м to go on foot
я о́чень не люблю́ I very much dislike
ра́но (*adv.*) early
е́здить (**II**) *hab.*; **е́зжу** (*pr.* **е́жжу**), **е́здишь, е́здят** to go (by conveyance), to ride (see ¶ 13-3)

* For the sake of clarity in presentation, the *actual* and *habitual* verbs are treated in one unit. The unit, however, is intended as a *double* unit, requiring approximately twice as much time as the average unit.
† *Hab.* designates *habitual* verbs.

96

конто́ра office
ка́ждый, -ая, -ое every, each
ей (*dat. of* она́) to her
нра́вится (*pr.* нра́вица) is pleasing
э́то ей нра́вится she likes it (*lit.* this is pleasing to her)
да́же even
сли́шком (*adv.*) too (much)
бли́зко (*adv. followed by* от) (*pr.* бли́ско) near

II

КАК ЖАЛЬ!

У нас в до́ме живёт наш ру́сский учи́тель, господи́н Смирно́в. У господи́на Смирно́ва есть но́вый, хоро́ший автомоби́ль, но он всегда́ предпочита́ет ходи́ть пешко́м в шко́лу. Сего́дня идёт дождь, но автомоби́ль господи́на Смирно́ва стои́т в гараже́, а господи́н Смирно́в идёт в шко́лу пешко́м. Почему́ он не е́дет? Я не понима́ю заче́м он купи́л автомоби́ль!

Господи́н Смирно́в зна́ет, что мне о́чень нра́вится его́ автомоби́ль, и он иногда́ даёт его́ мне. Оди́н раз он дал мне автомоби́ль на четы́ре дня. Но мне ну́жен автомоби́ль ка́ждый день! Сего́дня ве́чером я хочу́ е́хать с Ве́рой в теа́тр, но у меня́ нет автомоби́ля. Как жаль!

Слова́рь (Vocabulary)

как жаль! what a pity!
дождь (*m.*) rain
идёт дождь it is raining
гара́ж garage
заче́м why, wherefore
купи́л (*past of* купи́ть) bought
мне (*dat. of* я) to me
мне нра́вится I like
иногда́ sometimes
его́ (*acc. of* он) it, him
раз time (occasion)
оди́н раз once
дал (*past of* дать) gave
четы́ре four
на четы́ре дня for four days
ну́жен, нужна́, ну́жно necessary

мне ну́жен I need (see ¶ 13-6)
сего́дня ве́чером tonight, this evening
теа́тр theater

Грамма́тика (Grammar)

Part I

13-1. Possessive Phrases in the Negative

a. The present tense of the verb *to have* in the negative is rendered thus:

SINGULAR		PLURAL	
у меня́ нет		у нас нет	
у тебя́ нет	+ genitive	у вас нет	+ genitive
у него́ нет		у них нет	
у неё нет			

b. Compare the negative construction with the affirmative:

AFFIRMATIVE (see ¶ 9-2)

У меня́ **есть** газе́та.   I have a newspaper.
У меня́ **есть** автомоби́ль.   I have an automobile.

NEGATIVE

У меня́ **нет** газе́ты.   I have no newspaper.   (I do not have any newspaper.)

У меня́ **нет** автомоби́ля.   I have no automobile. (I do not have any automobile.)

13-2. Verbs of Motion

a. Verbs of motion in Russian do not indicate direction.   Direction is indicated by prepositions or by prefixes.   For example:

Я иду́ **в** конто́ру.   I am *going* to the office.
                               (**в** = *into*)

Я иду́ **из** конто́ры.   I am *coming* from the office.
                               (**из** = *out of*)

Я **прихожу́*** в конто́ру.   I *arrive* at the office.
                               (**при** = *arrival at*)

Я **ухожу́*** из конто́ры.   I *leave* the office.
                               (**у** = *departure from*)

* In the grammar, unfamiliar words are used only as illustrations, and are not to be memorized.

b. The distinction is always made in Russian between motion on foot, and motion by means of a conveyance.   For example:

Я **иду́** в конто́ру.	I am going (*on foot*) to the office.
Я **е́ду** в конто́ру.	I am going (*not on foot*) to the office.

13-3. Actual and Habitual Forms of Verbs :
идти́ and   ходи́ть
е́хать and е́здить

Verbs of motion have two distinct forms: the *actual* and the *habitual.*

a. The *actual* verb implies *actual* performance at a *given time,* not merely *possible* performance at unspecified times.   It is specific with regard to:

1. The *direction* of the motion.

Я е́ду в конто́ру	I am going (by conveyance) to the office. (I am bound for the office.)

2. The *time* the action *actually* takes place.

Я тепе́рь е́ду домо́й.	I am going home now. (I am actually on my way home.)
Я за́втра е́ду домо́й.	I am going home tomorrow. (I will actually be on my way home tomorrow.)

b. The *habitual* verb implies *possible* performance at an unspecified time or at various times.   It is *general* and *indefinite* with regard to:

1. The direction of the motion.

Я хожу́, когда́ у меня́ нет автомоби́ля.	I walk when I have no car. (Walking could be in any direction, or aimless.)

2. Time of possible performance.

In the sentence above, the action takes place when no car is available.   But we do not know when this happens.   A car may always be available and the action may never actually take place, and only remain *possible* forever.

c. Present tense of   { идти́ (I) — ходи́ть (II) *to go (on foot)*
                         { éхать (I) — éздить (II) *to go (by conveyance)*

ACTUAL	HABITUAL	ACTUAL	HABITUAL
идти́ (I)	**ходи́ть** (II)	**éхать** (I)	**éздить** (II)
я иду́	я хожу́	я éду	я éзжу
ты идёшь	ты хо́дишь	ты éдешь	ты éздишь
он идёт	он хо́дит	он éдет	он éздит
мы идём	мы хо́дим	мы éдем	мы éздим
вы идёте	вы хо́дите	вы éдете	вы éздите
они́ иду́т	они́ хо́дят	они́ éдут	они́ éздят

Part II

13-4. Dative of Personal Pronouns

SINGULAR

nom.	*dat.*	*meaning*
я	мне	to me
ты	тебé	to you
он	емý	to him
она́	ей	to her
оно́	емý	to it

PLURAL

мы	нам	to us
вы	вам	to you
они́	им	to them

13-5. "To like" in Russian

When the object liked is in the singular, the verb *to like* is rendered thus (see ¶14-4):

Мне нра́вится учи́тель.   I like the teacher (*lit.* the teacher is pleasing to me).

Тебé нра́вится моя́ сестра́.   You like my sister.
Им нра́вится наш дом.   They like our house.

Note: The direct object of the English sentence becomes the subject of the Russian sentence. Therefore, before translating into Russian such sentences as "I like the teacher," paraphrase it as "The teacher is pleasing to me."

13-6. Ну́жен, нужна́, and ну́жно

In constructions using **ну́жен**, **нужна́**, or **ну́жно** (meaning *necessary*), the subject of the English sentence must be expressed in the dative. For example:

Мне ну́жен автомоби́ль.	I need a car (*lit.* to me, a car is necessary).
Бра́ту нужна́ соба́ка.	Brother needs a dog.
Тебе́ ну́жно перо́.	You need a pen.
Им нужна́ ко́мната.	They need a room.
Что **ему́** ну́жно?	What does he need (want)?

Note: In this construction, the gender of the thing needed determines the gender of the word for *necessary*.

Упражне́ния (Exercises)

A. Supply the opposites of the words and phrases given, and use them in sentences. For example:

по́здно — Сего́дня я **ра́но** е́ду в парк.

1. далеко́ от 2. у неё есть 3. гро́мко 4. ме́дленно 5. краси́вое 6. но́вая 7. большо́й 8. всегда́ 9. там 10. хорошо́ 11. ма́ло 12. до свида́ния

B. Replace the words in parentheses with appropriate Russian equivalents.

1. У него́ есть (paper), но у него́ нет (pencil). 2. Она́ живёт (far), но у неё нет (automobile). 3. У нас нет (garage), но у нас есть (automobile). 4. У них нет (divan), но у них есть (armchair). 5. Мы ка́ждый день (go on foot) в (theater). 6. Куда́ ты тепе́рь (going on foot)? 7. Господи́н Смирно́в никогда́ не (walks) в (school). 8. (I need) газе́та, а (she needs) журна́л. 9. (We need) учи́тель, а (they need) учи́тельница. 10. (You need) кре́сло. 11. (Sister needs) рабо́та. 12. (Father needs) конто́ра.

C. Fill in the appropriate verb form. Make sure that you are using the correct verb of motion.

1. Сего́дня мы _____ (on foot) в парк. 2. Они́ всегда́ _____ (by conveyance) в го́род. 3. Куда́ она́

тепе́рь _____ (by conveyance)?   4. Они́ ка́ждый день
_____ (on foot) в го́род?   5. Вы сего́дня ве́чером
_____ (on foot) в теа́тр.   6. Куда́ вы ка́ждый день
_____ (by conveyance) так бы́стро?

D. Supply the personal pronoun in the proper case.

1. Он дал (me) _____ каранда́ш. Каранда́ш тепе́рь
у _____.   2. Я даю́ (her) кни́гу. Кни́га тепе́рь у
_____.   3. Вы даёте (them) _____ ла́мпу. Ла́мпа
тепе́рь у _____.   4. Они́ даю́т (you, *fam.*) _____
бума́гу. Бума́га тепе́рь у _____.   5. Мы даём (you, *pl.*)
_____ карти́ну. Карти́на тепе́рь у _____.
6. Они́ даю́т (us) _____ ка́рту. Ка́рта тепе́рь у·_____.

Перево́д (Translation)

A. Omit words in parentheses and include those in brackets:

1. My uncle has to be in the store every day.   2. He works (a
great deal) [much], but he likes it.   3. He even says that his work
in the store is interesting.   4. He lives near [from] the store and
always walks [on foot].   5. Why [wherefore] did you buy a car?
It stays [**стои́т**] in the garage, and you walk.   6. I prefer to walk,
but it is raining today.   What a pity!   7. Once you gave the car to
(your) brother for four days.   8. I need a car tonight because I am
going to the theater.

B. Omit words in parentheses and include those in brackets.
The corrected translation can be used for additional oral work—for
questions and answers, or as a dialogue between two students.

1. Where are you going (walking)?
2. I am going to the office.
3. Why aren't you riding?
4. I am not riding because I have no car.
5. I know that you (do) have a car.   Where is it now?
6. My wife has it now.   [It is now by (my) wife.]
7. It is raining now, but you are going on foot, and she is riding!
8. She always rides and I always walk.
9. I do not understand why you give her the car.   It is your car.
10. It is my car, but she is my wife and I love her.
11. Does she love you too?
12. Of course!

13. Why then [**Почему́ же**] does she not walk?

14. You have no wife and you do not understand anything [you nothing not understand].

15. I have no wife, but I always have a car!

Вопро́сы (**Questions**)

1. Вы живёте далеко́ и́ли бли́зко от го́рода? 2. Вы хо́дите и́ли е́здите в шко́лу? 3. Вы предпочита́ете ходи́ть пешко́м и́ли е́здить? 4. Когда́ ваш оте́ц до́лжен е́здить в конто́ру? 5. Кто живёт у вас в до́ме? 6. Когда́ идёт дождь, господи́н Смирно́в хо́дит и́ли е́здит в шко́лу? 7. Вы понима́ете заче́м господи́н Смирно́в купи́л автомоби́ль? 8. Вам нра́вится автомоби́ль господи́на Смирно́ва? 9. Заче́м вам сего́дня ну́жен автомоби́ль? 10. С кем (see ¶8-2) вы е́хали в теа́тр вчера́? 11. Как ча́сто (how often) вы е́здите в го́род? 12. Заче́м вам ну́жен автомоби́ль ка́ждый день? 13. Кто вам дал автомоби́ль на четы́ре дня? 14. Автомоби́ль господи́на Смирно́ва сли́шком большо́й и́ли сли́шком ма́ленький? 15. Когда́ вы бу́дете рабо́тать в конто́ре?

Pattern Drills

A. Study ¶**13-1**. Listen to the teacher (or the tape) and repeat the following sentences. Then read each sentence again giving the noun in the "Student" column in the genitive according to the model sentence.

Teacher	*Student*
У меня́ нет ка́рты.	У меня́ нет кни́ги.
У тебя́ нет газе́ты.	У тебя́ нет (бума́га).
У него́ нет пера́.	_____ (кре́сло).
У неё нет гаража́.	_____ (автомоби́ль).
У нас нет де́душки.	_____ (ба́бушка).
У вас нет сту́ла.	_____ (стол).
У них нет до́ма.	_____ (ко́мната).

B. 1. Study ¶**13-3** carefully and memorize ¶ **13-3c.** Listen to the teacher (or the tape) and repeat the following sentences.

Я всегда́ е́зжу в го́род, но сего́дня я иду́ пешко́м.

Ты всегда́ е́здишь в шко́лу, но сего́дня ты идёшь пешко́м.

Он всегда́ е́здит в теа́тр, но сего́дня он идёт пешко́м.

Мы всегда́ е́здим на уро́к, но сего́дгя, мы идём пешко́м.

Вы всегда́ е́здите на конце́рт, но сего́дня вы идёте пешко́м.

Они́ всегда́ е́здят на рабо́ту, но сего́дня они́ иду́т пешко́м.

2. Read the above sentences, substituting **ходи́ть** for **е́здить** and **е́хать на автомоби́ле** (*to ride in, to go by car*) for **идти́ пешко́м** according to the following model sentence:

Я всегда́ **хожу́** в го́род, но сего́дгя я **е́ду** на автомоби́ле.

C. Study **¶13-4.** Listen to the teacher (or the tape) and repeat the following sentences. Then read each sentence again substituting a possessive phrase according to the model in the "Student" column.

Teacher	*Student*	
Ты дал **мне** журна́л.	Ты дал **мне** журна́л.	Он тепе́рь у меня́.
Я дал **тебе́** газе́ту.	Я дал тебе́ газе́ту.	Она́ тепе́рь у тебя́.
Он дал **ей** перо́.	Он _____.	Оно́ _____ у неё.
Она́ дала́ **ему́** каранда́ш.	Она́ _____.	Он _____ у него́.
Вы да́ли **нам** ка́рту.	Вы _____.	Она́ _____ у нас.
Мы да́ли **вам** автомоби́ль.	Мы _____.	Он _____ у вас.
Они́ да́ли **им** кре́сло.	Они́ _____.	Оно́ _____ у них.

D. 1. Study **¶13-5.** Listen to the teacher (or the tape) and repeat the following questions. Then complete the answers in the "Student" column according to the model sentences.

Teacher	*Student*
Тебе́ нра́вится ко́мната?	Да, она́ **мне** нра́вится.
Ему́ _____ автомоби́ль?	Да, он ему́ нра́вится.
Ей _____ кре́сло?	Да, оно́ _____.
Вам _____ ба́бушка?	Да, она́ _____.
Им _____ де́душка?	Да, он_____.

2. Answer the above questions in the negative, according to the following model.

Тебе́ нра́вится ко́мната?   Нет, она́ **мне** не нра́вится.

E. 1. Study ¶13-6. Listen to the teacher (or the tape) and repeat the following.

m.	*f.*
Мне ну́жен дом.	**Мне нужна́** ко́мната.
Тебе́ _____ гара́ж.	**Тебе́** _____ конто́ра.
Ему́ _____ автомоби́ль.	**Ему́** _____ рабо́та.
Ей _____ дива́н.	**Ей** _____ ла́мпа.
Нам _____ учи́тель.	**Нам** _____ учи́тельница.
Вам _____ оте́ц.	**Вам** _____ мать.
Им _____ хозя́ин.	**Им** _____ хозя́йка.

n.

Мне ну́жно перо́.
Тебе́ _____.
Ему́ _____.
Ей _____.
Нам _____.
Вам _____.
Им _____.

2. Read the following sentences aloud, supplying the required gender of **ну́жен, нужна́, ну́жно.**

1. Мне _____ кре́сло, а вам _____ дива́н.
2. Тебе́ _____ ка́рта, а не карти́на.
3. Ему́ _____ учи́тель, а ей _____ учи́тельница.
4. Ей _____ перо́, а вам _____ каранда́ш.
5. Нам _____ бума́га, а ей _____ тетра́дь.
6. Вам _____ автомоби́ль, а им _____ гара́ж.
7. Им _____ дом, а вам _____ ко́мната.

3. Listen to the teacher (or the tape) and repeat the following questions and answers.

1. Что тебе́ ну́жно? Мне ну́жен каранда́ш.
2. Что ему́ ну́жно? Ему́ нужна́ доска́.
3. Что ей ну́жно? Ей ну́жно перо́.
4. Что вам ну́жно? Нам ну́жен автомоби́ль.
5. Что им ну́жно? Им ничего́ не ну́жно.
6. Что нам ну́жно? Нам то́же ничего́ не ну́жно.

U N I T 14

ДА́ЧА НА БЕРЕГУ́ МО́РЯ

1. — Где вы тепе́рь живёте?
2. — Я живу́ на да́че.
1. — Кто ещё там живёт?
2. — Вся на́ша семья́ там живёт.
1. — Когда́ вы живёте на да́че?
2. — Весно́й и ле́том.
1. — А где вы живёте о́сенью и зимо́й?
2. — О́сенью и зимо́й мы живём в го́роде.
1. — Вам нра́вится ва́ша да́ча?
2. — Она́ нам о́чень нра́вится, потому́ что она́ о́чень краси́вая и нахо́дится на берегу́ мо́ря.
1. — Кто купи́л э́ту краси́вую да́чу, вы и́ли ваш оте́ц?
2. — Оте́ц купи́л её.
1. — Како́го она́ цве́та?
2. — Она́ си́него цве́та.
1. — Вам наве́рно нра́вится э́тот цвет?
2. — Что зна́чит "наве́рно"? Я не зна́ю э́того сло́ва.
1. — Наве́рно зна́чит "surely."
2. — О да! Си́ний цвет мне о́чень нра́вится. Моя́ ко́мната то́же си́няя. Неда́вно я купи́л си́нюю ва́зу и си́нее кре́сло.
1. — Вы наве́рно лю́бите смотре́ть на мо́ре, потому́ что оно́ си́нее.
2. — Коне́чно. Я ча́сто сижу́ у окна́ и смотрю́ на си́нее мо́ре. Э́то ваш после́дний вопро́с?
1. — Да.
2. — Сла́ва Бо́гу!

Слова́рь (Vocabulary)

да́ча summer house
бе́рег (when governed by **в** or **на**, the *prep.* **берегу́** is used) shore
на берегу́ on the shore
мо́ре (*n.*) (*gen.* **мо́ря**) sea
на да́че (**на** is used instead of **в** with **да́ча**) at a summer house
весно́й (*adv.*) in the spring
ле́том (*adv.*) in the summer
о́сенью (*adv.*) in the fall
зимо́й (*adv.*) in the winter
нахо́дится (*pr.* **нахо́дица**) is situated
э́тот, э́та, э́то (*pron.*) this (see ¶ 14-1)
краси́вую *acc. of* **краси́вая** (see ¶ 14-2)
цвет color
како́й, кака́я, како́е what kind of
како́го (*pr.* **како́во**) **цве́та?** (of) what color?
си́ний, си́няя, си́нее blue
си́него цве́та (of) blue color
наве́рно surely, most likely
зна́чит means
сло́во word
ва́за vase
смотре́ть (II); **смотрю́, смо́тришь, смо́трят** to look
смотре́ть на (+ *acc.*) to look at
после́дний, после́дняя, после́днее last, final
вопро́с question
ну well!
сла́ва Бо́гу! thank goodness! (*lit.* Glory to God!)

часто - often

О́ЧЕНЬ ПРИЛЕ́ЖНЫЙ УЧЕНИ́К

1. **Учи́тель:** Почему́ вы сего́дня не зна́ете уро́ка?

2. **Учени́к:** Я не зна́ю уро́ка, потому́ что у меня́ нет кни́ги.

3. **Уч:** Почему́ у вас нет кни́ги?

4. **У:** У меня́ нет кни́ги, потому́ что у меня́ нет автомоби́ля.

5. **Уч:** Что э́то за отве́т: "Не зна́ю уро́ка, потому́ что у меня́ нет автомоби́ля"? Что́бы знать уро́к вам не ну́жен автомоби́ль, вам нужна́ кни́га!

6. **У:** Коне́чно мне нужна́ кни́га. Но кни́га в автомоби́ле, а автомоби́ль тепе́рь в Нью-Йо́рке.

7. **Уч:** Ничего́ не понима́ю.

8. **У:** У меня́ но́вый автомоби́ль, и оте́ц ча́сто берёт его́.

9. **Уч:** Хорошо́! А где ва́ше сочине́ние?

10. **У:** Тетра́дь с сочине́нием то́же в автомоби́ле.

11. **Уч:** Како́й приле́жный учени́к!

Слова́рь (Vocabulary)

прилѐжный, -ая, -ое diligent
отве́т answer
что э́то за отве́т? what kind of an answer is that?
что́бы in order to
ча́сто often
брать (I) ; **беру́, берёшь, беру́т** ; *past* **брал, -ла́, -ло, -ли** to take
сочине́ние (*n.*) (*instr.* **сочине́нием**) composition
тетра́дь (*f.*) notebook
како́й, -а́я, -о́е what a . . .

Konerha — of course

Грамма́тика (Grammar)

14-1. The Demonstrative Pronoun: э́тот, э́та, э́то

	m.	*f.*	*n.*
nom.	э́тот	э́та	э́то
gen.	э́того★	э́той	э́того★
acc.	э́тот *or* э́того★	э́ту	э́то

Note: In the masculine, pronouns and adjectives modifying *inanimate* objects are identical in the nominative and accusative; those modifying *animate* objects are identical in the genitive and accusative.

14-2. Declensions of Adjectives

a. Adjectival endings: *hard and soft.*

1. The last two letters of the adjective constitute its ending.
2. Compare the endings of the following two adjectives :

m.	*f.*	*n.*	*endings*
краси́вый	краси́вая	краси́вое	(-ый, -ая, -ое)
после́дний	после́дняя	после́днее	(-ий, -яя, -ее)

3. The last letter for each gender is the same in both adjectives (**-й, -я**, and **-е**), whereas the letter *next to the last* in the first adjective is a hard vowel (**-ы-, -а-**, and **-о-**), and in the second adjective a soft vowel (**-и-, -я-**, and **-е-**). These vowels determine the nature of the ending, which is accordingly *hard* or *soft*.

b. There are three declensions of adjectives, depending upon the nature of their endings:

★ **-ого** is pronounced **-ово.**

1 *Hard* adjectives, having hard endings throughout.

но́в**ый**	но́в**ая**	но́в**ое**	(new)
молод**о́й**	молод**а́я**	молод**о́е**	(young)

2. *Soft* adjectives, having soft endings throughout.

си́н**ий**	си́н**яя**	си́н**ее**	(blue)

3. *Mixed* adjectives, having some soft and some hard endings.

ру́сск**ий**	ру́сск**ая**	ру́сск**ое**	(Russian)

Note: The masculine form is soft, whereas the feminine and neuter forms are hard.

c. Adjectives ending in **-о́й, -а́я, -о́е** (e.g., молод**о́й, -а́я, -о́е**) are always stressed on the ending; all others on the stem.

Never stressed on ending	✷*Always stressed on ending*
hard: **-ый, -ая, -ое**	*hard:* **-о́й, -а́я, -о́е**
soft: **-ий, -яя, -ее**	
mixed: **-ий, -ая, -ое**	

d. See page 9͞3 for a table of case endings in the singular.

14-3. Direct Object of a Negative Verb

The direct object of a verb in the negative is usually in the genitive instead of in the accusative:

Я не зна́ю уро́к**а**.	I do not know the lesson.
Я не зна́ю э́т**ой** де́вушк**и**.	I do not know this girl.
Она́ не изуча́ла англи́йск**ого** язык**а́**.	She did not study English.

However, with verbs in the affirmative the direct object is in the accusative:

Я зна́ю уро́к.	I know the lesson.
Я зна́ю э́ту де́вушку.	I know this girl.

14-4. Мне нра́вится and я люблю́

a. **мне нра́вится** means *I like,* and refers to an object or a person producing a favorable impression, especially on first acquaintance:

Мне **нра́вится** Нью-Йо́рк.	I *like* New York. (I am favorably impressed — without knowing New York well.)
Мне **нра́вится** Ве́ра.	I *like* Vera.

CASE ENDINGS OF ADJECTIVES IN THE SINGULAR

Case	Hard		
	masculine	*feminine*	*neuter*
nom.	но́в**ый** журна́л но́в**ый** учени́к	но́в**ая** газе́та но́в**ая** учени́ца	но́в**ое** сло́во
gen.	но́в**ого** журна́ла но́в**ого** ученика́	но́в**ой** газе́ты но́в**ой** учени́цы	но́в**ого** сло́ва
acc.	но́в**ый** журна́л но́в**ого** ученика́	но́в**ую** газе́ту но́в**ую** учени́цу	но́в**ое** сло́во
	Soft		
nom.	после́дн**ий** журна́л после́дн**ий** учени́к	после́дн**яя** газе́та после́дн**яя** учени́ца	после́дн**ее** сло́во
gen.	после́дн**его** журна́ла после́дн**его** ученика́	после́дн**ей** газе́ты после́дн**ей** учени́цы	после́дн**его** сло́ва
acc.	после́дн**ий** журна́л после́дн**его** ученика́	после́дн**юю** газе́ту после́дн**юю** учени́цу	после́дн**ее** сло́во
	Mixed		
nom.	ру́сск**ий** журна́л ру́сск**ий** учени́к	ру́сск**ая** газе́та ру́сск**ая** учени́ца	ру́сск**ое** сло́во
gen.	ру́сск**ого** журна́ла ру́сск**ого** ученика́	ру́сск**ой** газе́ты ру́сск**ой** учени́цы	ру́сск**ого** сло́ва
acc.	ру́сск**ий** журна́л ру́сск**ого** ученика́	ру́сск**ую** газе́ту ру́сск**ую** учени́цу	ру́сск**ое** сло́во

b. **я люблю́** means *I am fond of* or *I love*, and implies some attachment or <u>emotion</u>:

Я люблю́ Нью-Йо́рк.	I *am fond* of New York (as a result of knowledge or habit).
Я люблю́ Ве́ру.	I *love* Vera (with deep emotion, irrespective of knowledge).

c. When "liking" refers to a verb, it is rendered by **люби́ть**:

Я люблю́ смотре́ть на мо́ре.	I *like to look* at the sea.

Упражнéния (Exercises)

A. Decline the following phrases in the *nominative, genitive,* and *accusative.*

1. э́тот отвéт   2. э́та вáза   3. э́то слóво   4. э́тот дóктор
5. приле́жный учени́к   6. приле́жная учени́ца   7. у́мный человéк   8. си́няя бумáга   9. си́нее окнó   10. ру́сская дéвушка
11. си́ний цвет   12. ру́сский теáтр   13. какáя рабóта   14.
мáленький брат   15. плохáя кóмната

B. Translate the following phrases.   *послéднее слóво*

1. blue notebook   2. good answer   3. last word   4. diligent
student (*f.*)   5. blue sea   6. beautiful summer house   7. good
hostess   8. this girl   9. interesting lesson   10. What a clever
dog!   11. last big town   12. last small village   13. What a good
composition!   14. What kind of a question is this?   15. Thank
goodness!   *Си́нии тетрáд   Хорóшо отвéт*

C. Change the following affirmative sentences to negative ones.
For example: *Си́нее мáре послéднее слóва*

Я пишу́ урóк. — Я **не** пишу́ урó**ка.**

У меня́ **есть** ру́сск**ая** кни́га. — У меня́ **нет** ру́сск**ой** кни́ги.

1. Ты берёшь кни́гу.   2. У негó есть гарáж.   3. Мы
изучáем ру́сский язы́к (*gen.* **языкá**).   4. Онá купи́ла по-
слéднюю вáзу.   5. Я знáю э́ту стáрую учи́тельницу.   6. Они́
пóмнят секрéт.   7. У них есть дáча.   8. Вы понимáете вопрóс.
9. Вы пóмните э́того человéка.   10. У них есть си́ний дивáн.

Перевóд (Translation)

A. Omit words in parentheses and include words in brackets.

1. I do not know this town.   2. They did not know the last
lesson.   3. She did not remember this Russian word.   4. We do
not like her room.   5. She does not like blue [color].   6. They
do not like your family.   7. You surely like to sit at the window
and look at the new summer house.

B. Omit words in parentheses and include words in brackets.

1. We shall live at the summer house in the spring.   2. In the
summer grandfather and grandmother will also live at our house.
3. They like the sea very (much).   4. They often go (by conveyance) to the summer house, even in the winter.   5. Our summer

house is situated on the sea shore [on the shore of the sea].   6. It
(the summer house) is far from town, and we need a car [in order to]
to go (drive) to the store.   7. I often take father's car [in order to]
to drive to town in the evening.   8. I like to drive (go by conveyance) in the evening or at night.

Вопро́сы (**Questions**)

1. Где вы живёте зимо́й?   2. Вы то́же живёте там ле́том?
3. Что вы де́лаете в го́роде?   4. Что вы де́лаете на да́че?
5. Где нахо́дится ва́ша да́ча?   6. Мо́ре далеко́ от да́чи?
7. Вы лю́бите смотре́ть на мо́ре?   8. Како́го цве́та мо́ре?
9. Вам нра́вится э́тот цвет?   10. Вам нра́вится ва́ша да́ча?
11. Кто купи́л э́ту да́чу?   12. Что оте́ц ча́сто берёт у вас?
13. Где ва́ша тетра́дь с сочине́нием?   14. Вы ча́сто е́здите в
Нью-Йо́рк?   15. Вы приле́жный учени́к?   16. Вам нра́вится
э́тот вопро́с?

Pattern Drills

A. 1. Study ¶14-1.   Listen to the teacher (or the tape) and
repeat the following.

m.	*f.*	*n.*
э́тот бе́рег	э́та да́ча	э́то мо́ре
э́тот дом	э́та дверь	э́то окно́
э́тот журна́л	э́та тетра́дь	э́то сочине́ние
э́тот дива́н	э́та ла́мпа	э́то кре́сло
э́тот каранда́ш	э́та бума́га	э́то перо́
э́тот день	э́та ночь	э́то у́тро
э́тот челове́к	э́та де́вушка	э́то сло́во

2. Supply **э́тот, э́та,** and **э́то** to agree with the following
nouns and read the phrases aloud.   For example, **э́тот учи́тель,
э́та учи́тельница.**

оте́ц, мать, учени́ца, учени́к, семья́, брат, сестра́, де́душка,
ба́бушка, господи́н, госпожа́, хозя́ин, хозя́йка, журна́л, газе́та,
Москва́, го́род, дере́вня, стена́, доска́, кре́сло, потоло́к, ве́чер,
день, у́тро.

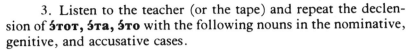

3. Listen to the teacher (or the tape) and repeat the declension of **этот, эта, это** with the following nouns in the nominative, genitive, and accusative cases.

	m.	*f.*	*n.*
nom.	этот человéк	эта красáвица	это слóво
gen.	этого человéка	этой красáвицы	этого слóва
acc.	этого человéка	эту красáвицу	это слóво

4. Decline the following aloud, as in A.3 above.

> этот дом, эта кóмната, это окнó
> этот муж, эта женá, это перó

B. 1. Study **¶14-2.** Listen to the teacher (or the tape) and repeat the following.

m.	*f.*	*n.*
крас**ивый** бéрег	крас**ивая** дáча	крас**ивое** мóре
нóв**ый** журнáл	нóв**ая** книга	нóв**ое** сочинéние
послéдн**ий** урóк	послéдн**яя** тетрáдь	послéдн**ее** слóво
син**ий** потолóк	син**яя** стенá	син**ее** окнó
хорóш**ий** день	хорóш**ая** ночь	хорóш**ее** утро
русск**ий** гóрод	русск**ая** дерéвня	русск**ое** слóво
плох**óй** ученик	плох**áя** ученица	плох**óе** сочинéние

2. Decline aloud the following phrases in the *nominative*, *genitive*, and *accusative* cases using exercise A.3 as your model.

> нóвый дом, нóвая кóмната, нóвое окнó
> синий мел, синяя бумáга, синее перó
> хорóший стол, хорóшая лáмпа, хорóшее крéсло

3. Decline the above phrases in B.2 adding **этот, эта, это** as in the following model:

этот нóвый дом, эта нóвая кóмната, это нóвое окнó

C. 1. Study **¶14-3.** Listen to the teacher (or the tape) and repeat the following sentences. Then read each sentence in the negative according to the model sentences in the ''Student'' column.

Teacher	*Student*
Я знáю урóк.	Я не знáю урóка.
Ты читáешь книгу.	Ты не читáешь книги.
Он даёт перó сестрé.	Он не даёт перá сестрé.

Онá пи́шет брáту отвéт.	Онá _____.
Мы понимáем вопрóс.	Мы _____.
Вы пóмните секрéт.	Вы _____.
Они́ берýт э́ту карти́ну.	Они́ _____.

2. Read the affirmative and negative sentences above, inserting the following before each noun in the required gender and case.

э́тот, э́та, э́то, нóвый, нóвая, нóвое, and последний, послéдняя, послéднее

D. Study ¶14-4. Listen to the teacher (or the tape) and repeat the following. Then replace **мне нрáвится** with **люби́ть** according to the model sentences.

Teacher	*Student*
Мне нрáвится Вашингтóн.	Я люблю́ Вашингтóн.
Тебé нрáвится э́та карти́на.	Ты лю́бишь э́ту карти́ну.
Емý _____ э́то крéсло.	Он _____.
Нам _____ Вéра.	Мы _____.
Вам _____ рýсский язы́к.	Вы _____.
Им _____ э́та хозя́йка.	Они́ _____.

E. Study ¶14-4c. Listen to the teacher (or the tape) and repeat the following. Then conjugate **люби́ть** with **читáть, рабóтать, писáть, жить в дерéвне,** and **смотрéть на мóре.**

Я люблю́ гуля́ть.
Ты лю́бишь _____.
Он лю́бит _____.
Мы лю́бим _____.
Вы лю́бите _____.
Они́ лю́бят _____.

UNIT 15

I

МАКСИ́М ИВА́НОВИЧ БО́ЛЕН

Макси́м Ива́нович бо́лен. У него́ нет аппети́та. Он почти́ ничего́ не ест и о́чень ма́ло спит. У него́ боли́т голова́. Иногда́ он пьёт немно́го воды́ и́ли молока́ и ест немно́го су́па. Э́то всё, что он мо́жет пить и́ли есть.

Он уже́ це́лую неде́лю сиди́т до́ма и не хо́дит в конто́ру. Весь день он лежи́т на дива́не и ничего́ не де́лает. Почему́ он не идёт к до́ктору?

Слова́рь (Vocabulary)

Макси́м Maxim
Ива́нович Ivanovich (*lit.* son of Ivan) (see **¶ 15-1**)
бо́лен (*adj., m.*), **больна́** (*f.*) sick
аппети́т appetite
почти́ almost
ест eats
есть (*irr.*) to eat (see **¶ 15-2**)
боли́т aches
голова́ (*gen.* **головы́**) head
у него́ боли́т голова́ his head aches
пить (I); пью, пьёшь, пьют; *past* **пил, -ла́, -ло, -ли;** *imper.* **пей, пе́йте** to drink
немно́го a little
вода́ water
молоко́ milk
суп soup
э́то всё that is all
це́лый, -ая, -ое whole (integral, complete)
неде́ля (*f.*) week
це́лую неде́лю a whole week (see **¶ 15-3 & 15-4**)
лежа́ть (II); лежу́, лежи́шь, лежа́т to lie
к (with *dat.*) to, towards (see **¶ 15-5**)

115

II

ТЕБЕ́ НУ́ЖЕН СПЕЦИАЛИ́СТ

Áнна Никола́евна, жена́ Макси́ма Ива́новича, ду́мает, что её муж серьёзно бо́лен.   Она́ зна́ет, что у него́ всегда́ мно́го эне́ргии, когда́ он здоро́в.   Тепе́рь же он весь день лежи́т на дива́не и ничего́ не де́лает.   Он да́же не слу́шает ра́дио и не смо́трит телеви́зор.

— Макси́м, — говори́т Áнна Никола́евна — вот хоро́ший суп.   Ку́шай, пожа́луйста.

— Нет, спаси́бо — отвеча́ет Макси́м Ива́нович — ничего́ не могу́ есть.

— Почему́ же ты не идёшь к до́ктору?   Ты уже́ це́лую неде́лю не рабо́таешь, ничего́ не ешь и почти́ не спишь.

— Я уже́ был у до́ктора две неде́ли тому́ наза́д, и мне тепе́рь ху́же, а не лу́чше.

— Тебе́ ну́жен специали́ст.   Бори́с Никола́евич большо́й специали́ст.   Пожа́луйста, Макси́м . . .

— Хорошо́! хорошо́!   Я зна́ю, что мне ну́жен специали́ст. За́втра у́тром иду́ к Бори́су Никола́евичу.   Он живёт о́коло университе́та, и э́то о́чень бли́зко.

— Ну, спаси́бо, Макси́м!   Я о́чень ра́да, что ты за́втра бу́дешь у специали́ста.

Слова́рь (Vocabulary)

специали́ст specialist
Никола́евна Nikolaevna (see ¶ 15-1)
ду́мать (I); **ду́маю, -ешь, -ют** to think
серьёзно seriously
эне́ргия (*pr.* эне́ргия) energy
же however, but; then (emphatic)
слу́шать (I); **слу́шаю, -ешь, -ют** to listen to
ра́дио (*n.*) (*not decl.*) radio
телеви́зор television set
смотре́ть телеви́зор to watch television
ку́шать (I); **ку́шаю, -ешь, -ют** to eat (see ¶ 15-6)
две (*f.*) two
тому́ наза́д ago
ху́же (*adv.*) worse
мне ху́же I feel worse
мне лу́чше I feel better
хорошо́! O.K., all right
за́втра у́тром tomorrow morning
университе́т university
рад (*m.*), **ра́да** (*f.*) glad

хлеб = bread
де́лать - to do
соль - salt

Грамма́тика (Grammar)

Part I

15-1. Patronymics

a. Patronymics are names formed by the addition of a suffix to the father's first name.

b. The following are common suffixes:

> *m.*   **-ович,**   **-евич**
> *f.*   **-овна,**   **-евна**

c. Patronymics are formed thus:

Ива́н + **ович** = Ива́н**ович**	(*lit.* son of Ivan)
Никола́(й) + **евич** = Никола́**евич**	(*lit.* son of Nicholas)
Ива́н + **овна** = Ива́н**овна**	(*lit.* daughter of Ivan)
Никола́(й) + **евна** = Никола́**евна**	(*lit.* daughter of Nicholas)

d. The first name and the patronymic are used by Russians in addressing each other, unless they are relatives or close friends. For example: **Макси́м Ива́нович, Ве́ра Ива́новна.**

Note: **Господи́н** or **госпожа́** can never be used alone as a form of address. The surname must always accompany it.

15-2. Infinitive: есть (*irr.*) *to eat*

Note: Do not confuse **е́хать** with **есть.**

a. Present tense.

я ем	мы еди́м
ты ешь	вы еди́те
он ест	они́ едя́т

b. Past tense.

> ел, е́ла, е́ло, е́ли

c. Compound future.

> я бу́ду есть, *etc.* (see ¶ 11-3)

15-3. Expressions of Time with the Accusative

To express length of time or recurrence in time, the accusative without a preposition is used:

весь день	the whole day
це́лую неде́лю	a whole week
ка́ждое у́тро	every morning

15-4. Present Tense Used as English Present Perfect

The present tense is used to indicate an action which has been going on and is continued in the present. For example:

Я уже́ в Москве́ три дня.	I have been in Moscow three days (*i.e.*, have been and am *now* in Moscow).
Он уже́ це́лую неде́лю не рабо́тает.	He has not been working for a whole week (*i.e.*, has not been and is not *now* working).

15-5. The Dative with Verbs of Motion

The preposition **к** + dative is used to indicate:

a. Motion toward an object (*up to it, but not inside it*).

Я иду́ к окну́.	I am going to the window (*up to it*).
Я иду́ к доске́.	I am going to the board.

b. A person as the destination.

Я иду́ к сестре́.	I am going to my sister's (*i.e.*, to her *place*, or to *see* her).
Я иду́ к до́ктору.	I am going to the doctor.

Note: In the above examples, motion is not to the interior of the object; otherwise **в** (*into*) would have to be used. Compare:

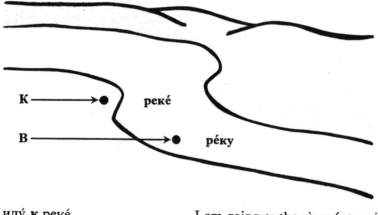

Я иду́ к реке́.	I am going *to* the river (*up to it*).
Я иду́ в ре́ку.	I am going *into* the river.

Part II

15-6. The Verbs "to eat": есть and ку́шать

a. **Есть** is the conversational form.   It should be used in the first person.

b. Politeness requires the use of **ку́шать** instead of **есть** in the second person, especially in the imperative.

15-7. Declension of Nouns

There are three declensions of nouns in Russian.   These are determined on the basis of gender.

a. First Declension — membership.

1. All feminine nouns ending in **-а**, **-я**, or **-ия** in the nominative singular belong to the First Declension.   For example:

ка́рта, неде́ля, а́рмия (army).

2. A few masculine nouns with feminine endings, such as де́душка, дя́дя, or Ва́ня, also belong to the First Declension. Although they are declined as feminine nouns, they are otherwise treated as masculine.   For example:

Мой де́душка хоро́ший учи́тель.
My grandfather is a good teacher.

b. The declensions are subdivided into two classes of nouns: *hard* and *soft.*

1. Nouns ending in **-а** are *hard*; those in **-я** or **-ия** are *soft.*

2. The inflection of soft nouns in **-я** differs from that of the hard vowels in **-а** only in the substitution of soft vowels for the corresponding hard ones.

c. First Declension in the singular.

	Hard	Soft		-ия
	-а	**-я**		**-ия**
nom.	ка́рта	неде́ля	дя́дя	а́рмия
gen.	ка́рты	неде́ли	дя́ди	а́рмии
dat.	ка́рте	неде́ле	дя́де	а́рмии
acc.	ка́рту	неде́лю	дя́дю	а́рмию
instr.	ка́ртой (-ою)	неде́лей (-ею)	дя́дей (-ею)	а́рмией (-ею)
prep.	о ка́рте	о неде́ле	о дя́де	об а́рмии

1. The preposition **о**, meaning _about_ or _concerning_, is used so frequently with the prepositional that it is usually included in declension tables. Before the vowels **а, э, о, у,** and **и, об** is used instead of **о**.

2. In the singular, the accusative endings of animate and inanimate nouns are identical. Compare: дя́дю with неде́лю.

Упражне́ния (Exercises)

A. Put the words in parentheses in the appropriate case, and fill in the blanks with appropriate words.

1. (Я) тепе́рь ху́же. 2. (Макси́м Ива́нович) ху́же, а не _____. 3. Почему́ вы не идёте к (до́ктор), е́сли вам _____? 4. Вы пьёте мно́го (вода́), но ничего́ не _____. 5. Мы говори́м с (дя́дя) об (а́рмия). 6. Она́ ча́сто _____ к (ба́бушка). 7. Ба́бушка уже́ четы́ре (неде́ля) живёт на (да́ча). 8. Да́ча нахо́дится на _____ мо́ря. 9. У отца́ боли́т _____. 10. Мы лю́бим смотре́ть на (си́няя ва́за). 11. У них нет (аппети́т). 12. Она́ уже́ (це́лая неде́ля) сиди́т _____.

B. Decline the following in the singular.

1. ко́мната	5. эне́ргия
2. кни́га	6. ва́за
3. тётя	7. ко́нтора
4. де́душка	8. дя́дя

C. Conjugate the following verbs in the present, past, and compound future.

1. есть	6. смотре́ть
2. ку́шать	7. ду́мать
3. пить	8. ходи́ть
4. лежа́ть	9. е́здить
5. слу́шать	10. брать

Перево́д (Translation)

Include words in brackets.

1. Anna Nikolaevna is sick [**больна́**]. 2. She always has a headache. 3. She eats almost nothing. 4. Yesterday she drank a little water, but ate nothing. 5. She has no energy, and she lies all day on the divan. 6. Her husband thinks that she needs a

doctor.   7. Every day he asks her [её] why she does not go to a
doctor.   8. Every day she answers that she is well, and that she does
not need a doctor.   9. But she stays home and does not go to the
office.   10. She likes very much to listen to the radio or to look at
television.   11. Now, however [же], she does nothing all day.
12. She likes very much to go to the theater, but now she does not
even want to talk about the theater.   13. Nothing pleases her now
[**Ничего́ ей тепе́рь не нра́вится**].   14. Her husband thinks
that she is seriously ill, but what can [**мо́жет**] he do?

Вопро́сы (Questions)

1. Кто бо́лен?   2. Почему́ у Макси́ма Ива́новича нет
аппети́та?   3. Его́ жена́, А́нна Никола́евна, то́же больна́?
4. У неё есть аппети́т?   5. Что боли́т у Макси́ма Ива́новича?
6. Что он мо́жет есть и пить?   7. Э́то всё что он мо́жет есть?
8. Как до́лго он уже́ сиди́т до́ма?   9. Что он де́лает весь день?
10. Он слу́шает ра́дио?   11. Он смо́трит телеви́зор?   12. Вы
ду́маете, что он серьёзно бо́лен?   13. Почему́ он не идёт к
до́ктору?   14. У кого́ он уже́ был две неде́ли тому́ наза́д?
15. Кто большо́й специали́ст?   16. Где живёт э́тот специа-
ли́ст?   17. Жена́ ра́да, что её муж за́втра идёт к специали́сту?

Pattern Drills

A. 1. Study ¶**15-2** and **15-6.**   Listen to the teacher (or the tape)
and repeat the following.

есть	ку́шать	*Polite usage of* есть *and* ку́шать
я ем	я ку́шаю	я ем
ты ешь	ты ку́шаешь	ты ку́шаешь
он ест	он ку́шает	он ест *or* ку́шает
мы еди́м	мы ку́шаем	мы еди́м
вы еди́те	вы ку́шаете	вы еди́те
они́ едя́т	они́ ку́шают	они́ едя́т *or* ку́шают

2. Review ¶**10-9.**   Listen to the teacher (or the tape) and
repeat the following sentences.   Then read each sentence substituting **молока́** for **воды́.**

Teacher	*Student*
Я ем немно́го су́па и пью нем-но́го воды́.	Я ем немно́го су́па и пью немно́го молока́.
Ты ку́шаешь немно́го су́па и пьёшь немно́го воды́.	Ты _____ .

Он ест немно́го су́па и пьёт   Он_____
немно́го воды́.   _____.
Мы еди́м немно́го су́па и пьём   Мы _____
немно́го воды́.   _____.
Вы ку́шаете немно́го су́па и   Вы _____
пьёте немно́го воды́.   _____.
Они́ едя́т немно́го су́па и пьют   Они́ _____
немно́го воды́.   _____.

B. 1. Study ¶15-3 and 15-4. Listen to the teacher (or the tape) and repeat the following questions. Then read each answer aloud supplying the missing words according to the model answer in the ''Student'' column.

Teacher	*Student*
1. Почему́ ты **весь день** сиди́шь до́ма? Why have you been staying home all day?	1. Я **весь день** сижу́ до́ма, потому́ что у меня́ боли́т голова́.
2. Почему́ Ма́ша **всё у́тро** лежи́т на дива́не? Why has Masha been lying on the divan all morning?	2. Ма́ша **всё у́тро** лежи́т на дива́не, потому́ что у _____ то́же _____ голова́.
3. Почему́ вы **це́лую неде́лю** не хо́дите в шко́лу?	3. Я **це́лую неде́лю** не _____ в _____, потому́ что я бо́лен.
4. Почему́ ва́ша сестра́ **всю ночь** смо́трит телеви́зор?	4. Она́ **всю ночь** _____, потому́ что она́ не мо́жет спать.
5. Почему́ вы **у́тром** ничего́ не ку́шаете?	5. Мы _____ ничего́ не еди́м, потому́ что у _____ нет аппети́та.
6. Почему́ они́ хо́дят в го́род **ка́ждый ве́чер,** а не е́здят на автомоби́ле?	6. Они́ хо́дят **ка́ждый ве́чер,** а не е́здят, потому́ что у _____ нет _____.

C. Study ¶15-5. Listen to the teacher (or the tape) and repeat the following sentences. Then read aloud each sentence in the ''Student'' column supplying the required case of the nouns in parentheses.

Teacher	*Student*
Я иду́ к кре́слу. Ты идёшь к стене́.	Я иду́ к окну́. Ты _____ (доска́).

Он идёт к телефо́ну.   Он _____ (стол).
Мы идём к отцу́.   Мы _____ (брат).
Вы идёте к до́ктору.   Вы _____ (специали́ст).
Они́ иду́т к де́душке.   Они́ _____ (ба́бушка).

D. Study ¶15-6.   Listen to the teacher (or the tape) and repeat the following sentences.   Then read aloud each sentence in the ''Student'' column replacing **дя́дя** with **сестра́** in the required case.

Teacher	Student
У меня́ есть дя́дя.	У меня́ есть сестра́.
У тебя́ нет дя́ди.	У тебя́ нет сестры́.
Он идёт к дя́де.	Он _____.
Мы лю́бим дя́дю.	Мы _____.
Вы гуля́ете с дя́дей.	Вы _____.
Они́ говоря́т о дя́де.	Они́ _____.

U N I T   16

I

ИЗ ДНЕВНИКА́ МОЛОДО́Й ДЕ́ВУШКИ—У́тром

Сего́дня о́чень плоха́я пого́да. Не́бо се́рое. Идёт дождь. Хо́лодно. В ко́мнате темно́. Мне ску́чно. Чита́ть не хочу́. Игра́ть на роя́ле не хочу́. За́втра у меня́ экза́мен, но я ничего́ не де́лаю. То́лько сижу́ у окна́ и смотрю́ на се́рое не́бо, на дождь и на пусту́ю у́лицу.

Всё у́тро ду́маю об Аки́ме. Почему́ его́ ещё нет? Мо́жет быть он забы́л, что я его́ жду . . . Нет, не мо́жет быть! Он тако́й ми́лый и так меня́ лю́бит! . . . Он ча́сто говори́т мне: "Кака́я ты краса́вица, Ма́ша!"

Слова́рь (Vocabulary)

из (*with gen.*) from, out of
дневни́к (*gen.* **дневника́**) diary
молодо́й, -а́я, -ое young
пого́да weather
не́бо sky
се́рый, -ая, -ое gray
хо́лодно it is cold (see ¶ 16-1)
темно́ it is dark
мне ску́чно (*pr.* **ску́шно**) I am bored
роя́ль (*m.*) piano
игра́ть на роя́ле to play the piano (see ¶ 16-2)
экза́мен examination
пусто́й, -а́я, -ое empty, deserted
у́лица street
Аки́м Joachim

то́лько - only
смотре́ть - to look at
за́втра - tomorrow
ча́сто - often

124

егó ещё нет he is not here yet (see ¶ 16-3)
забы́л (*past of* **забы́ть**) forgot
ждать (I); **жду, ждёшь, ждут** to wait
не мóжет быть (it is) impossible
такóй, -áя, -óе such a . . .
ми́лый, -ая, -ое nice, dear, lovely
он такóй ми́лый he is such a dear
так (*adv.*) so

II

ИЗ ДНЕВНИКÁ МОЛОДÓЙ ДÉВУШКИ—Днём

Урá! Аки́м приéхал!

Он приéхал так пóздно, потомý что всё ýтро шёл дождь, и нýжно бы́ло éхать óчень мéдленно. Нет, он не забы́л меня́! Он ничегó не говори́т, но я знáю, что он меня́ лю́бит.

Погóда тепéрь óчень харóшая. Нéбо я́сное. Теплó и светлó. Я пишý óчень бы́стро, потомý что скóро мы éдем купáться, а потóм бýдем игрáть в тéннис.

Ах, как Аки́м мне нрáвится! Какóй он ýмный, ми́лый, интерéсный! . . . Мой млáдший брат, Бори́с, говори́т, что Аки́м мне так нрáвится, потомý что у негó нóвый автомоби́ль. Но э́то непрáвда! Бори́с глýпый мáльчик.

Словáрь (Vocabulary)

урá hurrah
приéхал (*past of* **приéхать**) arrived (by conveyance)
шёл дождь it rained
нýжно бы́ло it was necessary (see ¶ 16-5)
я́сный, -ая, -ое clear
теплó it is warm
светлó it is bright
скóро soon
купáться (*pr.* **купáца**) (I); **купáюсь, купáешься** (*pr.* **купáешса**), **купáются** (*pr.* **купáюца**) to bathe (oneself) (see ¶ 16-6)
тéннис tennis
игрáть в тéннис to play tennis (see ¶ 16-2)
какóй он ýмный how clever he is!
интерéсный, -ая, -ое attractive (of a person)
млáдший, -ая, -ее younger, junior
прáвда truth
э́то непрáвда this is not true
глýпый, -ая, -ое stupid
мáльчик boy

Грамма́тика (Grammar)

Part I

16-1. Impersonal Expressions in the Present Tense

a. Impersonal expressions like *it is cold*, *it is boring*, are rendered by one word: **хо́лодно**, **ску́чно**. The subject *it* and the verb *is* of the English sentence are understood. For example:

хо́лодно	*it is* cold
ску́чно	*it is* boring
лу́чше	*it is* better
ху́же	*it is* worse
ну́жно	*it is* necessary

b. When such impersonal expressions refer to persons, the latter must be in the dative in Russian. For example:

Мне хо́лодно.	*I am cold (lit. to me it is cold).*
Ученику́ ску́чно.	The *pupil* is bored (*lit. to the pupil it is boring*).
Сестре́ тепе́рь лу́чше.	*Sister* is now better (*lit. to sister it is now better*).
Ему́ ну́жно.	*He* has to (*lit. it is necessary to him*).

16-2. Idioms with игра́ть

a. **игра́ть** + **на** + *prep.* = to play an instrument.

Она́ игра́ет на роя́ле.	She plays (is playing) the piano.
Ты игра́ешь на гита́ре.	You play (are playing) the guitar.

b. **игра́ть** + **в** + *acc.* = to play a game.

Мы игра́ем в те́ннис.	We play tennis.
Они́ игра́ют в ка́рты.	They play cards.

16-3. Expressions of Absence or Lack

a. **Есть** means *there is, there are.* It asserts the existence or presence of an object. For example:

В го́роде **есть** теа́тр.	There is a theater in town.
На да́че **есть** вода́.	There is water at the summer house.

gen

b. **Нет** is a contraction of **не** + **есть**. It means *there is not, there are not,* or *there is no, there are no.* It expresses *absence, lack,* or the *non-existence* of an object—in effect, the opposite of **есть**.

Ивáна **нет** в клáссе.	Ivan *is not* in class. (*Absence*)
Егó ещё **нет**.	He *is not* here yet. (*Absence*)
В гóроде **нет** теáтра.	There *is no* theater in town. (*Non-existence*)
На дáче **нет** вод
ы.	There *is no* water at the summer house. (*Non-existence or temporary lack*)

Note: The subject of such negative sentences must be in the *genitive.*

c. Do not confuse possessive phrases in the negative (see ¶ **13-1**) with expressions of absence or lack.

Compare:

У нас **нет** автомобúля.	We have no car.
Автомобúля **нет**.	The car is not here. (It is gone, or has not arrived; it is absent from a certain place.)

Note: In the first sentence, *car* is rendered in English as the *direct object*; in the second sentence, it is the *subject.*

16-4. Direct Object with ждать

a. **Ждать** means *to wait.*

b. *To wait for* is rendered thus:

1. **ждать** + *gen.* of a thing. For example:

Онá ждёт **журнáла**.	She is waiting *for* a magazine.
Онú ждут **отвéта**.	They are waiting *for* an answer.

2. **ждать** + *acc.* of a person, when definite. For example:

Я жду **сестрý**.	I am waiting *for* my sister.
Ты **егó** ждёшь.	You are waiting *for* him.

Part II

16-5. Impersonal Expressions—Present, Past, and Future

a. The present tense consists of the adverb alone (see ¶ **16-1**). The past is formed by adding **бы
ло**, and the future by adding **бýдет**.

b. Examples. (*Note* position of **не** for the negative, and the stress on **нé** in the past tense.)

PRESENT TENSE

Affirmative	хóлодно it *is* cold	мне тебé емý ей } хóлодно	I am you are he is she is } cold	
		нам вам им } хóлодно	we are you are they are } cold	
Negative	**не** хóлодно it *is not* cold	мне **не** хóлодно I am not cold, *etc.*		

PAST TENSE

Affirmative	бы́ло хóлодно it *was* cold	мне тебé емý ей } бы́ло хóлодно	I was you were he was she was } cold	
		нам вам им } бы́ло хóлодно	we were you were they were } cold	
Negative	**нé** было хóлодно it *was not* cold	мне **нé** было хóлодно	I was not cold, *etc.*	

FUTURE TENSE

Affirmative	бýдет хóлодно it *will be* cold	мне тебé емý ей } бýдет хóлодно	I shall be you will be he will be she will be } cold	
		нам вам им } бýдет хóлодно	we shall be you will be they will be } cold	
Negative	**не** бýдет хóлодно it *will not* be cold	мне **не** бýдет хóлодно	I shall not be cold, *etc.*	

16-6. Reflexive Verbs

a. A *reflexive verb* denotes action which the subject is performing upon himself. Compare:

купа́ть	to bathe (*someone else*)
купа́ться	to bathe (*oneself*)

b. Reflexive verbs are formed by adding **-ся** or **-сь** to regular verb endings.

1. **-ся** is added after a *consonant*, **ь**, or **й**.
2. **-сь** is added after a *vowel*.

c. Infinitive: **купа́ться (I)** (*pr.* **купа́ца**) *to bathe (oneself)*

PRESENT TENSE

я купа́юсь	
ты купа́ешься	(*pr.* купа́ешьса)
он, она́, оно́ купа́ется	(*pr.* купа́еца)
мы купа́емся	(*pr.* купа́емса)
вы купа́етесь	
они́ купа́ются	(*pr.* купа́юца)

PAST TENSE

я, ты, он купа́лся	мы ⎫
я, ты, она́ купа́лась	вы ⎬ купа́лись
оно́ купа́лось	они́ ⎭

FUTURE TENSE

я бу́ду купа́ться, *etc.*

IMPERATIVE

купа́йся (*fam. sing.*)   купа́йтесь (*pl.*, or *pol. sing.*)

Упражне́ния (Exercises)

A. Translate. (Review ¶ 5-2.)

1. Се́рое не́бо; не́бо се́рое.   2. Пуста́я у́лица; у́лица пуста́я.
3. Ми́лая де́вушка; де́вушка ми́лая.   4. Плоха́я пого́да; пого́да плоха́я.   5. Ма́ленький ма́льчик; ма́льчик ма́ленький.
6. Глу́пая жена́; жена́ глу́пая.   7. Приле́жная учени́ца; учени́ца приле́жная.   8. У́мная соба́ка; соба́ка у́мная.   9. Хоро́ший телеви́зор; телеви́зор хоро́ший.   10. Си́нее мо́ре; мо́ре си́нее.

B. Conjugate the following in the *present*, *past*, and *future*, using ❡ 16-5 as a sample.

1. ску́чно; мне ску́чно.
2. тепло́; мне тепло́.
3. ну́жно; мне ну́жно.
4. лу́чше; мне лу́чше.
5. ху́же; мне ху́же.

C. Supply the proper forms of **купа́ться** and translate.

1. Я не люблю́ _____, когда́ идёт дождь.
2. Ты о́чень ча́сто _____ в мо́ре.
3. Заче́м вы живёте на берегу́ мо́ря, е́сли вы никогда́ не _____?
4. Вчера́ А́нна до́лго _____ с бра́том и с сестро́й.
5. Мы ещё никогда́ не _____ в мо́ре.
6. Ле́том она́ бу́дет _____ ка́ждый день.
7. Ско́ро мы то́же бу́дем _____.

D. Supply the proper equivalents for words in parentheses.

1. Аки́м забы́л (her) и она́ забы́ла (Joachim).
2. Она́ не зна́ет (this Russian word).
3. Вы всё у́тро ду́маете (about the book).
4. Кого́ вы ждёте? Я жду (for sister).
5. Они́ ждут (for an answer) от учи́тельницы.
6. Они́ до́лго смотре́ли (at this picture).
7. (I was not cold) на берегу́ мо́ря.
8. (You will be bored) в дере́вне.
9. За́втра в го́роде (it will be very warm).
10. (Do not bathe) так ча́сто.

Перево́д (Translation)

A.   Omit words in parentheses and include words in brackets.

1. Joachim was at Masha's (home) two weeks ago.   2. He did not come [arrive by conveyance] today, because he is sick.   3. Masha has been waiting for him all morning.   4. She thinks [that] he has forgotten her.   5. Masha lives in the country, and is very bored when the weather is bad.   6. She likes to play the piano when it rains.   7. When the weather is good, she prefers to play tennis.

B. Omit words in parentheses and include those in brackets.

1. I am cold because it is so cold today.   2. It was very dark, and it was necessary [**нýжно бы́ло**] to go (by vehicle) very slowly. 3. It was very late when we got [arrived] home.   4. Is there a school in the village? (See **¶ 16-3**.)   5. No, there is no school in the village.   6. There is no water in the house.   7. Is Boris in school?   No, Boris is not in school (absent).   8. The teacher (*f.*) is not here yet.   Why is she not here (absent)?   9. We are not waiting for a car.   We have one [a car].   We are waiting for Vera. 10. The car is not here (missing).   Who has [**у когó**] it?

C. Translate.

1. Yesterday the weather was very good.   2. The sky was clear, and it was bright and warm.   3. Yesterday Masha had no examination, and today she also has no examination.   4. Yesterday she bathed in the sea [**в мóре**], and today she will play tennis with Joachim.   5. She is very fond of Joachim, because he plays tennis so well, plays the piano well, and has a new car.

Вопрóсы (**Questions**)

1. Какáя сегóдня погóда?   2. Какóго цвéта нéбо сегóдня? 3. Какóго цвéта онó бы́ло вчерá?˙   4. Какóго цвéта онó бýдет зáвтра?   5. Что вы предпочитáете дéлать, когдá идёт дождь? 6. Тепéрь темнó или светлó?   7. Óсенью хóлодно или теплó? 8. О ком (of whom) дýмает Мáша?   9. Когó онá ждёт всё ýтро?   10. Почемý Акúма ещё нет?   11. Как вы дýмаете, (What do you think) Акúм забы́л молодýю дéвушку?   12. Почемý Акúм так нрáвится Мáше?   13. Что он ей чáсто говорúт? 14. Почемý Акúм приéхал так пóздно?   15. Что говорúт Борúс, млáдший брат Мáши?   16. Это прáвда или не прáвда? 17. Как вы дýмаете, Борúс ýмный или глýпый мáльчик? 18. Как вам нрáвится дневнúк Мáши?   Почемý?

Pattern Drills

A. 1. Study **¶16-1a** and **16-5b**.   Listen to the teacher (or the tape) and repeat the following sentences.   Then make up similar sentences with the words in the "Student" column.

Teacher	*Student*
Сегóдня хóлодно.	теплó, я́сно,
Вчерá бы́ло хóлодно.	тúхо, скýчно,
Зáвтра тóже бýдет хóлодно.	темнó, светлó

2. Use drill A.1 as your model.

Сего́дня не ску́чно.	хо́лодно, я́сно,
Вчера́ **не́** бы́ло ску́чно.	ти́хо, тепло́,
За́втра то́же не бу́дет ску́чно.	светло́

B. Study **¶16-1b**. Then turn to **¶16-5b**. Listen to the teacher (or the tape) and repeat the second column in full. Drill on the impersonal expressions **мне тепло́, мне ску́чно, мне ху́же, мне лу́чше.**

C. Drill on the following, using the table in **¶16-5b** as a model (see **¶16-1b**).

Present	Past	Future
Мне ну́жно рабо́тать.	Мне ну́жно бы́ло рабо́тать.	Мне ну́жно бу́дет рабо́тать.

Мне ну́жно отдыха́ть.
Мне ну́жно лежа́ть.
Мне ну́жно спать.
Мне ну́жно писа́ть.

D. 1. Study **¶16-1** and **16-5**. Listen to the teacher (or the tape) and repeat the following questions. Then read aloud the answers in the "Student" column.

Teacher	Student
Хо́лодно сего́дня. Здесь всегда́ так хо́лодно?	Здесь всегда́ о́чень хо́лодно зимо́й.
А вам не хо́лодно?	Нет, мне тепло́.
Вам нра́вится ва́ша да́ча?	Да, она́ мне о́чень нра́вится.
А вам не ску́чно на да́че?	Мне никогда́ не ску́чно на да́че.
Почему́ вам не ску́чно?	Мне не ску́чно, потому́ что мне всегда́ ну́жно рабо́тать.
Челове́ку ну́жно отдыха́ть?	Я зна́ю. Но мой оте́ц бо́лен и не мо́жет рабо́тать.
Ему́ тепе́рь лу́чше и́ли ху́же?	Спаси́бо. Ему́ тепе́рь лу́чше, но он ещё до́лжен сиде́ть до́ма.

2. Memorize the above dialogue and practice it with a classmate. Then make up a similar dialogue together and recite it in class.

E. Study ¶16-3. Listen to the teacher (or the tape) and repeat
the following sentences. Then read each sentence in the negative
according to the model in the ''Student'' column.

Teacher	Student
В го́роде **есть** университе́т.	В го́роде **нет** университе́та.
В дере́вне **есть** теа́тр.	В _____.
В конто́ре **есть** дива́н.	В _____.
В ко́мнате **есть** окно́.	В _____.
Учи́тельница до́ма.	Учи́тельниц**ы нет** до́ма.
Ива́н в кла́ссе.	Ива́н**а нет** в кла́ссе.
А́нна в шко́ле.	_____.
Автомоби́ль в гараже́.	_____.

F. Study ¶16-2. Listen to the teacher (or the tape) and repeat
the following questions. Then answer each question according
to the models in the ''Student'' column.

Teacher	Student
Кто хорошо́ игра́ет **на роя́ле**?	Бори́с хорошо́ игра́ет **на роя́ле**.
А кто хорошо́ игра́ет на гита́ре?	Ма́ша _____.
Вы лю́бите игра́ть **в те́ннис**?	Да, я люблю́ _____.
Пра́вда, что Ма́ша предпочи-та́ет игра́ть в ка́рты?	Это непра́вда. Она́ предпочи-та́ет игра́ть в те́ннис.
Но она́ лю́бит игра́ть в ка́рты?	Да, она́ лю́бит _____, когда́ плоха́я пого́да.

G. 1. Study ¶16-4*b*.1. Listen to the teacher (or the tape) and
repeat the following sentences.

Я жду журна́ла.
   I am waiting for a magazine.
Ты ждёшь газе́ты.
Он ждёт кни́ги.

Мы ждём автомоби́ля.

Вы ждёте экза́мена.
Они́ ждут отве́та.

2. Study ¶16-4*b*.2. Listen to the teacher (or the tape) and
repeat the following sentences. Then conjugate **ждать** with the
nouns in the ''Student'' column.

Teacher	Student
Я жду профе́ссора.	А́нна, ма́льчик, специали́ст
I am waiting for the professor.	
Ты ждёшь до́ктора.	
Он ждёт хозя́ина.	

Мы ждём хозя́йку.
Вы ждёте сестру́.
Они́ ждут отца́.

H. Turn to ¶16-6c. Listen to the teacher (or the tape) and repeat the conjugation of **купа́ться.**

U N I T 17

REVIEW LESSON

Vocabulary and Grammar Review

A. Place the nouns in parentheses in the appropriate case, supply required case endings for adjectives and pronouns, and translate at sight. For example:

Я не зна́ю эт_____ (де́вушка).
Я не зна́ю **э́той де́вушки**.

1. Далеко́ от (го́род). 2. У (оте́ц) нет (автомоби́ль). 3. Мы бу́дем рабо́тать в (конто́ра). 4. У меня́ нет ру́сск_____ (учи́тельница). 5. Они́ нам да́ли (телеви́зор) на четы́ре (день). 6. Оте́ц купи́л краси́в_____ (да́ча). 7. Наш_____ семья́ живёт на (да́ча) весно́й и ле́том. 8. Моё кре́сло син_____ (цвет). 9. Вы лю́бите смотре́ть на син_____ (мо́ре)? 10. Э́то мой после́дн_____ вопро́с. 11. Ты не зна́ешь эт_____ (сло́во). 12. Они́ живу́т на (бе́рег) (мо́ре). 13. Мы купи́ли после́дн_____ (ва́за). 14 Они́ уже́ цел_____ (неде́ля) сидя́т до́ма. 15. Почему́ вы не идёте к (специали́ст)? 16. У (Макси́м Ива́нович) боли́т голова́. 17. Ма́ша смо́трит на пуст_____ (у́лица). 18. Вы не чита́ли (дневни́к) молод_____ (де́вушка). 19. Сего́дня о́чень хоро́ш_____ (пого́да). 20. У (Ма́ша) за́втра нет (экза́мен).

B. Here is a list of verbs given in Lessons XIII–XVI. Supply their English meanings, and conjugate them orally in the *present*, *past*, and *compound future*. When in doubt, refer to the vocabulary section or to the individual lessons.

135

1. ходи́ть	6. есть
2. е́здить	7. пить
3. смотре́ть	8. лежа́ть
4. брать	9. ждать
5. слу́шать	10. купа́ться

C. Supply the imperatives for the above verbs, except for **е́здить** and **есть** which will be studied later.

Reading and Comprehension Drill

A. Read the following affirmative sentences aloud and translate them; then change them to the negative in Russian.

1. У вас есть ру́сская газе́та.
2. Мы купи́ли после́днюю ва́зу.
3. Они́ изуча́ли англи́йский язы́к.
4. Мне нра́вится Нью-Йо́рк.
5. Вчера́ мне бы́ло ску́чно на да́че.
6. За́втра мы бу́дем купа́ться.

B. Translate the following sentences into idiomatic English.

1. У него́ боли́т голова́.   2. У них нет да́чи.   3. Она́ должна́ ходи́ть в шко́лу пешко́м.   4. Ты игра́ешь на роя́ле ка́ждый день.   5. Ба́бушка живёт у нас.   6. Вчера́ шёл дождь.   7. Мы тепе́рь идём к сестре́.   8. Мне ну́жно перо́. 9. Вы хорошо́ игра́ете в те́ннис.   10. Ты дал ей кни́гу то́лько на две неде́ли.   11. Их да́ча нахо́дится на берегу́ мо́ря. 12. Что э́то за отве́т?   13. У меня́ нет эне́ргии.   14. Как жаль, что до́ктора нет.   15. В го́роде нет теа́тра.   16. Моя́ ко́мната си́него цве́та.   17. Заче́м вы купи́ли дом в го́роде? 18. Они́ ча́сто е́здят в дере́вню?   19. Бори́с глу́пый ма́льчик и ничего́ не понима́ет.   20. Мы ждём сестру́ и бра́та.

C. Supply the words in parentheses; read and translate at sight.

Бори́с и Ма́ша

1. Бори́с (diligent) ма́льчик.   2. Он о́чень лю́бит (school). 3. Ча́сто он (is obliged) (to walk) в шко́лу пешко́м, но (he likes it).   4. Он (every day) зна́ет уро́к и о́чень хорошо́ (answers) в кла́ссе.

5. Ма́ша, (the younger) сестра́ Бори́са, (likes) сиде́ть до́ма. 6. Ча́сто её нет в кла́ссе.   7. Она́ (does not go on foot) в шко́лу,

когда́ (it is cold) и́ли когда́ (it rains).   8. (She is very bored)
в шко́ле.   9. До́ма же (she is never bored).   10. Она́ игра́ет
(the piano), (listens to the) ра́дио, и́ли (watches) телеви́зор.

11. В кла́ссе у Ма́ши никогда́ нет (paper) и о́чень ча́сто нет
(a pen).   12. Е́сли учи́тель (her) спра́шива́ет:—Почему́ вы
(are looking at the street) и не пи́шете?   13. Она́ отвеча́ет —
Я ду́маю.   14. — О чём [about what] вы ду́маете?   15. —
Э́то (a secret).   16. — (Please write) — говори́т учи́тель.   17. —
(I have no paper and no pen) — отвеча́ет Ма́ша.   18. — Вот
перо́ и бума́га.   19. — Спаси́бо — говори́т Ма́ша, но ничего́ не
пи́шет.   20. — Почему́ же вы ничего́ не де́лаете? — ещё раз
спра́шивает учи́тель.   21. — Я о́чень (want to sleep).

D. Rewrite the text of Exercise C above, substituting **Ма́ша**
for **Бори́с**, **де́вушка** for **ма́льчик**, **учени́к** for **учени́ца**, and
vice versa.   For example: Ма́ша приле́жная де́вушка.

Перево́д (Translation)

Include the words in brackets.

1. Such a nice boy!   2. What a beautiful street!   3. We have
no energy.   4. Sister has no work.   5. They have no appetite.
6. We have a picture.   7. The picture is now at our house.   8. I
need a map.   9. I am taking the map.   10. They need a piano.
11. This is all [that] I know.   12. I do not remember this person.
13. She likes to play tennis.   14. We like your dog.   15. Drink
[**пе́йте**] a little milk.   16. Thank goodness, this is my last examination.   17. Do you know this pupil?

Вопро́сы (Questions)

1. Где вы живёте, в го́роде и́ли в дере́вне?   2. Вы хо́дите
и́л и е́здите в го́род?   В дере́вню?   3. У вас есть автомоби́ль?
4. Вам нра́вится ваш автомоби́ль?   5. Како́го он цве́та?
6. Вам ну́жен автомоби́ль ка́ждый день?   7. Когда́ вы живёте
на да́че?   8. Где нахо́дится ва́ша да́ча?   9. Почему́ Макси́м
И ва́нович сиди́т до́ма?   10. Почему́ у него́ так ма́ло эне́ргии
те́ перь?   11. Кого́ ждёт Ма́ша?   12. Почему́ Аки́м прие́хал
та к по́здно?   13. Почему́ Ма́ша так ра́да, что он прие́хал?
1 . Почему́ Ма́ша так нра́вится Аки́му?   15. Когда́ Аки́м и
Ма́ша е́дут купа́ться?

U N I T 18 *

I

ПИСЬМÓ

Дорогóй Вáся!

Вчерá я поéхал в дерéвню к Мáше. Всё ýтро шёл дождь, и я дóлжен был éхать óчень мéдленно. Отéц купил мне нóвый автомобиль, и Мáша óчень хотéла егó видеть. Онá, конéчно, хотéла видеть не тóлько автомобиль, но и меня. Ты навéрно хорошó её пóмнишь. Онá óчень ýмная, красивая и милая дéвушка. Онá мне óчень нрáвится, и я знáю, что я ей тóже нрáвлюсь.

Лéтом семья Мáши живёт на дáче, котóрая нахóдится на берегý большóго óзера. Мáша купáется в óзере кáждый день, и вчерá мы тóже поéхали купáться. Пóсле дождя водá былá довóльно холóдная, но я óчень люблю плáвать в холóдной водé. Мы были на óзере цéлый час, а потóм поéхали в парк игрáть в тéннис. Мáша óчень лю́бит спорт и прекрáсно игрáет в тéннис, в волейбóл, и дáже в бейзбóл.

Ужé óчень пóздно, а зáвтра, рáно ýтром, я дóлжен быть в гóроде. У меня не бýдет автомобиля, и нýжно бýдет éхать на трамвáе. Итáк, спокóйной нóчи!

Словáрь (Vocabulary)

письмó letter
дорогóй, -áя, -óе dear
Вáся (*m.*) Basil
поéхал (*past of* **поéхать**) went (by conveyance)
я дóлжен был I had to

* This unit is intended as a *double* unit, requiring approximately twice as much time as the average unit.

138

ви́деть (II); **ви́жу, ви́дишь, ви́дят;** (*no imperative*) to see
её (*acc. of* **она́**) her
нра́виться (II); **нра́влюсь, нра́вишься, нра́вятся** to like, to please (see
  ¶ **18-1**)
кото́рый, -ая, -ое (*rel. & interr. pron.*) which, who (see ¶ **18-2**)
о́зеро lake
дово́льно (*adv.*) quite, rather
холо́дный, -ая, -ое cold
пла́вать (I) *hab.*; **пла́ваю, -ешь, -ют** to swim
на о́зере at the lake
час hour
спорт sport
прекра́сно very well, excellently
волейбо́л volleyball
бейзбо́л baseball
трамва́й (*m.*) streetcar
е́хать на трамва́е to go by streetcar
ита́к well then
споко́йной но́чи! (*idiom*) good night!

II

ПИСЬМО́ (Continued)

Дорого́й Ва́ся!

Я весь день был в го́роде и прие́хал домо́й дово́льно по́здно, но продолжа́ю письмо́.

Мать Ма́ши пригото́вила прекра́сный обе́д: борщ, котле́ты, и сала́т, а на десе́рт — компо́т. Аппети́т у меня́, сла́ва бо́гу, всегда́ о́чень хоро́ший, и я мно́го ел и пил. Бы́ло о́чень ве́село. Все гро́мко разгова́ривали и смея́лись.

На столе́ стоя́л большо́й самова́р, и все пи́ли чай. Оте́ц Ма́ши ру́сский и всегда́ пьёт чай из стака́на. Но мне да́ли ча́шку, потому́ что я америка́нец.

Я пло́хо рису́ю, но зна́ю, что ты никогда́ не́ был в ру́сском до́ме и никогда́ не ви́дел самова́ра.

Вот самова́р!

По́сле обе́да я пое́хал домо́й. Ну, э́то всё. А ты, как живёшь и что де́лаешь? Жду отве́та.

Твой друг Аки́м.

Слова́рь (Vocabulary)

продолжа́ть (I); **продолжа́ю, -ешь, -ют** to continue
пригото́вила (*past of* **пригото́вить**) she prepared
прекра́сный, -ая, -ое excellent
обе́д dinner
борщ (*gen.* **борща́**) borshch, beet soup
котле́ты (*pl. of* **котле́та**) Russian hamburgers
сала́т salad
десе́рт dessert
на десе́рт for dessert
компо́т stewed fruit
ве́село it is cheerful, gay
разгова́ривать (I); **разгова́риваю, -ешь, -ют** to converse
смея́ться (I); **смею́сь, смеёшься, смею́тся** to laugh (see ¶ 18-1)
самова́р samovar (a Russian urn for making tea)
чай (*m.*) tea
стака́н glass
ча́шка cup
америка́нецᶠˡ (*noun, m.*) (*gen.* **америка́нца**) American (see ¶ 18-5)
рисова́ть (I); **рису́ю, рису́ешь, рису́ют** to draw
твой, твоя́, твоё (*adj. & pron.*) your, yours (*fam. sing.*)
друг (*m.*) friend (*used for man or woman*)

Грамма́тика (Grammar)

Part I

18-1. Intransitive Verbs in -ся

a. Intransitive verbs do not take a direct object.

b. Many intransitive verbs have the ending **-ся** in the infinitive and are conjugated as reflexives even though they do not have a reflexive meaning. For example: **нра́виться, смея́ться**.

c. Note the conjugation of **смея́ться**:

PRESENT	PAST
я смею́сь	я, ты, он смея́лся
ты смеёшься	я, ты, она́ смея́лась
он смеётся	оно́ смея́лось
мы смеёмся	мы, вы, они́ смея́лись
вы смеётесь	
они́ смею́тся	FUTURE
	я бу́ду смея́ться, *etc.*

IMPERATIVE

сме́йся   сме́йтесь

d. The use of **нра́виться** requires the normal English subject in the *dative*, and the normal English object in the *nominative*.   (See ¶ **13-5** and **14-4**.)

PRESENT

я нра́**влюсь** учи́тельнице
{ The teacher likes me (*lit.* I am
  pleasing to the teacher).

ты нра́**вишься** учи́тельнице
{ The teacher likes you (*lit.* you
  are pleasing to the teacher).

он нра́**вится** учи́тельнице
etc.

мы нра́**вимся** учи́тельнице
вы нра́**витесь** учи́тельнице
они́ нра́**вятся** учи́тельнице

18-2. The Relative Pronoun: кото́рый

a. The relative pronoun **кото́рый** introduces a subordinate clause.   For example:

Я зна́ю де́вушку, **кото́рая** пи́шет кни́гу.
I know the girl *who* is writing a book.

b. **Кото́рый** agrees in *number* and *gender* with the noun in the main clause to which it refers.   The *case* of **кото́рый**, however, is determined by its own function in the relative clause.   For example:

Мы живём на **да́че** (*sing., fem., prep.*), **кото́рая** (*sing., fem., nom.*) нахо́дится на берегу́ о́зера.

Note: In both examples above, **кото́рая** is the *subject* of the subordinate clause and is therefore in the *nominative* case, although **де́вушку** is in the *accusative* in the first example, and **да́че** is in the *prepositional* in the second.

18-3. Prepositional Case of Adjectives in the Singular

Declension	Case	Masculine	Feminine	Neuter
Hard	*nom.*	но́в**ый**	но́в**ая**	но́в**ое**
	prep.	о но́в**ом**	о но́в**ой**	о но́в**ом**
Soft	*nom.*	после́дн**ий**	после́дн**яя**	после́дн**ее**
	prep.	о после́дн**ем**	о после́дн**ей**	о после́дн**ем**
Mixed	*nom.*	ру́сск**ий**	ру́сск**ая**	ру́сск**ое**
	prep.	о ру́сск**ом**	о ру́сск**ой**	о ру́сск**ом**

after O always prepositional

Part II

18-4. Second Declension of Nouns in the Singular*

a. Membership consists of:

1. Masculine nouns ending in a *consonant*, **-ь**, or **-й** in the nominative singular. For example:

> *inanimate:* журна́л   автомоби́ль   трамва́й
> *animate:* студе́нт   учи́тель   геро́й (hero)

2. Neuter nouns ending in **-о**, **-е**, or **-ие**. For example:

> сло́во, мо́ре, сочине́ние.

b. Classes: *hard* and *soft*.

1. Nouns ending in a *consonant* or in **-о** are *hard*.
2. Those ending in **-ь**, **-й**, or **-е** are *soft*.

Note: In the case of adjectives, the designations *hard*, *soft*, and *mixed* refer to the declensions themselves, whereas in the case of nouns, *hard* and *soft* refer to classes which are subdivisions within the declensions of nouns.

c. Stress.

1. All the cases, except the nominative, are called *oblique*.
2. In the singular, the stress in the *genitive* determines the pattern for the other oblique cases. It is therefore necessary to know the *genitive* as well as the *nominative* of every noun. Compare:

nom.	стул	стол	учени́к	челове́к	сло́во	перо́
gen.	сту́ла	стола́	ученика́	челове́ка	сло́ва	пера́
dat.	сту́лу	столу́	ученику́	челове́ку	сло́ву	перу́
	etc.	*etc.*	*etc.*	*etc.*	*etc.*	*etc.*

3. Henceforth, the *genitive* of a noun will be given in the vocabulary if it is not stressed on the same syllable as the nominative. The same applies to the Russian-English vocabulary at the end of the book.

d. Masculine nouns.

1. Masculine *inanimate* nouns are identical in the *nominative* and *accusative*. Note also that, when stressed, the ending **-ем** becomes **-ём**.

---

* See ¶ **15-7** for the First Declension of nouns in the singular.

	Hard	Soft		
	Consonant	**-ь**		**-й**
		Stress on stem	Stress on ending	
nom.	журна́л	автомоби́ль	дождь	трамва́й
gen.	журна́ла	автомоби́ля	дождя́	трамва́я
dat.	журна́лу	автомоби́лю	дождю́	трамва́ю
acc.	журна́л	автомоби́ль	дождь	трамва́й
instr.	журна́лом	автомоби́лем	дождём	трамва́ем
prep.	о журна́ле	об автомоби́ле	о дожде́	о трамва́е

2. Masculine *animate* nouns are identical in the *genitive* and *accusative*; otherwise, they are declined as above.

nom.	студе́нт	учи́тель	царь (tsar)	геро́й (hero)
acc.	студе́нта	учи́теля	царя́	геро́я

e. Neuter nouns are identical in the *nominative* and the *accusative*.

	Hard	Soft	
	-о	**-е**	**-ие**
nom.	сло́во	мо́ре	сочине́ние
gen.	сло́ва	мо́ря	сочине́ния
dat.	сло́ву	мо́рю	сочине́нию
acc.	сло́во	мо́ре	сочине́ние
instr.	сло́вом	мо́рем	сочине́нием
prep.	о сло́ве	о мо́ре	о сочине́нии

18-5. Capitalization of Terms of Nationality

Nouns and adjectives that designate nationality are not capitalized except at the beginning of a sentence. For example:

nouns:	америка́нец (*m.*)	American
	ру́сская (*f.*)	Russian
adjectives:	америка́нский, -ая, -ое	American
	ру́сский, -ая, -ое	Russian

Упражнéния (Exercises)

A. Translate the following nouns and adjectives, and decline them in the *genitive*, *accusative*, and *prepositional* cases (review ¶ 14-2). For example:

nom.	стáрый дом	old house
gen.	стáрого дóма	
acc.	стáрый дом	
prep.	о стáром дóме	

1. молодóй человéк.   2. дорогáя тётя.   3. холóдный дождь.   4. ясное нéбо.   5. пустóй гóрод.   6. глýпый мáльчик. 7. прекрáсный обéд.   8. рýсский чай.   9. большóе óзеро. 10. послéднее письмó.   11. мúлый учúтель.   12. сúнее мóре. 13. интерéсное сочинéние.   14. послéдний трамвáй.   15. плохóй хозяин.

B. Decline the following nouns in the singular, and indicate the stress.

Group I (oblique cases stressed like the nominative):

1. друг   2. суп   3. дóктор   4. студéнт   5. чай   6. учúтель 7. крéсло   8. мóре   9. самовáр   10. Ивáн   11. стакáн   12. рояль

Group II (oblique cases stressed on endings):

1. язык   2. стол   3. борщ   4. карандáш   5. гарáж   6. дождь   7. ученúк   8. окнó   9. потолóк   10. отéц   11. дневнúк 12. письмó

C. Conjugate the following verbs in all the forms studied thus far (i.e., *present, past, compound future, imperative*).

1. плáвать	5. разговáривать
2. рисовáть	6. смеяться
3. вúдеть (no imperative)	7. лежáть
4. продолжáть	8. смотрéть

D. Supply the proper cases of the Russian words in parentheses and replace the English words with Russian equivalents. For example: Я *lived* в (большóй гóрод). **Я жил в большóм гóроде**.

1. Вчерá *there was no* (дождь).   2. Зáвтра *it will not be* хóлодно.   3. Мáша *wanted* вúдеть (учúтель).   4. В (гóрод) нет (трамвáй).   5. *We do not like* éздить на (трамвáй).   6. Онá не *bathed* вчерá в (óзеро).   7. Онú тепéрь *are walking* к (мóре). 8. Мы весь вéчер *talked* о (сочинéние).   9. Я дóлго *conversed* с (учúтель).   10. Все грóмко *laughed*, тóлько мой друг не

laughed. 11. Де́вушка, (кото́рая) вы *saw* неде́лю тому́ наза́д, моя́ сестра́. 12. Она́ никогда́ не *drank* (чай) из (стака́н). 13. Аки́му *they gave* (ча́шка), потому́ что он америка́нец. 14. Он *does not see* (не́бо), потому́ что темно́. 15. Никола́й *eats* с (аппети́т), когда́ он у (тётя). 16. Вы *are not conversing* и *are not laughing,* потому́ что (вы) ску́чно. 17. Они́ ча́сто *swim* в (холо́дная вода́). 18. Вы прекра́сно *played* на (роя́ль). 19. Ты хорошо́ *draw* (дере́вня). 20. По́сле (обе́д) мы пое́хали к (оте́ц), но его́ не́ было в (го́род).

Перево́д (Translation)

Omit the words in parentheses and include the words in brackets.

1. It rained yesterday and it is also raining today.   2. I have to continue the letter which I have been writing [уже́ пишу́] (for) two days.   3. It is quite late now, but I do not want to sleep. 4. He knows that Masha likes him [that he is pleasing to Masha], and that she wants to see him.   5. Do not bathe and do not swim in cold water.   6. Basil went [пое́хал] to town by streetcar and arrived at the office very late.   7. They conversed about volleyball and baseball (for) a whole hour.   8. My mother prepared an excellent dinner.   9. I do not like to drink tea out of a glass. 10. Tanya never listens (to the) teacher, and only laughs and talks [converses] in class.   11. They had no borshch, but they gave us tea and stewed fruit.   12. Here is paper.   Draw a summer home on the shore of a big lake.   13. They gave the American a small cup. 14. You have never been in a Russian home [house], 15. That is all.   Good night.

Вопро́сы (Questions)

1. Кто пи́шет письмо́?   2. Кому́ он пи́шет э́то письмо́? 3. Где был Аки́м и кого́ он ви́дел?   4. Почему́ Аки́м до́лжен был е́хать ме́дленно?   5. Что оте́ц купи́л Аки́му?   6. Где живёт семья́ Ма́ши?   7. Где нахо́дится э́та да́ча?   8. О́зеро большо́е и́ли ма́ленькое?   9. Ма́ша ча́сто купа́ется в о́зере? 10. Как до́лго Аки́м и Ма́ша бы́ли на о́зере?   11. Где они́ пото́м игра́ли в те́ннис?   12. Почему́ Аки́м до́лжен е́хать в го́род на трамва́е?   13. Аки́му нра́вился обе́д, кото́рый пригото́вила мать Ма́ши?   14. Вы лю́бите борщ?   15. Что вы ку́шаете на десе́рт?   16. Вы уже́ ви́дели самова́р?   17. Куда́ Аки́м пое́хал по́сле обе́да у Ма́ши?

Pattern Drills

A. 1. Turn to page   . Listen to the teacher (or the tape) and repeat the conjugation of **смея́ться**.

2. Turn to page   . Listen to the teacher (or the tape) and repeat the conjugation of **нра́виться**.

3. Repeat the conjugation of **смея́ться** and **нра́виться** until you can tape-record them without errors.

B. 1. Read aloud (or tape-record) the following sentences supplying the required tense and person of **смея́ться**.

Мой друг Аки́м всегда́ _____.
А Ва́ся и Никола́й никогда́ не _____.
Аки́м, почему́ вы всегда́ _____.
Я вчера́ не _____ и тепе́рь я то́же не _____.
Мы то́же вчера́ не _____ и тепе́рь мы не _____.
Сего́дня ве́чером все _____.
Ва́ся и Никола́й, пожа́луйста не _____. Ве́ра, ты то́же, пожа́луйста, не _____.

2. Read aloud (or tape-record) the following sentences supplying the required persons of **нра́виться** in the present tense.

Мне **нра́вится** Аки́м.   Я **нра́влюсь** Аки́му.
  I like Akim.   Akim likes me.
Тебе́ **нра́вится** профе́ссор.   Ты _____ профе́ссору.
Ему́ **нра́вится** А́нна.   Он _____ А́нне.
Ей **нра́вится** де́душка.   Она́ _____ де́душке.
Нам **нра́вится** ма́льчик.   Мы _____ ма́льчику.
Вам **нра́вится** де́вушка.   Вы _____ де́вушке.
Им **нра́вится** хозя́йка.   Они́ _____ хозя́йке.

C. Study ¶18-2.   Listen to the teacher (or the tape) and repeat the following sentences.   Then read aloud each corresponding sentence in the "Student" column supplying the appropriate gender and case of **кото́рый** according to the model sentence.

Teacher	*Student*
Учи́тель, **кото́рый** живёт у нас в до́ме, мой дя́дя.	Учи́тельница, **кото́рая** живёт у нас в до́ме, моя́ тётя.
Студе́нт, **кото́рого** мы ви́дели в па́рке, мой брат.	Студе́нтка, _____ мы ви́дели в па́рке, моя́ сестра́.
Газе́та, **кото́рую** они́ вчера́ чита́ли лежи́т на полу́.	Кни́га, _____ они́ вчера́ чита́ли, _____.

Мы не ви́дим кре́сла, **кото́рое**   Мы не ви́дим пера́, _____
всегда́ стои́т о́коло стола́.   всегда́ лежи́т на столе́.
Мы зна́ем ученика́, кото́рый   Мы зна́ем учени́цу, _____.
пи́шет сочине́ние.   _____.

D. Turn to ¶18-4*d*. Listen to the teacher (or the tape) and
repeat the Second Declension of nouns in the table and in the
"Teacher" column. Then decline similarly the corresponding
nouns in the "Student" column.

| *Teacher* | *Student* |

1. Oblique cases stressed like the nominative.
    a. Inanimate nouns
        журна́л   уро́к, стака́н, шокола́д, дом, го́род

    b. Animate nouns
        студе́нт   профе́ссор, челове́к, хозя́ин, гос-
                          поди́н

2. Oblique cases stressed on endings.
    a. Inanimate nouns
        дневни́к   каранда́ш, гара́ж, борщ, язы́к

    b. Animate nouns
        учени́к

3. Oblique cases stressed like the nominative.
        автомоби́ль   роя́ль, учи́тель (animate)

4. Oblique cases stressed on endings.
        дождь   царь (animate)

5.   трамва́й   чай, геро́й (animate)

6. Oblique cases stressed like the nominative.
        сло́во   кре́сло, о́зеро

7. Oblique cases stressed on endings.
        письмо́   перо́ окно́

8.   мо́ре   по́ле (field)

9.   сочине́ние   зда́ние (building)

U N I T 19

ОТВÉТ ВÁСИ

Дорогóй Акúм!

Большóе спасúбо за длúнное письмó, в котóром ты так мнóго пúшешь о Мáше и так мáло о себé.

Вот замечáтельная дéвушка! — прекрáсно игрáет в тéннис, в волейбóл и дáже в бейзбóл, прекрáсно игрáет на роя́ле, плáвает как ры́ба и поёт как птúца. А отéц Мáши рýсский и пьёт чай из стакáна. А мать её умéет приготовля́ть борщ, котлéты и компóт! И какáя у Мáши мúлая семья́! — все сидя́т вокрýг самовáра, пьют чай, грóмко разговáривают и смею́тся. Ну, почемý ты дýмаешь, что всё э́то интерéсно? Ты прекрáсно знáешь, что дéвушки меня́ не интересýют.

У тебя́ тепéрь нóвый автомобúль — вот э́то интерéсно! Тепéрь ты мóжешь éздить к нам чáще. У нас, конéчно, нет дáчи на берегý большóго óзера, но у нас есть прекрáсная фéрма.

Ты пóмнишь нáшу сéрую лóшадь? Ты чáсто давáл ей сáхар и онá тебя́ за э́то óчень любúла. Когдá бýдешь на фéрме, бýдем вмéсте éздить верхóм, ты на сéрой лóшади, а я на бéлой.

Мы все тебя́ ждём: и я, и моя́ сестрá Ирúна, и нáша сéрая лóшадь.

Итáк, до свидáния!

Твой друг Вáся.

Словáрь (Vocabulary)

большóе спасúбо many thanks
за (*with acc.*) for

дли́нный, -ая, -ое long
себя́ (*reflex. pron.*) self, oneself (see ¶ 19-1)
замеча́тельный, -ая, -ое remarkable
ры́ба fish
петь (I); пою́, поёшь, пою́т to sing
пти́ца bird
уме́ть (I); уме́ю, уме́ешь, уме́ют to know how (see ¶ 19-3)
приготовля́ть (I); приготовля́ю, -ешь, -ют to prepare
вокру́г (*with gen.*) around
интере́сно it is interesting
де́вушки (*pl. of* де́вушка) girls
интересова́ть (I); интересу́ю, интересу́ешь, -ют to interest
ча́ще (*comp. of* ча́сто) more frequently
фе́рма farm
ло́шадь (*f.*, *third decl.*) horse (see ¶ 19-2)
са́хар sugar
вме́сте (*adv.*) together
верхо́м (*adv.*) astride
е́здить верхо́м
е́здить на ло́шади $\Big\}$ to ride horseback
е́здить верхо́м на ло́шади
бе́лый, -ая, -ое white
Ири́на Irene

АКИ́М НА ФЕ́РМЕ

Ве́чер. Ва́ся у себя́ в ко́мнате. Он чита́ет рома́н "Война́ и мир." Рома́н о́чень интере́сный, и Ва́ся ничего́ не слы́шит. Вдруг в ко́мнату вхо́дит Аки́м, но Ва́ся продолжа́ет чита́ть. Аки́м стои́т в ко́мнате це́лую мину́ту, смо́трит на Ва́сю и ждёт. Но Ва́ся ничего́ не ви́дит и не слы́шит. Наконе́ц Аки́м говори́т:

— Слу́шай, Ва́ся! Э́то я . . .

— Ах, Аки́м! Како́й прия́тный сюрпри́з! Когда́ ты прие́хал?

— То́лько что.

— Как до́лго ты бу́дешь у нас на фе́рме?

— Неде́лю.

— То́лько одну́ неде́лю! Почему́ не две и́ли три?

— Че́рез неде́лю я е́ду в дере́вню к Ма́ше.

— Как жаль, что ты до́лжен е́хать к Ма́ше . . . Но об э́том бу́дем говори́ть пото́м. А тепе́рь идём у́жинать. Моя́ сестра́, Ири́на, пригото́вила прекра́сный у́жин. Она́ не игра́ет в бейзбо́л, но она́ о́чень хоро́шая хозя́йка.

Словáрь (Vocabulary)

на фéрме at the farm
Вáся у себя́ в кóмнате Basil is in his (own) room
ромáн novel
войнá war
мир peace
слы́шать (II); слы́шу, слы́шишь, слы́шат to hear
вдруг suddenly
входи́ть (II); вхожý, вхóдишь, вхóдят to go in; to enter
минýта minute
наконéц at last
прия́тный, -ая, -ое pleasant
сюрпри́з surprise
тóлько что just now
однý (*acc. of* **однá**) **недéлю** one week
чéрез (*with acc.*) in (*lit.* after the lapse of)
чéрез недéлю in a week
идём let's go
ýжинать (I); ýжинаю, -ешь, -ют to have supper
ýжин supper
хозя́йка *here:* housekeeper

Граммáтика (Grammar)

19-1. The Reflexive Pronoun: себя́

a. **Себя́** (*self*) can be used with all genders, persons, and numbers, but must always refer to the subject of the sentence. It has no *nominative* form and cannot itself be the subject.

b. **Себя́** is declined as follows:

DECLENSION		EXAMPLES	
nom.	none		
gen.	себя́	Он у **себя́** в кóмнате.	He is in his (own) room.
dat.	себé	Онá купи́ла **себé** кни́гу.	She bought (for) herself a book.
acc.	себя́	Я ви́жу **себя́**.	I see myself.
instr.	собóй (-óю)	Мы берём сестрý с со-**бóй**.	We are taking sister along (with ourselves).
prep.	о себé	Ты мáло пи́шешь о **себé**.	You are writing little about yourself.

19-2. Third Declension in the Singular

a. Soft feminine nouns in **-ь** belong to the Third Declension.

nom.	ло́шадь	*acc.*	ло́шадь
gen.	ло́шади	*instr.*	ло́шадью
dat.	ло́шади	*prep.*	о ло́шади

b. Animate and inanimate nouns of this declension are identical in the nominative and accusative singular.

Note: The *genitive*, *dative*, and *prepositional* are alike.

19-3. Мочь and уме́ть

Note the difference in the meaning of these verbs.

a. **Мочь** means *to be able physically, to be in a position to*.   For example:

Я не **могу́** писа́ть, потому́ что темно́.   *I cannot* write because it is dark (*i.e.*, I know how, but *am physically unable* to do it now).

b. **Уме́ть** means *to know how* as a result of acquired knowledge, skill, or training.   For example:

Он не **уме́ет** писа́ть по-ру́сски, потому́ что никогда́ не изуча́л ру́сского языка́.   He *cannot* (*does not know how to*) write Russian because he has never studied Russian (*i.e., has never acquired such knowledge, has never had such training*).

c. Conjugation of **мочь** in the

> *Present Tense: see* ¶ 9-6.
> *Past Tense:* **мог, могла́, могло́, могли́**
> *Compound Future:* none.
> *Imperative:* none.

Упражне́ния (Exercises)

A. Replace the English words with the required case of **себя́**, and supply the proper case endings for the Russian words in parentheses.   Refer to the examples in ¶ 19-1b.

1. Они́ купи́ли *themselves* (фе́рма).   2. В э́том (дли́нное письмо́) они́ ничего́ не пи́шут *about themselves*.   3. Она́ всегда́ сиди́т у *her (own)* в (ко́мната).   4. Он ду́мает то́лько *about him-self*.   5. Почему́ вы никогда́ не берёте (соба́ка) *with you?*   6. Она́ *herself* не зна́ет.   7. Челове́к никогда́ *himself* не зна́ет.

себя

8. Они́ хорошо́ *themselves* ви́дят в (вода́). 9. Бери́те меня́ *along (with you)* когда́ вы е́здите на (да́ча). 10. Она́ приго-
то́вляет (*for*) *herself* у́жин.

себе dat   *be able   to know how*

B. Supply the proper forms of **мочь** or **уме́ть** as required,
according to ¶ 19-3.

1. Она́ тепе́рь больна́ и не _____ рабо́тать. 2. Она́
_____ рабо́тать, когда́ она́ была́ здоро́ва. 3. Вчера́ шёл
дождь и мы не _____ е́хать о́чень бы́стро. 4. Мой
друг Ва́ся не лю́бит спо́рта и не _____ игра́ть в те́ннис.
5. У меня́ никогда́ не́ было ло́шади и я не _____
е́здить верхо́м. 6. Четы́ре го́да тому́ наза́д он _____
говори́ть по-ру́сски, но тепе́рь он всё забы́л. 7. Мы не
_____ чита́ть, когда́ все говоря́т так гро́мко. 8. Вы
не _____ пла́вать, потому́ что никогда́ не жи́ли о́коло
мо́ря и́ли о́зера.

C. Supply the proper case ending for the words in parentheses.
(Memorize ¶ 19-2 before doing this exercise.)

1. У меня́ нет (ло́шадь). 2. Она́ купи́ла себе́ но́вую (те-
тра́дь). 3. Пиши́те сочине́ние в (тетра́дь). 4. Сего́дня он
прие́хал в шко́лу с (кни́га), с (тетра́дь) и с (перо́). 5. Но он
ча́сто е́здит в шко́лу без* (кни́га), без (тетра́дь), и без (перо́).
6. Ты лю́бишь е́здить на (ло́шадь). 7. Ты всегда́ даёшь
са́хар (ло́шадь), но (соба́ка) ты ничего́ не даёшь. 8. Кого́ вы
ждёте? Я жду (мать). 9. Я ви́дел (америка́нец) верхо́м на
(ло́шадь). 10. Че́рез (неде́ля) Аки́м е́дет в (дере́вня) к (Ма́ша).

D. Conjugate the following verbs in the present, past, and compound future.

1. уме́ть   4. интересова́ть
2. петь   5. входи́ть
3. приготовля́ть   6. у́жинать

E. Translate the following sentences, and *memorize* the forms of
the imperative.

1. **По́йте,** пожа́луйста, вме́сте.
2. **Живи́те** на фе́рме.
3. **Слу́шайте** ра́дио.
4. **У́жинай** ра́но.
5. **Входи́те** в ко́мнату ти́хо, когда́ все спят.

* **Без** (*with gen.*) without.

6. Она́ тепе́рь поёт.   Пожа́луйста, **слу́шайте**.

7. **Уме́йте** нра́виться учи́телю.

8. **Жди** меня́.

9. **Приготовля́йте** тако́й обе́д ча́ще.

Перево́д (Translation)

Translate, omitting the words in parentheses and including the words in brackets. Note that a girl is writing this letter to her friend. Therefore, use *feminine* and *familiar* forms where necessary.

1. Dear Irene,

2. Today I was all day at the office, and did not know that your letter (was) [is] lying on my [**у меня́ на**] table.   3. What a pleasant surprise!   4. At last I know where you are and what you are doing.   5. Many thanks for such a long and interesting letter. 6. I have been waiting for this letter (for) four weeks.   7. Thank goodness [that] you are well!

8. You write too little about Boris, but he interests me very (much).   9. Who is he, where does he live, and what is he doing? 10. You write that girls are fond of him [**его́ лю́бят**], but you do not say [**говори́шь**] why.

11. We just bought an excellent farm, which is situated on the shore of a beautiful lake.   12. In a week we shall have on (our) farm a white horse.   13. I know that you like to ride horseback. 14. When you (are) [will be] here, we shall do everything together— we shall swim in the lake, ride horseback, and play tennis.   15. In the evening we shall play the piano and sing.

16. How glad I am (to have) [that I have] a friend who can [knows how to] do everything so well.   17. Please write more frequently.

18. Your friend Vera.

Вопро́сы (Questions)

1. Кому́ Ва́ся пи́шет письмо́?   2. Аки́м мно́го пи́шет о себе́?   3. О ком он мно́го пи́шет?   4. Ва́ся ду́мает, что Ма́ша замеча́тельная де́вушка?   5. Кто пла́вает как ры́ба?   6. Кто поёт как пти́ца?   7. Вы уме́ете пла́вать?   8. А купа́ться вы уме́ете?   9. Что мать Ма́ши уме́ет приготовля́ть?   10. **Что**

семья́ Ма́ши де́лает вокру́г самова́ра?   11. Кто ждёт Аки́ма?
12. Что Ва́ся чита́ет у себя́ в ко́мнате?   13. Кто вдруг вхо́дит
в ко́мнату Ва́си?   14. Почему́ Ва́ся ничего́ не ви́дит и не
слы́шит?   15. Что де́лает Аки́м, когда́ Ва́ся продолжа́ет
чита́ть?   16. Ва́ся рад, что Аки́м прие́хал?   17. Как до́лго
Аки́м бу́дет на фе́рме?   18. Куда́ он е́дет че́рез неде́лю?
19. Кто приготови́л прекра́сный у́жин?   20. Ири́на хоро́шая
хозя́йка?   Почему́ вы так ду́маете?

Pattern Drills

A. Study **¶19-1.**   Listen to the teacher (or the tape) and repeat
the following questions.   Then read aloud the answers in the
"Student" column.

Teacher	*Student*
Где Ва́ся? Он **у себя́** в ко́мнате?	Да, он **у себя́** в ко́мнате.
Что он купи́л **себе́** в го́роде сего́дня?	Он купи́л **себе́** но́вый рома́н.
Кто пое́хал с ним в го́рол?	Его́ сестра́ пое́хала с ним в го́род.
Он ча́сто берёт её **с собо́й**?	Да, он о́чень ча́сто берёт её **с собо́й.**
А вы ча́сто е́здите с ним в го́род?	Я никогда́ не е́зжу с ним в го́род.
Почему́ нет?	Потому́ что мне с ним ску́чно. Он всегда́ говори́т то́лько **о себе́.**
А он э́то зна́ет?	Да, он э́то зна́ет. Он **себя́** хорошо́ зна́ет.

B. Study **¶19-2.**   Listen to the teacher (or the tape) and repeat
the declension of **тетра́дь.**   Then decline **ло́шадь** and **дверь.**
(*Note:* Always name the cases aloud to associate them automatically
with their respective endings.)

nom.	тетра́дь	*acc.*	тетра́дь
gen.	тетра́ди	*instr.*	тетра́дью
dat.	тетра́ди	*prep.*	о тетра́ди

C. Study ¶**19-2.** Read aloud (or tape-record) the following sentences giving the proper case endings of the nouns in parentheses.

Пишите сочинение в (тетрадь).
Почему у вас нет (лошадь)?
Вася хорошо ездит на (лошадь).
Маша сидела около (дверь).
Аким шёл с (лошадь) к озеру.
Павел приехал в школу без (тетрадь).

D. Study ¶**19-3.** Listen to the teacher (or the tape) and repeat the following questions.   Then read each answer in the ''Student'' column supplying the proper form of **мочь** or **уметь**, depending upon the meaning of the sentence.

Teacher	*Student*
Вы умеете играть на рояле?	Да, я умею играть на рояле. Но сегодня я не могу играть.
Почему вы сегодня не можете играть?	Не могу играть сегодня, потому что у меня болит голова.
А на гитаре вы умеете играть?	Нет, не умею.
Вы умеете писать по-русски?	Да, умею.
Почему же вы ничего не пишете?	Я не могу теперь писать, потому что темно и я ничего не вижу.
А читать по-русски вы умеете?	Конечно умею. Но теперь темно, и я не могу читать.
Почему ваша мать сегодня не работает?	Она больна и не может работать.
Но вчера она работала!	Конечно. Вчера она была здорова и могла работать.

U N I T 20

I

ПИСЬМО́ АКИ́МА К МА́ШЕ

Ми́лая Ма́ша!

Я тепе́рь у Ва́си на фе́рме. Ты зна́ешь, что мы хоро́шие
това́рищи и о́чень лю́бим друг дру́га. Ва́ся о́чень у́мный,
до́брый и весёлый ю́ноша, но немно́го стра́нный. Де́вушки
его́ не интересу́ют. Он ре́дко хо́дит в кино́ и ре́дко смо́трит
телеви́зор. Он чита́ет дли́нные и серьёзные рома́ны, как
наприме́р: "Отцы́ и де́ти," "Война́ и мир" и́ли "Америка́нская
траге́дия."

Ва́ся о́чень лю́бит иностра́нные языки́. Он чита́ет по-
францу́зски, по-неме́цки и по-ру́сски и тепе́рь та́кже изуча́ет
испа́нский язы́к. На столе́ у него́ лежа́т: испа́нские словари́,
неме́цкие журна́лы, ру́сские рома́ны и францу́зские газе́ты.
Он уже́ хорошо́ зна́ет испа́нскую грамма́тику, по́мнит са́мые
тру́дные слова́ и да́же пи́шет дли́нные сочине́ния по-испа́нски.
Но Ва́ся та́кже хоро́ший спортсме́н. Он прекра́сно игра́ет в
футбо́л и в баскетбо́л и о́чень хорошо́ е́здит верхо́м.

Сестра́ Ва́си, Ири́на, то́же прекра́сная спортсме́нка и ча́сто
е́здит с на́ми купа́ться, игра́ет с на́ми в те́ннис и е́здит верхо́м.

Слова́рь (Vocabulary)

това́рищ comrade, friend
друг дру́га each other
весёлый, -ая, -ое cheerful, gay
ю́ноша (*m.*) youth, young man
стра́нный, -ая, -ое strange, odd

156

ре́дко (*adv.*) rarely, seldom
кино́ (*n.*) (*not decl.*) movies, movie theater
серьёзный, -ая, -ое serious
наприме́р for instance
как наприме́р as for instance
де́ти (*pl. of* **дитя́**) children
америка́нский, -ая, -ое American
траге́дия tragedy
иностра́нный, -ая, -ое foreign
по-францу́зски (*adv.*) French (in French)
по-неме́цки (*adv.*) German (in German)
испа́нский, -ая, -ое Spanish
слова́рь (*m.*) (*gen.* **словаря́**) dictionary
неме́цкий, -ое German
францу́зский, -ая, -ое French
грамма́тика grammar
са́мый, -ая, -ое (*used with adj. to form superlative*) the most
тру́дный, -ая, -ое difficult
по-испа́нски (*adv.*) Spanish (in Spanish)
спортсме́н (*m.*) sportsman
футбо́л football
баскетбо́л basketball
спортсме́нка (*f.*) sportswoman
с на́ми (*instr. of* **мы**) with us

II

ПИСЬМО́ АКИ́МА К МА́ШЕ (Continued)

Ах, как хорошо́ жить на фе́рме! Всё мне здесь нра́вится: и роди́тели Ва́си, и его́ сестра́ Ири́на, и коро́вы, и ло́шади, и чёрная соба́ка, и бе́лая ко́шка, и пти́цы, кото́рые ве́село пою́т в саду́.

Все здесь встаю́т о́чень ра́но. Роди́тели Ва́си встаю́т в пять часо́в утра́, Ва́ся и Ири́на встаю́т в шесть, а я встаю́ в семь часо́в. Я умыва́юсь, одева́юсь и иду́ в столо́вую. Ва́ся уже́ ждёт меня́ в столо́вой, и мы за́втракаем вме́сте.

Ири́на всегда́ приготовля́ет за́втрак. Она́ не то́лько хоро́шая спортсме́нка, но и прекра́сная хозя́йка . . .

Вдруг Ма́ша начина́ет пла́кать и не мо́жет чита́ть да́льше.

Слова́рь (Vocabulary)

здесь here
роди́тели (*m. pl.*) parents, father and mother
коро́ва cow
чёрный, -ая, -ое black

ко́шка cat
ве́село (*adv.*) cheerfully, gaily
сад garden
в саду́ in the garden (see ¶ 20-6)
встава́ть (I); встаю́, встаёшь, встаю́т to get up, to rise
пять five
часы́ (*gen. pl.* часо́в) hours
в пять часо́в утра́ at five o'clock in the morning
шесть six
семь seven
умыва́ться (I); умыва́юсь, -ешься, -ются to wash oneself
одева́ться (I); одева́юсь, -ешься, -ются to dress oneself
столо́вая (*noun, f.*) dining room
за́втракать (I); за́втракаю, -ешь, -ют to have breakfast
за́втрак breakfast
начина́ть (I); начина́ю, -ешь, -ют to begin
пла́кать (I); пла́чу, пла́чешь, пла́чут; *imper.* плачь, пла́чьте to weep
(see ¶ 20-10)
да́льше (*adv.*) further

Грамма́тика (Grammar)

Part I

20-1. Position of Adverbs

a. Adverbs modifying adjectives or other adverbs precede the word they modify, as in English. For example:

Он **о́чень** хоро́ший учени́к.	He is a *very* good pupil.
Он **о́чень** хорошо́ чита́ет.	He reads *very* well.
Он **сли́шком** мно́го говори́т.	He talks *too* much.
Не встава́йте **так** по́здно.	Do not get up *so* late.

b. The position of adverbs modifying verbs is not rigidly fixed.

1. Usually such adverbs precede the verb. They may, however, follow the verb for the sake of emphasis. For example:

Он хорошо́ чита́ет.	He reads well.
Он чита́ет **хорошо́**.	He reads *well*.

2. The adverbs **по-ру́сски**, **по-англи́йски**, and the like generally follow the verb. When emphasis is desired, they are placed before the verb. For example:

Я хорошо́ говорю́ по-испа́нски.	I speak Spanish well.
По-испа́нски я говорю́ хорошо́.	*Spanish* I speak well.

3. Often, the position of the adverb in the sentence does not affect the meaning, any more than in English.

Я сего́дня иду́ в го́род.
Сего́дня я иду́ в го́род. } Today I am going to town.

Я иду́ в го́род сего́дня.   I am going to town today.

20-2. Nominative Plural of Nouns*

a. Hard feminine and masculine nouns of the First and Second Declensions take **-ы**.

sing.	*pl.*
ка́рт**а**	ка́рт**ы**
журна́л	журна́л**ы**

1. After **г, к,** or **х,** they take **-и**.

| кни́**га** | кни́**ги** |
| учени́**к** | учени**ки́** |

2. After **ж, ч, ш,** or **щ,** they take **-и**.

| да́**ча** | да́**чи** |
| това́ри**щ** | това́ри**щи** |

b. Soft feminine and masculine nouns of the First, Second, and Third Declensions take **-и**.

неде́л**я**	неде́л**и**
а́рми**я**	а́рми**и**
автомоби́л**ь**	автомоби́л**и**
дожд**ь**	дожд**и́**
трамв**а́й**	трамв**а́и**
тетра́д**ь**	тетра́д**и**
ло́шад**ь**	ло́шад**и**

c. Neuter nouns in **-o** take **-a** in the nominative plural, and usually shift the stress.

| сло́в**о** | слов**а́** |
| письм**о́** | пи́сьм**а** |

d. Neuter nouns in **-e** or **-ие** take **-я** or **-ия** in the nominative plural.

| мо́р**е** | мор**я́** |
| сочине́ни**е** | сочине́ни**я** |

* Nouns whose stress shifts in the plural are given in the Vocabulary at the end of the book.

20-3. Accusative Plural of Inanimate Nouns

The accusative plural of inanimate nouns, regardless of gender, is the same as the nominative plural:

	f.	*m.*	*f.*	*m.*	*n.*
nom.	ка́рты	журна́лы	неде́ли	словари́	моря́
acc.	ка́рты	журна́лы	неде́ли	словари́	моря́

20-4. Nominative Plural of Adjectives

The plural endings are the same for all three genders.

a. Hard adjectives take **-ые**:

SINGULAR	PLURAL (*m., f., n.*)
но́в**ый**, но́в**ая**, но́в**ое**	но́в**ые**
молодо́**й**, молода́**я**, молодо́**е**	молод**ы́е**

b. Soft adjectives take **-ие**:

после́дн**ий**, после́дн**яя**, после́дн**ее**	после́дн**ие**

c. Mixed adjectives whose stems end in **г, к, х,** or **ж, ч, ш, щ** take **-ие**:

ру́сск**ий**, ру́сск**ая**, ру́сск**ое**	ру́сск**ие**
хоро́ш**ий**, хоро́ш**ая**, хоро́ш**ее**	хоро́ш**ие**

20-5. Accusative Plural of Adjectives with Inanimate Nouns

Adjectives of all three genders modifying inanimate nouns are identical in the nominative and accusative plural.

nom. & *acc.* но́в**ые** карти́н**ы**
nom. & *acc.* ру́сск**ие** журна́л**ы**
nom. & *acc.* си́н**ие** кре́сл**а**

Part II

20-6. Nouns with Prepositional in -ý

Some masculine nouns ending in a consonant in the *nominative* take the stressed **-ý** in the *prepositional* when governed by the prepositions **в** or **на**.

nom.	*prep.*	
пол	на полу́	*on* the floor
бе́рег	на берегу́	*on* the shore
сад	в саду́	*in* the garden
лес	в лесу́	*in* the forest

20-7. Genitive Plural of Nouns Ending in a Consonant

Masculine nouns ending in a *consonant* in the nominative singular take **-ов** in the genitive plural.

nom. sing.	*nom. plural*	*gen. plural*	
журна́л	журна́лы	журна́лов	
час	часы́	часо́в	
учени́к	ученики́	учени́ков	*only sibilants*

Exceptions: Nouns ending in **-ж, -ч, -ш,** or **-щ** take **-ей** instead of **-ов** in the genitive plural.

гара́ж	гаражи́	гараже́й
каранда́ш	карандаши́	карандаше́й
това́рищ	това́рищи	това́рищей

20-8. Genitive Plural with the Numbers 5 through 20

The cardinal numerals 5 through 20 govern the genitive plural.* (For the numerals 2, 3, and 4, which govern the genitive singular, see ¶9-3.)

пять журна́лов	five magazines
шесть часо́в	six hours; six o'clock
семь това́рищей	seven friends

20-9. Adjectives Used as Nouns

Some adjectives are also used as nouns, but they are always declined as adjectives. For example:

nom. sing.	столо́вая	dining room
gen. sing.	столо́вой	of a dining room
nom. pl.	столо́вые	dining rooms

20-10. The Imperative in -ь and -ьте

The imperative endings are **-ь** and **-ьте** instead of **-и** and **-ите** when (1) the first person singular in the present is stressed on the stem, *and* (2) the present stem ends in a consonant. For example:

INFINITIVE	PRESENT	IMPERATIVE
пла́кать	я пла́чу	
(to weep)	(*stressed on stem*)	
	ты пла́ч - ешь	{ пла́чь { пла́чьте

* The words for the numerals 8 through 20 will be given in ¶27-5.

INFINITIVE	PRESENT	IMPERATIVE
ста́вить (to put, place)	я ста́влю (*stressed on stem*)	
	ты ста́в - ишь	{ ставь { ста́вьте

Note: The imperative of **идти́** is **иди́, иди́те**, and the imperative of **люби́ть** is **люби́, люби́те** (see ¶11-5), because they do not meet both requirements of the rule above. Their present stems end in consonants, but the first person present is stressed on the ending, and not on the stem.

Упражне́ния (Exercises)

A. Give the plural of the following phrases and translate.

1. хоро́ший това́рищ. 2. чёрная коро́ва. 3. весёлый ю́ноша. 4. францу́зская траге́дия. 5. неме́цкий слова́рь. 6. тру́дный язы́к. 7. англи́йский трамва́й. 8. больша́я столо́вая. 9. прекра́сный за́втрак. 10. плохо́й у́жин. 11. прия́тный сюрпри́з. 12. молода́я де́вушка. 13. си́няя тетра́дь. 14. дли́нное письмо́. 15. после́днее сло́во.

B. Supply Russian equivalents for the English words in italics; then translate the sentences.

1. Ма́льчик лежи́т *on the floor*. 2. Де́ти сидя́т *in the garden*. 3. Ло́шади стоя́т *on the shore* о́зера. 4. Тепе́рь уже́ пять *o'clock*. 5. Он ка́ждый день рабо́тает семь *hours*. 6. В кла́ссе сего́дня то́лько шесть *pupils*. 7. Пять *friends* ждут Ва́сю. 8. *Do not cry*, Ма́ша. *Cry* то́лько ма́ленькие де́ти. 9. Роди́тели Аки́ма иду́т в *dining room*. 10. Ва́ся лю́бит *foreign languages*.

C. Count from 1 through 7 with each of the following masculine nouns, and indicate stress on the nouns throughout. (Refer to ¶20-7 and ¶20-8.) For example:

оди́н стол, два стола́, *etc.* . . . пять столо́в, *etc.* . . .

1. журна́л. 2. час. 3. учени́к. 4. гара́ж. 5. каранда́ш. 6. това́рищ. 7. рома́н. 8. стака́н (*pl.* стака́ны). 9. ма́льчик 10. оте́ц.

D. Memorize the nominative plural of the following nouns and adjectives, noting the stress. Then translate these phrases, and write them in the nominative singular. For example:

бе́лые да́чи: white summer homes; **бе́лая да́ча**

1. це́лые дни. 2. америка́нские чаи́. 3. ру́сские борщи́. 4. хоро́шие словари́. 5. холо́дные дожди́. 6. стра́нные пи́сьма. 7. испа́нские траге́дии. 8. после́дние пти́цы. 9. францу́зские супы́. 10. ми́лые ю́ноши. 11. замеча́тельные ло́шади. 12. интере́сные дневники́. 13. прекра́сные потолки́. 14. плохи́е кре́сла. 15. больши́е о́кна. 16. пусты́е стака́ны. 17. краси́вые полы́. 18. прия́тные часы́. 19. весёлые ма́льчики. 20. дли́нные во́йны. 21. чёрные до́ски. 22. се́рые ко́шки. 23. бе́лые сте́ны. 24. неме́цкие дере́вни. 25. си́ние моря́.

E. *Check yourself!* Close the book and rewrite Exercise D from your paper, changing the singular back to the plural. Then compare the results with the text.

Перево́д (Translation)

A. Omit the words in parentheses and include the words in brackets.

1. Please read on [further]. 2. You cried yesterday and are crying today. Please, do not cry. 3. We have on our farm [**У нас на фе́рме есть**] horses, cows, cats, and dogs. 4. The birds are singing gaily in the garden. 5. You dress (yourself) too late. 6. You wash (yourselves) too rarely. Please wash (yourselves) more frequently. 7. Go to [into] the dining room. Everybody [all] is waiting (for) you. 8. Vasya bought a new German grammar. 9. The new lessons are very difficult (ones). 10. The students of this university are good sportsmen. 11. The girls of this school are good sportswomen. 12. Do you want to play basketball with us in the garden? 13. Children like to watch television. 14. Masha's parents often go to the movies. 15. Vasya and Akim have breakfast together.

B. Translate at sight.

1. Here is our dining room. 2. Here we have breakfast and supper. 3. In the morning I prepare breakfast, and in the evening mother prepares supper. 4. We get up at six o'clock, and wash and dress quickly. 5. At seven o'clock we begin to work. 6. I like to work in the garden when the weather is good. 7. It is pleasant [**прия́тно**] to work when the birds are singing gaily in the garden.

C. Omit the words in parentheses and include the words in brackets.

1. I like [**люблю́**] foreign languages very (much).   2. I am now studying French.   3. Two years ago I studied German, and in a year [**че́рез год**] I shall be studying Spanish.   4. I want to speak Russian, French, Spanish, and German well.   5. My [**мой**] parents are Russians, but we rarely speak Russian at home.   6. My sister prefers to speak French, and my younger brother wants to speak only English.   7. But my friend Paul speaks Russian quite well, and we often converse in Russian (for) a whole hour.   8. We are very good friends and are very fond of each other.   9. Sometimes I think that he is too serious, and he thinks that I am too gay. 10. My parents think that I need such a friend.

Вопро́сы (Questions)

1. Кому́ Аки́м пи́шет э́то письмо́?   2. Где он тепе́рь? 3. Аки́м и Ва́ся лю́бят друг дру́га?   4. Почему́ Аки́м ду́мает, что Ва́ся немно́го стра́нный?   5. Каки́е рома́ны чита́ет Ва́ся? 6. Какой иностра́нный язы́к Ва́ся тепе́рь изуча́ет?   7. Каки́е иностра́нные языки́ вы тепе́рь изуча́ете?   8. Что лежи́т у Ва́си на столе́?   9. Каки́е сочине́ния он пи́шет?   10. Как Ва́ся игра́ет в футбо́л?   11. Сестра́ Ва́си хоро́шая спортсме́нка? 12. Ири́на, сестра́ Ва́си, уме́ет е́здить верхо́м?   13. Когда́ роди́тели Ва́си встаю́т у́тром?   14. Когда́ Аки́м встаёт? 15. Куда́ он идёт за́втракать?   16. С кем он за́втракает в столо́вой?   17. Кто всегда́ приготовля́ет за́втрак?   18. Почему́ Ма́ша начина́ет пла́кать, когда́ она́ чита́ет, что Ири́на прекра́сная хозя́йка?

Pattern Drills

A. 1. Study ¶20-2. Listen to the teacher (or the tape) and repeat the following feminine nouns in the nominative singular and in the nominative plural.

nom. sing.	nom. pl.	nom. sing.	nom. pl.
шко́ла	шко́лы	ча́шка	ча́шки
ла́мпа	ла́мпы	де́вушка	де́вушки
ва́за	ва́зы	студе́нтка	студе́нтки
мину́та	мину́ты	неде́ля	неде́ли
коро́ва	коро́вы	а́рмия	а́рмии

nom. sing.	*nom. pl.*	*nom. sing.*	*nom. pl.*
рыба	рыбы	траге́дия	траге́дии
пти́ца	пти́цы	тетра́дь	тетра́ди
да́ча	да́чи	дверь	две́ри
кни́га	кни́ги	ло́шадь	ло́шади

2. Study ¶20-7. Listen to the teacher (or the tape) and repeat the following masculine nouns in the nominative singular, in the nominative plural, and in the genitive plural.

nom. sing.	*nom. pl.*	*gen. pl.*
дива́н	дива́ны	дива́нов
телефо́н	телефо́ны	телефо́нов
у́жин	у́жины	у́жинов
теа́тр	теа́тры	теа́тров
уро́к	уро́ки	уро́ков
за́втрак	за́втраки	за́втраков
ма́льчик	ма́льчики	ма́льчиков
язы́к	языки́	языко́в
учени́к	ученики́	ученико́в
дневни́к	дневники́	дневнико́в
гара́ж	гаражи́	гараже́й
каранда́ш	карандаши́	карандаше́й
това́рищ	това́рищи	това́рищей
ю́ноша	ю́ноши	ю́ношей
автомоби́ль	автомоби́ли	автомоби́лей
роя́ль	роя́ли	роя́лей
словарь	словари́	словаре́й

3. Listen to the teacher (or the tape) and repeat the following neuter nouns in the nominative singular and in the nominative plural.

nom. sing.	*nom. pl.*
кре́сло	кре́сла
письмо́	пи́сьма
лицо́	ли́ца
сло́во	слова́
сочине́ние	сочине́ния
мо́ре	моря́

B. Study **¶20-6**.   Listen to the teacher (or the tape) and repeat the following questions.   Then read each answer aloud supplying the proper prepositional endings for the nouns in parentheses.

Teacher	*Student*
Где лежа́т ко́шки?	Ко́шки лежа́т на полу́.
Где роди́тели отдыха́ют тепе́рь?	Роди́тели тепе́рь отдыха́ют в (сад).
Где ма́льчики рабо́тают?	Ма́льчики рабо́тают в (лес).
Где нахо́дится ва́ша да́ча?	Она́ нахо́дится на (бе́рег) о́зера.

C. Review **¶9-3** and study **¶10-8**.   Read (or tape-record) the following nouns in the number and case required by the word they accompany according to the model for the first noun.

оди́н	уро́к	дневни́к	ма́льчик	каранда́ш
два	уро́ка	_____	_____	_____
три	уро́ка	_____	_____	_____
четы́ре	уро́ка	_____	_____	_____
пять	уро́ков	_____	_____	_____
шесть	уро́ков	_____	_____	_____
семь	уро́ков	_____	_____	_____

D. Study **¶20-10**.   Listen to the teacher (or the tape) and repeat the following verbs.   Then make up sentences using the imperative form of each verb.

Infinitive	**пла́кать**	**есть**	**быть**
Imper. sing.	плачь	ешь	будь
Imper. pl.	пла́чьте	е́шьте	бу́дьте

UNIT 21

МА́ЛЕНЬКАЯ ТРАГЕ́ДИЯ

Вдруг в ко́мнату вхо́дит А́нна Па́вловна, мать Ма́ши. Она́ ви́дит, что письмо́ Аки́ма лежи́т на полу́, и что Ма́ша сиди́т у стола́ и ти́хо пла́чет.

— Что с тобо́й? — спра́шивает А́нна Па́вловна. — Де́сять мину́т тому́ наза́д ты была́ так ра́да, когда́ я тебе́ дала́ письмо́ Аки́ма, а тепе́рь оно́ лежи́т на полу́, и ты пла́чешь.

Но Ма́ша ничего́ не отвеча́ет, кладёт го́лову на стол и продолжа́ет пла́кать. А́нна Па́вловна берёт письмо́ и чита́ет его́ о́чень внима́тельно. Вдруг она́ начина́ет смея́ться.

— Почему́ ты смеёшься, ма́ма? — кричи́т Ма́ша.—Аки́м лю́бит другу́ю де́вушку, Ири́ну, а меня́ он совсе́м забы́л! Он говори́т то́лько о ней: — Ири́на прекра́сная спортсме́нка, Ири́на замеча́тельная хозя́йка, Ири́на всегда́ приготовля́ет за́втрак . . . Это совсе́м не смешно́! А я ду́мала, что Аки́м меня́ лю́бит . . . — и Ма́ша опя́ть начина́ет пла́кать.

— Глу́пая де́вушка! — говори́т А́нна Па́вловна — ты не прочита́ла письма́ до конца́. Вот оно́. Чита́й!

— Не хочу́ чита́ть! — кричи́т Ма́ша — Аки́м меня́ не интересу́ет. Не хочу́ да́же ду́мать о нём.

А́нна Па́вловна ничего́ не отвеча́ет. Она́ берёт письмо́ Аки́ма и чита́ет его́ ме́дленно и гро́мко, а Ма́ша слу́шает о́чень внима́тельно.

Слова́рь (Vocabulary)

Па́вловна Pavlovna (*lit.* Paul's daughter)
ти́хо quietly
что с тобо́й? (*instr. of* **ты**) what is the matter with you?
де́сять ten

167

де́сять мину́т (*gen. pl. of* **мину́та**) ten minutes
дала́ (*f., past of* **дать**) gave
класть (**I**); **кладу́, кладёшь, кладу́т** to put
кладёт го́лову на стол (*acc. of* **стол** *indicates direction of motion*) puts her head on (*lit.* on to) the table
внима́тельно carefully, attentively
ма́ма mama
крича́ть (**II**); **кричу́, кричи́шь, крича́т** to shout, to scream
друго́й, -а́я, -о́е (*adj. & pron.*) other, another
совсе́м (*adv.*) entirely
о ней (*prep. of* **она́**) about her
совсе́м не not at all, not in the least
смешно́ it is funny
э́то совсе́м не смешно́! this is not at all funny!
опя́ть again
прочита́ла (*past of* **прочита́ть**) she read through
до (*with gen.*) to, up to, until
коне́цᴶᴵ (*gen.* **конца́**) end
о нём (*prep. of* **он**) about him

ВСЁ ХОРОШО́, ЧТО ХОРОШО́ КОНЧА́ЕТСЯ

. . . Мы обыкнове́нно еди́м компо́т, пото́м я́йца и хлеб с ма́слом и пьём ко́фе.*

Мы начина́ем рабо́тать в во́семь и́ли в де́вять часо́в. Иногда́ мы рабо́таем в саду́, а иногда́ в лесу́, кото́рый нахо́дится недалеко́ от фе́рмы. Мы берём с собо́й са́ндвичи и за́втракаем в оди́ннадцать и́ли в двена́дцать часо́в.

Мы обыкнове́нно конча́ем рабо́ту в пять часо́в дня, и в шесть вся семья́ обе́дает в большо́й столо́вой. Мы еди́м сли́шком бы́стро и ма́ло разгова́риваем. Э́то мне совсе́м не нра́вится. По́мнишь как до́лго мы разгова́ривали по́сле обе́да, когда́ я был у вас? Я тогда́ не знал как прия́тно сиде́ть вокру́г самова́ра, пить чай и разгова́ривать.

Ве́чером мы ча́сто е́здим в го́род. Ва́ся обыкнове́нно хо́дит в библиоте́ку, а мы с Ири́ной хо́дим в кино́ и́ли гуля́ем в па́рке.

Ири́на о́чень ми́лая де́вушка. У неё краси́вое лицо́, больши́е си́ние глаза́ и прия́тный го́лос, — но мне с ней ску́чно. Она́ ма́ло чита́ла, нигде́ не была́, и ма́ло зна́ет. То́лько с тобо́й, Ма́ша, мне никогда́ не ску́чно. Ско́ро мы бу́дем вме́сте.

Твой друг Аки́м.

Ма́ша, счастли́вая, весёлая, целу́ет ма́му. Всё хорошо́, что хорошо́ конча́ется!

* For the beginning of this paragraph, see p. 130.

✝ Слова́рь (Vocabulary)

что (*rel. pron.*) that
конча́ться (**I**) (*intrans., used mostly in third person*); конча́ется, конча́ются
   to end, to come to an end
всё хорошо́, что хорошо́ конча́ется all is well that ends well
обыкнове́нно usually
яйцо́ (*pl.* я́йца) egg
хлеб bread
ма́сло butter
ко́фе (*m.; not decl.*) coffee
во́семь eight
де́вять nine
лес (*prep. with* в = лесу́) forest
недалеко́ not far
са́ндвич sandwich
за́втракать (*when referring to noon meal*) to eat lunch
оди́ннадцать eleven
двена́дцать twelve
конча́ть (**I**); конча́ю, -ешь, -ют to finish
в пять часо́в дня at five o'clock in the afternoon
обе́дать (**I**); обе́даю, -ешь, -ют to dine, to have dinner
тогда́ then, at that time (see ¶ 21-5)
прия́тно it is pleasant
библиоте́ка library
мы с Ири́ной Irene and I (see ¶ 21-6)
лицо́ (*pl.* ли́ца) face
глаз (*pl.* глаза́) eye
го́лос (*pl.* голоса́) voice
счастли́вый, -ая, -ое (*pr.* щастли́вый) happy
целова́ть (**I**); целу́ю, целу́ешь, целу́ют to kiss

Грамма́тика (Grammar)

Part I

21-1. The Pronoun: что*

   a. Interrogative.

	DECLENSION		EXAMPLES
People	*things*		
Кто *nom.*	что? what?		Что лежи́т на столе́? Газе́та лежи́т на столе́.
Кого *gen.*	чего́? of what?		Чего́ вы не зна́ете? Я не зна́ю уро́ка.
Каму *dat*	чему		

* See ¶ 12-2.

Кого Асс что
Кем I чем
о ком P о чём

Кому dat. **чему?** to what? (often used idiomatically)

К **чему́** подхо́дит по́езд? По́езд подхо́дит к **ста́нции.** (То) what is the train approaching? The train is approaching the station.

Кого acc. **что?** what?

Что вы чита́ете? Я чита́ю га-зе́ту.

Кем instr. **чем?** with what?

Чем вы пи́шете? Я пишу́ пе-ро́м.

о Ком prep. **о чём?** about what?

О чём вы говори́те? Мы го-вори́м **о пого́де.**

b. Relative.

1. The relative pronoun **что** (*what, that, which*) is declined like the interrogative but is used without the question mark. For example:

Я зна́ю, **что** он чита́л. — I know *what* he was reading.

Всё хорошо́, **что** хорошо́ кон-ча́ется. — All is well *that* ends well.

Мы де́лаем всё, **что** мо́жем. — We do all (*that*) we can.

2. Do not confuse the subordinating conjunction **что** (see **¶7-4**) with the relative pronoun **что**. Compare:

Я зна́ю **что** он чита́л. — I know *what* he was reading.

Я зна́ю, **что** он чита́л э́ту кни́гу. — I know *that* he was reading this book.

21-2. The Declension of Personal Pronouns in the Singular

The nominative, genitive, dative, and accusative forms of the personal pronouns in the singular were given in **¶3-4, 9-1,** and **13-4.** The following tables summarize the singular declension of personal pronouns in *all* cases.

	FIRST PERSON (*m., f., & n.*)	SECOND PERSON (*m., f., & n.*)
nom.	я	ты
gen.	меня́	тебя́
dat.	мне	тебе́
acc.	меня́	тебя́
instr.	мной (мно́ю)	тобо́й (тобо́ю)
prep.	обо мне́	о тебе́

	THIRD PERSON (m. & n.)	With governing prepositions	THIRD PERSON (f.)	With governing prepositions
nom.	он оно́		она́	
gen.	его́	у него́	её	у неё
dat.	ему́	к нему́	ей	к ней
acc.	его́	на него́	её	на неё
instr.	им	с ним	ей, е́ю	с ней, с не́ю
prep.	о нём	о нём	о ней	о ней

Note: Pronouns of the third person take the prefix **н-** when they are governed by a preposition.

21-3. Possessives for the Third Person

a. The possessive adjective for the *first person* is **мой, моя́,** and **моё** in the singular, and **мои́** in the plural.

b. The possessive adjective for the *second person* is **твой, твоя́,** and **твоё** in the singular, and **твои́** in the plural.

c. There is no possessive adjective for the *third person.* To express such possession, the genitive forms of the corresponding personal pronouns are used.

SINGULAR

m.	(*nom.* он)	**его́**	his	(*lit.* of him)
f.	(*nom.* она́)	**её**	her	(*lit.* of her)
n.	(*nom.* оно́)	**его́**	its	(*lit.* of its)

PLURAL

m.
f. } (*nom.* они́)   **их**   their   (*lit.* of them)
n.

Note: When the above forms are used as possessive adjectives (that is, when they are used to answer the question *whose?*), they are *not* declined and they are *never* prefixed by **н-**. (The prefix **н-** thus indicates that **его́, её, его́,** and **их** are personal pronouns, not adjectives.) Compare:

PRONOUNS	ADJECTIVES
Я иду́ к **нему́**.	Я иду́ к **его́** бра́ту.
I am going to *him* (his home).	I am going to *his* brother.
Я иду́ к **ней**.	Я иду́ к **её** бра́ту.
I am going to *her* (her home).	I am going to *her* brother.
Э́то письмо́ от **него́**.	Э́то письмо́ от **его́** отца́.
This letter is from *him*.	This letter is from *his* father.
Мы бы́ли у **них**.	Мы бы́ли у **их** сестры́.
We were at *their* house.	We were at *their* sister's.

Part II

21-4. Time of Day—On the Hour

Memorize this paragraph, which is largely a matter of review. The table will greatly help your memory.

CARDINAL NUMERALS (1 to 12)	TIME OF DAY	
	P.M.	A.M.
1. оди́н, одна́, одно́	1:00 час дня	час но́чи
2. два (*m. & n.*), две (*f.*)	2:00 два часа́ дня	два часа́ но́чи
3. три	3:00 три часа́ дня	три часа́ но́чи
4. четы́ре	4:00 четы́ре часа́ дня	четы́ре часа́ утра́
5. пять	5:00 пять часо́в дня	пять часо́в утра́
6. шесть	6:00 шесть часо́в ве́чера	шесть часо́в утра́
7. семь	7:00 семь часо́в ве́чера	семь часо́в утра́
8. во́семь	8:00 во́семь часо́в ве́чера	во́семь часо́в утра́
9. де́вять	9:00 де́вять часо́в ве́чера	де́вять часо́в утра́
10. де́сять	10:00 де́сять часо́в ве́чера	де́сять часо́в утра́
11. оди́ннадцать	11:00 оди́ннадцать часо́в ве́чера	оди́ннадцать часо́в утра́
12. двена́дцать	12:00 двена́дцать часо́в но́чи	двена́дцать часо́в дня

Note: The afternoon hours 1:00–5:00 are regarded as hours of the *day* = **дня**; 6:00–11:00 p.m. as hours of the *evening* = **ве́чера**; 12:00 midnight–3:00 a.m. as hours of the *night* = **но́чи**; and 4:00–11:00 a.m. as hours of the *morning* = **утра́**. Twelve noon is considered an hour of the *day* = **дня**.

21-5. Тогда́ and пото́м

Note the difference in the meanings of тогда́ and пото́м: *then* *later*

a. **Тогда́** refers to a specific point in time, past or future, but *not* present. For example:

Я **тогда́** был здоро́в.	I was well *then* (at that time).
Ско́ро мы бу́дем в СССР и **тогда́** бу́дем говори́ть то́лько по-ру́сски.	Soon we shall be in the U.S.S.R. and shall *then* speak only Russian.

b. **Пото́м** refers to an event or situation in a series of successive events or situations. For example:

Сего́дня я иду́ в шко́лу, **пото́м** в библиоте́ку, а **пото́м** в кино́.	Today I am going to school, *then* to the library, and *then* to the movies.

21-6. Plural Subjects with the Instrumental

To express a plural subject, especially in the first person, **с** with the instrumental is often used thus:

Мы **с Ири́ной** хо́дим в кино́.	Irene and I go to the movies.
Мы **с отцо́м** слу́шаем ра́дио.	Father and I are listening to the radio.

21-7. Verbs in -овать and -авать

a. Verbs in **-овать** lose the syllable **-ов** in the *present tense* and in the *imperative*. For example:

INFINITIVE	PRESENT	IMPERATIVE
рисова́ть	рису́ю	рису́й
to draw	рису́ешь	рису́йте

b. Verbs in **-авать** lose the syllable **-ва** only in the present; their imperative is formed from the infinitive stem, *not* from the present stem. For example:

встава́ть	вста́ю	встава́й
	встаёшь	встава́йте

- get up

Упражне́ния (Exercises)

A. The following sentences are all affirmative. Use the interrogative **что ?** to form questions to which these sentences can serve as answers. (Master **¶21-1** before doing this exercise. **Чему́**, which is used idiomatically, is not included here.) For example:

Учи́тель пи́шет ме́лом на доске́.

Question: **Чем учи́тель пи́шет на доске́ ?**

1. Я чита́ю рома́н. 2. Ма́ша ду́мает о письме́. 3. Мы говори́м о войне́. 4. Он пи́шет сочине́ние перо́м. 5. Она́ не уме́ет приготовля́ть борщ. 6. Оте́ц пьёт чай из стака́на. 7. Я никогда́ не пью воды́. 8. Лес нахо́дится недалеко́ от фе́рмы.

B. Replace the words in parentheses with the proper form of the pronoun or with an appropriate possessive, as required by the sentence. (Master **¶21-2** and **21-3** before doing this exercise.) For example:

Я иду́ к (она́). — Я иду́ к **ней**.

Вот письмо́ от (она́) бра́та. — Вот письмо́ от **её** бра́та.

1. Ты сиди́шь о́коло (он). 2. Он стои́т о́коло (я). 3. Мы сиди́м о́коло (она́) отца́. 4. Мы разгова́риваем с (она́). 5. Вы говори́ли о (он). 6. Она́ была́ с (он) в теа́тре. 7. Вот сочине́ние (он) ученика́. 8. Мать дала́ (она́) письмо́. 9. Письмо́ бы́ло у (она́). 10. Что с (ты)? 11. Почему́ вы так смо́трите на (он)? 12. Я е́ду к (ты). 13. Они́ сего́дня бу́дут у (ты). 14. О ком вы говори́ли, о (он) и́ли о (она́)? 15. Что вы (он) пи́шете обо (я)? 16. Вот ва́ше письмо́, чита́йте (оно́). 17. Здесь темно́. Ты (я) ви́дишь? 18. Да, я (ты) ви́жу, но (она́) я не ви́жу. 19. Мы е́дем в го́род и берём (ты) с собо́й. 20. Учи́тельница то́лько что говори́ла о (ты).

C. Supply Russian equivalents for the English words in italics. Then translate the sentences. (Refer to **¶21-4**.)

1. Мы встаём в *8:00 a.m.* 2. В *9:00 o'clock* мы за́втракаем. 3. *Then* мы идём в *garden*. 4. Мы рабо́таем *in the garden* пять и́ли шесть *hours*. 5. At *6:00 o'clock* мы конча́ем рабо́ту. 6. В *8:00 p.m.* мы обе́даем. 7. В Аме́рике *usually* обе́дают в *6:00 p.m.*, но мы обе́даем в *8:00*. 8. Мы обе́даем так по́здно, потому́ что всегда́ ждём *father*. 9. Он рабо́тает но́чью и спит днём *six or seven hours*. 10. Он начина́ет рабо́тать в *2:00 a.m.*

Перево́д (Translation)

A. Omit the words in parentheses and include the words in brackets.

1. Why are you laughing? This is not at all funny! 2. What do you want to know about him? 3. He does not interest me in the least [совсе́м не]. 4. You did not read the end of her letter. 5. We read the book through [прочита́ли] to [up to] the end. I shall read again and you listen carefully. 6. The boy again puts (his) head on the table and begins to cry. 7. What is the matter with you? Why are you screaming? 8. Who is on the phone? You are talking too quietly, and I do not hear anything [and I hear nothing]. 9. Who shouted so loudly in the forest? 10. She was not talking about you (*fam.*), but about another girl.

B. Omit the words in parentheses and include the words in brackets. (See ¶ 21-6.)

1. My brother and I usually have breakfast at seven o'clock in the morning. 2. We eat eggs, bread [with] and butter, and drink milk or coffee. 3. We never drink tea in the morning. 4. My sister and I often eat lunch in town. 5. We usually eat sandwiches and drink cold milk. 6. After lunch [по́сле за́втрака] we often go to the library. 7. We have a new library in town, and it is very pleasant to work there. 8. Four years ago we lived in the country, and I did not know then how pleasant (it was) to live in a big town. 9. At 6:00 p.m. the whole family has dinner [dines] in the big dining room. 10. I also have a little brother, Vanya, whom everybody loves very much. 11. He has an intelligent [smart] face, big blue eyes, and a pleasant voice. 12. His teacher (*f.*) says that he is the most diligent pupil in school. 13. He always enters the dining room, gay and happy, and kisses mother and father. 14. He never kisses me, but always wants to sit near me. 15. What a fine [прекра́сный] boy!

Вопро́сы (Questions)

1. Кто вдруг вхо́дит в ко́мнату Ма́ши? 2. Что она́ ви́дит? 3. Почему́ Ма́ша была́ так ра́да де́сять мину́т тому́ наза́д? 4. Почему́ она́ тепе́рь пла́чет? 5. Она́ прочита́ла письмо́ до конца́? 6. Почему́ Ма́ша не хо́чет чита́ть да́льше? 7. Э́то пра́вда, что Аки́м её не интересу́ет? 8. Как Ма́ша слу́шает, когда́ её мать чита́ет письмо́ Аки́ма?

9. Когда́ Аки́м и его́ друг начина́ют рабо́тать? 10. Где они́ ча́сто рабо́тают? 11. Когда́ они́ конча́ют рабо́ту? 12. Когда́ вся семья́ обе́дает? 13. Семья́ Ва́си мно́го разгова́ривает в столо́вой? 14. Э́то нра́вится Аки́му? 15. Что Ва́ся обыкнове́нно де́лает в го́роде? 16. А что де́лают Аки́м и Ири́на? 17. Како́е у Ири́ны лицо́? 18. Каки́е у неё глаза́ и како́й го́лос? 19. Почему́ Аки́му ску́чно с Ири́ной? 20. А с Ма́шей ему́ то́же ску́чно? 21. Почему́ Ма́ша целу́ет ма́му? 22. А́нна Па́вловна хоро́шая мать? Почему́?

Pattern Drills

A. 1. Study ¶21-1c. Listen to the teacher (or the tape) and repeat the following questions. Then read aloud each answer in the "Student" column.

Teacher	*Student*
Что (*nom.*) лежи́т на полу́?	Письмо́ лежи́т на полу́.
Чего́ (*gen.*) вы не понима́ете сего́дня?	Я сего́дня не понима́ю вопро́са.
К чему́ (*dat.*) подхо́дит* по́езд? (*to*) what is the train approaching?	По́езд подхо́дит к го́роду.
Что (*acc.*) вы тепе́рь де́лаете?	Мы тепе́рь одева́емся.
Чем (*instr.*) она́ тепе́рь пи́шет?	Она́ тепе́рь пи́шет карандашо́м.
О чём (*prep.*) вы ду́маете?	Я ду́маю об экза́мене.

2. Listen to the teacher (or the tape) and repeat the following sentences. Then make up questions with the appropriate cases of **что** to correspond to the sentences in the "Teacher" column according to the model sentences.

Teacher	*Student*
Автомоби́ль стои́т в гараже́.	**Что** стои́т в гараже́?
Я сего́дня не зна́ю уро́ка.	_____?
По́езд подхо́дит к дере́вне.	_____?
Мы пи́шем сочине́ние.	_____?
Учи́тель пи́шет ме́лом на доске́.	_____?
Он всегда́ говори́т о футбо́ле.	_____?

B. Turn to ¶21-2. Listen to the teacher (or the tape) and repeat the declension of personal pronouns until you know them by heart.

* Idiomatic usage.

C. 1. Study ¶21-3. Listen to the teacher (or the tape) and repeat the following sentences. Then replace the nouns with the appropriate possessive adjectives, as in the model sentences. (*Note:* Make sure that you distinguish between pronouns and possessive adjectives.)

Teacher	*Student*
Вот автомобиль **учителя**.	Вот **егó** автомобиль.
Это роя́ль **учительницы**.	Это **её** роя́ль.
Вот кре́сло **бáбушки**.	Вот _____ кре́сло.
А э́то кре́сло **дя́ди**.	А э́то _____ кре́сло.
Вот кóмната **мáльчиков**.	Вот _____ кóмната.
А э́то кóмната **Ве́ры** и **Áнны**.	А э́то _____ кóмната.

2. Listen to the teacher (or the tape) and repeat the following sentences. Then replace the nouns with the appropriate pronouns, as in the model sentences. (*Note:* Make sure that you distinguish between pronouns and possessive adjectives.)

Teacher	*Student*
Мы е́дем к **учи́телю**.	Мы е́дем к **нему́**.
А мы идём к **учи́тельнице**.	А мы идём к **ней**.
Вот письмó от **отцá**.	Вот письмó от _____.
А э́то письмó от **товáрищей**.	А э́то письмó от _____.
Мы говори́ли о **Вáсе**.	Мы говори́ли о _____.
Мы обе́дали с **Ве́рой**.	Мы с _____ обе́дали.

3. Turn to page 174 . Practice reading exercise B aloud several times. Then tape-record it.

D. Turn to ¶21-4. Listen to the teacher (or the tape) and repeat the numerals and phrases in the three columns of the table.

E. Turn to page 174. Practice reading exercise C aloud several times. Then tape-record it.

F. Study ¶21-6. Listen to the teacher (or the tape) and repeat the following questions. Then read each answer aloud supplying the proper case of the noun in parentheses.

Teacher	*Student*
С кем ты читáешь нóвый ромáн?	Мы с Ири́ной читáем нóвый ромáн.
С кем ты приготовля́ешь у́жин?	Мы с (мáма) _____.
С кем ты е́дешь на дáчу?	Мы с (дя́дя) _____.

С кем вы гуля́ли в саду́? Мы с (брат) _____.
С кем вы хо́дите в теа́тр? Мы с (Ка́тя) _____.

G. Study ¶21-7. Listen to the teacher (or the tape) and repeat the conjugations of **целова́ть** and **встава́ть**. Then conjugate **рисова́ть** and **дава́ть**.

Teacher	Student		Teacher	Student
целова́ть	**рисова́ть**		**дава́ть**	**встава́ть**
		Present Tense		
Я целу́**ю**	я рису́**ю**		я да**ю́**	я вста**ю́**
ты целу́**ешь**	_____		ты да**ёшь**	_____
он целу́**ет**	_____		он да**ёт**	_____
мы целу́**ем**	_____		мы да**ём**	_____
вы целу́**ете**	_____		вы да**ёте**	_____
они́ целу́**ют**	_____		они́ да**ю́т**	_____
		Imperative		
целу́**й**	_____		дава́**й**	_____
целу́**йте**	_____		дава́**йте**	_____

U N I T **22**

REVIEW LESSON

Grammar and Vocabulary Review

A. Supply the proper form of the verb in parentheses and the Russian equivalent for English words, and translate at sight. When two verbs are given, select the one required by the meaning of the sentence.

1. Они́ всегда́ (смея́ться), но вчера́ они́ не (смея́ться).

2. Ма́ша, почему́ ты (смея́ться)? Это совсе́м не (funny)!

3. Мой това́рищ мне о́чень (люби́ть, нра́виться), и я зна́ю, что я ему́ то́же (нра́виться, люби́ть).

4. Она́ о́чень (likes) (ходи́ть, е́здить) верхо́м на чёрной (horse).

5. Ма́ша о́чень (хоте́ть) ви́деть (Joachim).

6. Здесь так (dark), что мы ничего́ не (уме́ть, мочь) ви́деть.

7. Три го́да тому́ наза́д он (уме́ть, мочь) говори́ть (Spanish), но тепе́рь он всё забы́л.

8. Она́ тепе́рь больна́ и не (уме́ть, мочь) игра́ть на (piano).

9. Ва́ша тетра́дь всегда́ (лежа́ть) (on the floor). Кто (класть) её (on the floor)?

10. Я вас прекра́сно (слы́шать). Пожа́луйста, не (крича́ть)!

11. Уро́к (конча́ться) в (12:00 noon). По́сле уро́ка (we shall eat lunch).

12. Не (пла́кать) де́ти! Ско́ро (we shall have dinner).

13. Мы (купа́ться) в (lake) ка́ждый день, но вчера́ (идти́, ходи́ть) дождь и мы не (купа́ться).

14. Ма́льчик (встава́ть) в (7:00 a.m.) ка́ждый день и бы́стро (умыва́ться) и (одева́ться).

15. Семья́ (за́втракать) в (dining room) в (1:00 p.m.) и (у́жинать) в (8:00 p.m.).

B. Translate the following infinitives, conjugate them in the present, past, and future, and give the imperative.

Group I. (Note that these verbs lose the syllable **-ов** or **-ва**—see **¶ 21-7**.)

1. рисова́ть	3. целова́ть
2. интересова́ть	4. дава́ть
	5. встава́ть

Group II.

1. класть*	5. входи́ть	9. продолжа́ть
2. пла́кать	6. одева́ться	10. приготовля́ть
3. крича́ть	7. умыва́ться	11. уме́ть
4. конча́ть	8. смея́ться	12. петь

C. Give the time of the day:

1. From 1:00 p.m. through 12:00 midnight.
2. From 1:00 a.m. through 12:00 noon.

D. Decline the following nouns in the singular and give their plural in the *nominative* and the *accusative*.

1. да́ча. 2. дождь. 3. кре́сло. 4. мо́ре. 5. сочине́ние. 6. окно́. 7. письмо́. 8. потоло́к. 9. коне́ц. 10. тетра́дь. 11. столо́вая. 12. неде́ля.

E. Give the nominative and genitive plural of the following nouns. (See **¶ 20-7**.)

1. час. 2. учени́к. 3. журна́л. 4. го́лос. 5. обе́д. 6. са́ндвич. 7. това́рищ. 8. гара́ж. 9. за́втрак. 10. спортсме́н.

Reading and Comprehension Drill

A. Read the following sentences aloud and translate them orally into idiomatic English.

1. Идёт дождь, и я до́лжен е́хать о́чень ме́дленно.

2. Моя́ мать купи́ла мне но́вый неме́цкий слова́рь.

3. Мы берём её с собо́й, потому́ что она́ всегда́ предпочита́ет е́здить с на́ми.

4. Мой това́рищ прекра́сно игра́ет в те́ннис.

5. Ма́ша внима́тельно прочита́ла письмо́ Ва́си до конца́.

6. Профе́ссор, у кото́рого мы жи́ли три неде́ли, хоро́ший друг семьи́.

7. Он рабо́тал весь ве́чер и прие́хал домо́й дово́льно по́здно.

* *Past* клал, -ла, -ло, -ли.

8. Ты поéхала в гóрод в вóсемь часóв утрá.

9. Мы хотúм пить чай, но у нас нет стакáнов.

10. Мы ждём отвéта от товáрищей.

B. Supply the endings, read aloud, and translate.

1. Мой друг пúшет интерéсные сочинéн_____.

2. У негó никогдá нé было лóшад_____ и он не умéет éздить верхóм.

3. Вы всегдá сидúте у себ_____ в кóмнате и дýмаете тóлько о себ_____.

4. Чéрез недéл_____ мы éдем в дерéвн_____ к дя́д_____.

5. Большóе спасúбо за интерéсн_____ кнúгу.

6. Как вам нрáвятся инострáнн_____ язык_____?

7. Вы пóмните сáмые трýдн_____ францýзск_____, немéцк_____ и испáнск_____ слов_____.

8. Ирúна и Мáша ýмн_____ и красúв_____ рýсск_____ дéвушк_____.

9. Ýтром мы едúм я́йц_____, хлеб с мáсл_____ и пьём кóфе, а в час дня мы едúм сáндвич_____ и пьём холóдн_____ молокó.

10. Какúе у вас прекрáсн_____ чёрн_____ глазá!

11. Птúц_____ вéсело пéли в лес_____, котóр_____ нахóдится на берег_____ óзера.

12. Мы говорúли с учúтел_____ о послéдн_____ рýсск_____ урóк_____.

13. Мой товáрищи прекрáсн_____ спортсмéн_____.

14. У Ирúны мúл_____ лицó, больш_____ сúн_____ глазá, и прия́тн_____ гóлос.

15. Вáся читáет серьёзн_____ ромáны, как напримéр "Отц_____ и дéти" úли "Америкáнск_____ трагéдия."

Перевóд (Translation)

Omit the words in parentheses and include the words in brackets.

1. Boris wanted to see the teacher (*m.*), but he was not at home. 2. The little boy, whom you saw a week ago, is my younger brother. 3. We shall be very bored in the country. 4. After supper we went [**поéхали**] to grandfather's, but he was not in town. 5. Do not swim in the lake when it is raining. 6. Boris and Ivan are the most diligent pupils in school. 7. A week ago we saw a French tragedy at the new theater. 8. My sister went [**поéхала**] with us, and cried all evening. 9. She is a strange girl.

10. She cries when she is reading a novel, when our little brother is not well, and even when our dog is sick.

Discussion (Бесе́да)

The Russian translation of this text is given on the next page. Translate without looking at the Russian text; then compare your work with the printed version.

Omit the words in parentheses and include words in brackets.

Teacher: 1. "We read a great deal [much] about Joachim, Masha, Vasya, and Irene. 2. How do you like these [**э́ти**] young men and women [girls]? 3. What are they doing? 4. What interests Joachim, Vasya, or Masha?"

Ivan: 5. "Joachim writes long letters to Vasya. 6. Vasya is very fond of Joachim, but he thinks that Joachim writes too much about Masha and too little about himself."

Vera: 7. "Girls do not interest Vasya, and he does not like (it) that they interest his friend."

Petya: 8. "Masha, of course, does not sing like a bird, and does not swim like a fish. 9. Joachim wrote nothing about this [**об э́том**], and Vasya does not know how she swims, or how she sings."

Anne: 10. "Vasya is a serious youth. 11. He reads long novels and very often goes to the library, but his letters are not at all serious. 12. He writes, for instance, (to) Joachim, that everybody is waiting for him: [both] the horses and the cows, [and] the dogs and the cats, and (his) sister Irene. . . ."

Tanya: 13. "This is not true! 14. He writes only that the grey horse is waiting for Joachim!"

Teacher: 15. "Tanya, please do not shout!"

Fedya: 16. "It's not true. . . . Vasya is not an odd youth! 17. A person who reads serious novels, as for instance, *War and Peace, Fathers and Sons,* or *An American Tragedy,* is not at all odd, but very, very intelligent [**у́мный**]!"

Katya: 18. "I do not understand why Joachim is bored (when he is) with Irene. 19. She has a beautiful face, big black eyes, and a pleasant voice. 20. She is a beauty!"

Ivan: 21. "Her eyes are not black, but blue!"

Teacher: 22. "If you want (to), we can continue our conversation [**разгово́р**] tomorrow. 23. But for [**А на**] today—(that's) enough [**дово́льно**]!"

Pupils: 24. "Oh, what a pity!"

Бесе́да (Discussion)

(This section of the lesson could also be used as a skit to be put on by the Russian club or in class.)

Учи́тель: 1. Мы мно́го чита́ли об Аки́ме, Ма́ше, Ва́се и Ири́не. 2. Как вам нра́вятся э́ти (these) ю́ноши и де́вушки? 3. Что они́ де́лают? 4. Что интересу́ет Аки́ма, Ва́сю и́ли Ма́шу?

Ива́н: 5. Аки́м пи́шет Ва́се дли́нные пи́сьма. 6. Ва́ся о́чень лю́бит Аки́ма, но он ду́мает, что Аки́м сли́шком мно́го пи́шет о Ма́ше и сли́шком ма́ло о себе́.

Ве́ра: 7. Де́вушки не интересу́ют Ва́сю и ему́ не нра́вится, что они́ интересу́ют его́ дру́га.

Пе́тя: 8. Ма́ша, коне́чно, не поёт как пти́ца и не пла́вает как ры́ба. 9. Аки́м об э́том [about this] ничего́ не писа́л, и Ва́ся не зна́ет, как она́ пла́вает, и́ли как она́ поёт.

А́нна: 10. Ва́ся серьёзный ю́ноша. 11. Он чита́ет дли́нные рома́ны и о́чень ча́сто хо́дит в библиоте́ку, но его́ пи́сьма совсе́м не серьёзные. 12. Он, наприме́р, пи́шет Аки́му, что все его́ ждут: и ло́шади, и коро́вы, и соба́ки, и ко́шки и сестра́ Ири́на. . . .

Та́ня: 13. Э́то непра́вда! 14. Он пи́шет то́лько, что Аки́ма ждёт се́рая ло́шадь! . . . .

Учи́тель: 15. Та́ня, пожа́луйста, не кричи́те!

Фе́дя: 16. Непра́вда. . . . Ва́ся не стра́нный ю́ноша! 17. Челове́к, кото́рый чита́ет серьёзные рома́ны, как наприме́р: "Война́ и мир," "Отцы́ и де́ти" и́ли "Америка́нская траге́дия," совсе́м не стра́нный, а о́чень, о́чень у́мный!

Ка́тя: 18. Я не понима́ю, почему́ Аки́му ску́чно с Ири́ной. 19. У неё краси́вое лицо́, больши́е чёрные глаза́ и прия́тный го́лос. 20. Она́ краса́вица!

Ива́н: 21. Её глаза́ не чёрные, а си́ние! . . . .

Учи́тель: 22. Е́сли хоти́те, мы мо́жем продолжа́ть наш разгово́р (conversation) за́втра. 23. А на (for) сего́дня — дово́льно (enough)!

Ученики́: 24. Ах, как жаль!

U N I T **23**

THE ASPECTS

This unit presents the basic and most useful information on the aspects. The grammar in this unit should be covered before the reading exercises and is therefore given first.

The text is intended to illustrate and clarify grammatical principles rather than offer connected material. To simplify the study of the aspects, perfective forms of familiar verbs are used. Irregular perfective forms, especially of unfamiliar verbs, will be introduced very sparingly in the remaining units.

Грамма́тика (Grammar)

23-1. The Aspects

We have already learned that verbs of motion have two distinct forms in Russian: the *habitual* and the *actual*. (See ¶13-3.) However, there are two other forms that most Russian verbs—not simply those of motion—possess. These two forms are known as the *imperfective aspect* and the *perfective aspect*.

Both aspects designate the same action but they describe different types of performance with respect to the element of time. For example:

imp.	Он ви́дел.	He saw.
pf.	Он **уви́дел.**	He noticed.
imp.	Она́ пла́кала.	She was crying.
pf.	Она́ **запла́кала.**	She started crying.

184

a. The *imperfective* describes an action which is in progress and is unfinished.   Such an action is either:

1. continuous *or*
2. repeated *or*   } No *result* or *time limit* is indicated.
3. of unknown duration

b. The *perfective* describes an action which is either:

1. completed *or*
2. just begun *or*   } *Completion,   start,   result   or   time*
3. performed only once *or*   } *limit* is emphasized.
4. of limited duration

c. In English, ideas of continuity or completion of an action are conveyed by means of auxiliary verbs or other words, e.g., *was, used to, began to, finished, once, awhile.*   In Russian, instead of such additional words, the aspects are generally used to describe varieties of the same action.   The following table gives concrete examples of the way the aspects function in this respect.

		Imperfective	Perfective
Infinitive		1. писа́ть to write, to be writing	написа́ть to finish writing (*action completed*)
		2. пла́кать to cry, to be crying	запла́кать to start crying (*action begun*)
		3. крича́ть to shout, to be shouting	кри́кнуть to exclaim once (*single performance*)
		4. рабо́тать to work, to be working	порабо́тать to work awhile (*limited duration*)
Present		1. Он пи́шет кни́гу. He is writing a book. Он пи́шет. He is writing, he writes.	None
		2. Она́ пла́чет. She is crying. Она́ ча́сто пла́чет. She often cries.	
		3. Я кричу́. I shout, am shouting.	
		4. Ты рабо́таешь. You work, you are working.	

	Imperfective	Perfective
Past	1. Он писа́л кни́гу. He was writing a book (*action in progress and unfinished*).	Он написа́л кни́гу. He has written a book (*action completed in the past*).
	2. Она́ пла́кала. She was crying.	Она́ запла́кала. She started crying (*action begun in the past*).
	3. Я крича́л. I was shouting.	Я кри́кнул. I shouted once, I exclaimed (*single performance in the past*).
	4. Ты рабо́тал. You were working.	Ты порабо́тал. You worked awhile (*limited duration in the past*).
Future	1. Он бу́дет писа́ть. He will write, will be writing.	Он напи́шет. He will write (and finish) (*action will be completed*).
	2. Она́ бу́дет пла́кать. She will cry, will be crying.	Она́ запла́чет. She will start crying (*action will be begun*).
	3. Я бу́ду крича́ть. I shall shout, shall be shouting.	Я кри́кну. I shall shout once (*single performance in the future*).
	4. Ты бу́дешь рабо́тать. You will work, will be working.	Ты порабо́таешь. You will work awhile (*limited duration in the future*).
Imperative	1. пиши́! write!	напиши́! write (and finish)!
	2. плачь! cry!	запла́чь! start crying!
	3. кричи́! shout!	кри́кни! exclaim! shout (once)!
	4. рабо́тай! work!	порабо́тай! work awhile!

23-2. Perfective Forms of the Verb

a. Perfective infinitive.

1. All of the infinitives given in previous lessons have been *imperfective* infinitives. The perfective infinitive, however, closely resembles the imperfective infinitive and can be derived from it in one of the following ways:

	IMPERFECTIVE	PERFECTIVE
(a) by adding a prefix	писа́ть	**на**писа́ть (to finish writing)
(b) by dropping a syllable	встава́ть	встать (to get up once)
(c) by changing **-ать** or **-ять** to **-ить**	изуча́ть	изуч**и́ть** (to master something)
(d) irregularly (from different stems).	говори́ть	сказа́ть (to tell, say one thing)

2. Henceforth, perfective infinitives will be designated by the abbreviation *pf.* as they occur in the vocabulary.

b. Present tense—none.

The perfective aspect has no present tense since a completed action cannot be going on in the present. *Always* use the imperfective aspect to render the present tense.

c. The perfective past tense is formed from the perfective infinitive in the same way as the imperfective past is formed from its infinitive, and has the same endings. For example:

Imperfective		Perfective	
Infinitive	Past	Infinitive	Past
писа́ть	писа́л	написа́ть	написа́л
встава́ть	встава́ла	встать	вста́ла
изуча́ть	изуча́ли	изучи́ть	изучи́ли
говори́ть	говори́ло	сказа́ть	сказа́ло

d. Perfective future.

1. When the perfective is formed from the imperfective by adding a prefix, the *perfective future* is obtained by merely adding the prefix to the present tense. For example:

PRESENT TENSE	PERFECTIVE FUTURE	
я пишу́	я **на**пишу́	I shall write (and finish)
ты пи́шешь	ты **на**пи́шешь	you will write (and finish)
etc.	*etc.*	
я рабо́таю	я **по**рабо́таю	I shall work *awhile*
ты рабо́таешь	ты **по**рабо́таешь	you will work *awhile*
etc.	*etc.*	

2. All other perfectives form the future tense from the perfective infinitive in accordance with the same rules which determine the formation of the present tense from the imperfective infinitive (see ¶ **4-2**, **7-1**, and **8-1**). For example:

IMPERFECTIVE INFINITIVE	PERFECTIVE INFINITIVE
изуча́ть (I) to study	изучи́ть (II) to master
	(*study carried to completion*)

PRESENT	PERFECTIVE FUTURE	
я изуча́**ю**	я изучу́	I shall master
ты изуча́**ешь**	ты изу́**чишь**	
он изуча́**ет**	он изу́**чит**	
мы изуча́**ем**	мы изу́**чим**	
вы изуча́**ете**	вы изу́**чите**	
они́ изуча́**ют**	они́ изу́**чат**	

IMPERFECTIVE INFINITIVE	PERFECTIVE INFINITIVE
говори́ть (II) to speak,	сказа́ть (I) to have told or
to talk	said (once)

PRESENT	PERFECTIVE FUTURE	
я говор**ю́**	я скажу́	I shall tell, say
		(something once)
ты говор**и́шь**	ты ска́**жешь**	
он говор**и́т**	он ска́**жет**	
мы говор**и́м**	мы ска́**жем**	
вы говор**и́те**	вы ска́**жете**	
они́ говор**я́т**	они́ ска́**жут**	

Note: The imperfective of the verb **изуча́ть** belongs to the First Conjugation and the perfective to the Second; thus the present tense and the perfective future differ accordingly. On the other hand, **говори́ть** is of Conjugation II and **сказа́ть** of Conjugation I.

e. Perfective imperative.

The *perfective imperative* is formed from the *perfective future* in accordance with the same rules which apply to the formation of the *imperfective imperative* from the *present tense* (see ¶ 11-5 and 20-10.

For example:

PERFECTIVE FUTURE	PERFECTIVE IMPERATIVE	
ты напи́шешь	напиши́! напиши́те!	write (and finish)!
ты изу́чишь	изучи́! изучи́те!	master (something)!
ты ска́жешь	скажи́ скажи́те!	tell, say (one thing)!

23-3. Plural of Nouns in -á or -я́

A few masculine nouns take an accented **-á** or **-я́** in the nominative plural instead of the regular plural ending (see ¶ 20-2).

бе́рег	берега́	shores
ве́чер	вечера́	evenings
глаз	глаза́	eyes
го́лос	голоса́	voices
го́род	города́	towns
до́ктор	доктора́	doctors
дом	дома́	houses
лес	леса́	forests
профе́ссор	профессора́	professors
учи́тель	учителя́	teachers

Приме́ры (Examples)

The perfective verbs in these exercises are all formed from the imperfective by adding one of the following prefixes:

на-, про-, по-, or **с-.**

The sentences are given in pairs: the first one contains the *imperfective* and the second, the corresponding *perfective* form. Translate the following sentences. *Note:* The perfective meaning of the verbs is *to have done something* (completed action).

A. *Perfective Past*

1. Я две неде́ли ничего́ не писа́л.   2. Сего́дня я написа́л два письма́.   3. Учени́ца до́лго писа́ла сочине́ние.   4. Ва́ся написа́л коро́ткое, но о́чень хоро́шее сочине́ние.   5. Ле́том, когда́ она́ жила́ на да́че, она́ мно́го чита́ла.   6. Она́ прочита́ла трина́дцать рома́нов и четы́рнадцать и́ли пятна́дцать журна́лов.   7. Он всегда́ рисова́л то́лько берега́ Во́лги, города́, дома́, и леса́.   8. Сего́дня он в пе́рвый раз нарисова́л ю́ношу и де́вушку.   9. Они́ вчера́ весь день де́лали уро́ки.   10. Сего́дня они́ сде́лали уро́ки днём, а ве́чером смотре́ли телеви́зор.   11. Когда́ мы жи́ли у ба́бушки, мы всегда́ за́втракали в во́семь часо́в утра́.   12. Сего́дня мы поза́втракали в де́вять, а пото́м всё у́тро игра́ли в те́ннис.   13. Когда́ мы жи́ли в Чика́го, мы ча́сто обе́дали в рестора́не "Самова́р."   14. Мы то́лько что пообе́дали, а тепе́рь слу́шаем ра́дио.   15. Зимо́й мы ча́сто у́жинаем дово́льно по́здно.   16. Сего́дня мы поу́жинали о́чень ра́но и сейча́с же пое́хали в теа́тр.

B. *Perfective Future*

1. Мой друг пи́шет дли́нные пи́сьма.   2. За́втра я напишу́ ему́ коро́ткое письмо́.   3. Она́ тепе́рь чита́ет "Войну́ и мир."   4. Э́тот рома́н мне о́чень нра́вится и я прочита́ю его́ ещё раз.   5. Па́па рису́ет ка́ждый день.   6. Сего́дня ве́чером он нарису́ет портре́т ба́бушки.   7. Мы всегда́ за́втракаем в де́вять часо́в утра́ и де́лаем уро́ки в де́сять и́ли в оди́ннадцать.   8. За́втра же мы поза́втракаем в семь и сейча́с же сде́лаем все уро́ки.   9. Нам о́чень нра́вится рестора́н "Си́няя пти́ца" и мы там ча́сто обе́даем.   10. Е́сли хоти́те, мы снача́ла пообе́даем в рестора́не, а пото́м бу́дем пить чай и разгова́ривать у меня́ в ко́мнате.

C. *Perfective Imperative*

1. Большо́е спаси́бо за ми́лое письмо́, но пиши́те, пожа́луйста, ча́ще!   2. Напиши́те сочине́ние сего́дня!   3. Чита́йте, пожа́луйста, да́льше!   4. Прочита́йте письмо́ до конца́!   5. Рису́йте всё, что вы ви́дите!   6. Нарису́йте, пожа́луйста, самова́р!   7. Де́лайте уро́ки ка́ждый день!   8. Сде́лай уро́к до обе́да!   9. У́жинайте до́ма!   10. Поу́жинайте в рестора́не, кото́рый нахо́дится о́коло библиоте́ки, а пото́м жди́те меня́ в библиоте́ке.

✈ Слова́рь (Vocabulary)

Verbs are given first.

Prefix +	Imperfective	=	Perfective	(*To have done something*)
на-	писа́ть	=	написа́ть	to have written
про-	чита́ть	=	прочита́ть	to have read
на-	рисова́ть	=	нарисова́ть	to have drawn
с-	де́лать	=	сде́лать	to have done
по-	за́втракать	=	поза́втракать	to have had breakfast
по-	обе́дать	=	пообе́дать	to have dined
по-	у́жинать	=	поу́жинать	to have had supper

коро́ткий, -ая, -ое short
трина́дцать thirteen
четы́рнадцать fourteen
пятна́дцать fifteen
Во́лга Volga (river in the U.S.S.R.)
пе́рвый, -ая, -ое first
в пе́рвый раз for the first time
Чика́го (*not decl.*) Chicago
рестора́н restaurant
сейча́с now, presently
сейча́с же immediately, at once
ещё раз once again
па́па (*m.*) papa
портре́т portrait
снача́ла (*adv.*) at first
до *here:* before

Приме́ры (Examples)

The perfective verbs in these exercises are formed from the imperfective by adding the prefix **по-** or **за-**. Note that the same prefix may lend different meanings to a verb. Compare **по-обе́дать** (*to have had dinner*) with **погуля́ть** (*to walk awhile*). The first perfective denotes *completed action* whereas the second denotes *short duration*.

A. Translate. Note that in the following sentences all perfectives with **по-** indicate *short duration*.

1. Я немно́го погуля́ю в па́рке, а пото́м весь ве́чер бу́ду чита́ть.   2. Посиди́те ещё немно́го, мы так ре́дко ви́дим друг дру́га.   3. Вчера́ я немно́го порабо́тал в саду́, пото́м полежа́л на дива́не и поспа́л.   4. Ма́льчик постоя́л не́сколько мину́т о́коло две́ри рестора́на и ушёл.   5. Де́вочка поигра́ла с ко́шкой и ушла́.   6. Мы поговори́ли с хозя́йкой и ушли́. 7. Ты иди́ домо́й, а я ещё посижу́ немно́го и поговорю́ с тётей

и с дя́дей.   8. Ты немно́го поигра́ешь на роя́ле, а пото́м сде́лаешь уро́ки.   9. Мы ещё раз послу́шаем му́зыку, а пото́м бу́дем танцова́ть.   10. Снача́ла поду́май, а пото́м отвеча́й!

Слова́рь (Vocabulary)

Verbs are given first.

Prefix +	Imperfective	=	Perfective	(To do something for a short time)
по-	гуля́ть	=	погуля́ть	to walk awhile
по-	сиде́ть	=	посиде́ть	to sit awhile
по-	рабо́тать	=	порабо́тать	to work awhile
по-	лежа́ть	=	полежа́ть	to lie awhile
по-	спать	=	поспа́ть	to sleep a little, to take a nap
по-	стоя́ть	=	постоя́ть	to stand awhile
по-	игра́ть	=	поигра́ть	to play awhile
по-	говори́ть	=	поговори́ть	to have a chat
по-	слу́шать	=	послу́шать	to listen awhile
по-	ду́мать	=	поду́мать	to think awhile

не́сколько (*adv. with gen. pl.*) several, a few
мину́т (*gen. pl. of* **мину́та**)
ушёл, ушла́, ушло́, ушли́ (*past of pf.* **уйти́**) went away (once)
де́вочка little girl
му́зыка music
танцова́ть (**I**); **танцу́ю, -ешь, -ют** to dance

B. Translate.   Note that in the following sentences all perfectives with **за-** indicate the *beginning of an action*.

1. Все вдруг заговори́ли о войне́.   2. Студе́нты закрича́ли "ура́!"   3. Ученики́ запе́ли весёлую пе́сню.   4. Ве́ра чита́ла "Войну́ и мир" и вдруг запла́кала.   5. Де́вочка запла́чет, е́сли она́ прочита́ет письмо́ до конца́.   6. Учени́ца написа́ла упражне́ние, поду́мала немно́го и вдруг гро́мко засмея́лась.

Слова́рь (Vocabulary)

Verbs are given first.

Prefix +	Imperfective	=	Perfective	(To begin doing something)
за-	говори́ть	=	заговори́ть	to begin talking
за-	крича́ть	=	закрича́ть	to begin shouting, to exclaim
за-	петь	=	запе́ть	to begin singing
за-	пла́кать	=	запла́кать	to begin weeping
за-	смея́ться	=	засмея́ться	to burst into laughter

пе́сня song
упражне́ние exercise

Перево́д (Translation)

Omit the words in parentheses and include the words in brackets.

1. Write the exercise, please!   2. You have written a very short composition.   3. When will you read (and finish) the novel? 4. He has drawn a samovar for the first time.   5. They have already done the lessons for tomorrow [на за́втра].   6. We shall first have dinner, and then listen (for awhile) to the radio.   7. Read (through) your lesson once again.   8. Please write the exercises before [до] dinner.   9 There are fourteen or fifteen restaurants in town. 10. Mother began to cry, but father burst into laughter.   11. We listened (awhile) to the music, and then danced all evening. 12. We had a little chat with the host and left [went away].   13. He talked for a long time about Masha, but suddenly he began talking about Irene.   14. Everybody exclaimed: "We do not like this song!"   15. The little girl burst into laughter.   16. We shall sit awhile in the park and have a little chat.   17. This exercise is not difficult.   Think awhile and then write.

The aspects are learned easily when it is understood that describing an action must be more definite, more specific in Russian than it usually is in English.   Therefore, study carefully ¶23-1 and 23-2.   Then work on the pattern drills below.

Pattern Drills

A. Study **Приме́ры,** page 190.

Prefix + Imperfect = Perfective (To have done something).

Listen to the teacher (or the tape) and repeat the following sentences.   Then supply the *perfective* form of each verb in the same *person* and *tense* according to the model sentences in the "Student" column.

Teacher	*Student*
писа́ть	**на**писа́ть
Я писа́л упражне́ние.	Я написа́л упражне́ние.
Я писа́ла ———————.	Я написа́ла ———————.
Я бу́ду писа́ть ———————.	Я напишу́ ———————.
Пиши́ ———————.	Напиши́ ———————.

читáть	прочитáть
Вы читáли ромáн.	Вы прочитáли ромáн.
Вы бýдете читáть_____.	Вы _____.
Читáйте _____.	_____.

зáвтракать	позáвтракать
Онá зáвтракала рáно.	Онá позáвтракала рáно.
Онá бýдет зáвтракать _____.	Онá _____.
Зáвтракай _____.	_____.

дéлать	сдéлать
Мы дéлали урóки.	Мы сдéлали урóки.
Мы бýдем дéлать _____.	Мы _____.
Дéлайте _____.	_____.

B. Study **Примéры,** pages 191 – 192 .

Prefix + Imperfective = Perfective (To do something for a short time).

Teacher	*Student*
гуля́ть	погуля́ть
Ты гуля́л в садý.	Ты погуля́л в садý.
Ты бýдешь гуля́ть _____.	Ты _____.
Гуля́й _____.	_____.

сидéть	посидéть
Мы сидéли на дивáне.	Мы **по**сидéли на дивáне.
Мы бýдем сидéть _____.	Мы _____.
Сидúте_____.	_____.

говорúть	поговорúть
Онú говорúли о рабóте.	Онú **по**говорúли о рабóте.
Онú бýдут говорúть _____.	Онú_____.
Говорúте _____.	_____.

слу́шать   послу́шать

Вы слу́шали му́зыку.   Вы **по**слу́шали му́зыку.
Вы бу́дете слу́шать _____.   Вы _____.
Слу́шайте _____.   _____.

C. Study **Приме́ры,** page 192.

Prefix + *Imperfective* = *Perfective* (*To begin doing something*).

  Teacher   *Student*
  говори́ть   **за**говори́ть

Он говори́л о войне́.   Он **за**говори́л о войне́.
Он бу́дет говори́ть.   Он _____.

  петь   запе́ть

Они́ пе́ли ру́сскую пе́сню.   Они́ **за**пе́ли ру́сскую пе́сню.
Они́ бу́дут петь _____.   Они́_____.
По́йте_____.   _____.

  пла́кать   **за**пла́кать

Учени́к гро́мко пла́кал.   Учени́к гро́мко **за**пла́кал.
За́втра он бу́дет пла́кать в
 кла́ссе.   За́втра он _____.

U N I T 24

МОЙ ЗАНЯ́ТИЯ И МОЙ УЧИТЕЛЯ́

Обыкнове́нно я встаю́ в во́семь часо́в утра́, но сего́дня у меня́ экза́мен по ру́сской исто́рии и я встал в шесть. За́втра я опя́ть вста́ну о́чень ра́но, потому́ что у меня́ экза́мен по матема́тике.

Наш учи́тель, Фёдор Па́влович, говори́т, что матема́тика о́чень лёгкий предме́т, но я ду́маю, что а́лгебра, геоме́трия и да́же арифме́тика о́чень тру́дные предме́ты. Фёдор Па́влович большо́й специали́ст по матема́тике. Когда́ он объясня́ет уро́к в кла́ссе, я всё понима́ю, но че́рез пятна́дцать и́ли два́дцать мину́т я забыва́ю почти́ всё, что он объясни́л. К сча́стью, мы с Оле́гом ча́сто занима́емся вме́сте. Он прекра́сно зна́ет матема́тику и объясня́ет мне все тру́дные уро́ки, а я объясня́ю ему́ ру́сскую грамма́тику. О́чень прия́тно занима́ться с таки́м хоро́шим ученико́м.

Я беру́ уро́ки му́зыки у одно́й ста́рой да́мы. Вчера́, когда́ я шёл на уро́к к мое́й учи́тельнице, я уви́дел Фёдора Па́вловича, кото́рый шёл домо́й. Как то́лько он меня́ уви́дел, он закрича́л: "За́втра бу́дет о́чень тру́дный экза́мен. По́мни э́то, Ми́ша!" Я зна́ю, что он сказа́л пра́вду. Он всегда́ говори́т пра́вду и, к сожале́нию, всегда́ даёт о́чень тру́дные зкза́мены.

Слова́рь (Vocabulary)

Verbs are given first. When both aspects are presented, the *imperfective* comes first, then the *perfective* with associated forms.

вставать (I); *pf.* встать (I); *fut.* вста́ну, вста́нешь, -нут; *imper.* встань, вста́ньте to get up, to rise

объясня́ть (I); объясня́ю, -ешь, -ют; *pf.* объясни́ть (II); *fut.* объясню́, объясни́шь, -я́т to explain (see ¶ 10-В)

забыва́ть (I); забыва́ю, -ешь, -ют; *pf.* забы́ть (I); *fut.* забу́ду, -ешь, -ут; *imper.* забу́дь, забу́дьте to forget

занима́ться (I) *intrans.*; **занима́юсь, -ешься, -ются** to study, to busy oneself (with)
ви́деть (II) to see; *pf.* **уви́деть** (II); *fut.* **уви́жу, уви́дишь, -ят**; (*no imper.*) to notice
говори́ть (II); to speak, to say, to talk; *pf.* **сказа́ть** (I); *fut.* **скажу́, ска́жешь, -ут**; *imper.* **скажи́, -и́те** to say, to tell (once)
заня́тия (*n. pl.*) studies
по (*with dat.*) on, in
исто́рия history
по ру́сской исто́рии in Russian history
матема́тика (*sing. in Russian*) mathematics
Фёдор (*dim.* **Фе́дя**) Theodore
Па́влович Pavlovich (*lit.* Paul's son)
лёгкий, -ая, -ое (*pr.* **лёхкий**) easy
предме́т subject
а́лгебра algebra
геоме́трия geometry
арифме́тика arithmetic
два́дцать twenty
сча́стье luck, happiness
к сча́стью fortunately
Оле́г Oleg
таки́м *instr. of* **тако́й**
да́ма lady
я беру́ уро́ки у одно́й да́мы I am taking lessons *from a* lady
как то́лько as soon as
Ми́ша (*m.*) Misha
сожале́ние regret
к сожале́нию unfortunately

Грамма́тика (Grammar)

24-1. Full Declension of Adjectives in the Singular

The following tables are largely a matter of review, except for the *dative* and the *instrumental*. (See ¶ **14-2** and **18-3**.)

a. Hard adjectives.

Group I (**-ый, -ая, -ое**)

	masculine	*feminine*	*neuter*
nom.	но́в**ый**	но́в**ая**	но́в**ое**
gen.	но́в**ого**	но́в**ой**	но́в**ого**
dat.	но́в**ому**	но́в**ой**	но́в**ому**
acc.	но́в**ый** *or* но́в**ого**	но́в**ую**	но́в**ое**
instr.	но́в**ым**	но́в**ой (ою)**	но́в**ым**
prep.	о но́в**ом**	о но́в**ой**	о но́в**ом**

Какой Какая Какое - what kind
ручка - pen

Group II (-ой, -áя, -óе)

	masculine	feminine	neuter
nom.	молодóй	молодáя	молодóе
gen.	молодóго	молодóй	молодóго
dat.	молодóму	молодóй	молодóму
acc.	молодóй	молодýю	молодóе
	or молодóго		
instr.	молоды́м	молодóй (óю)	молоды́м
prep.	о молодóм	о молодóй	о молодóм

b. Soft adjectives.

	masculine	feminine	neuter
nom.	послéдний	послéдняя	послéднее
gen.	послéднего	послéдней	послéднего
dat.	послéднему	послéдней	послéднему
acc.	послéдний or	послéднюю	послéднее
	послéднего		
instr.	послéдним	послéдней (ею)	послéдним
prep.	о послéднем	о послéдней	о послéднем

c. Mixed adjectives.

accent not on ending !

Group I (-г, -к, -х + -ий, -ая, -ое)

	masculine	feminine	neuter
nom.	рýсский	рýсская	рýсское
*gen.	рýсского	рýсской	рýсского
*dat.	рýсскому	рýсской	рýсскому
*acc.	рýсский	рýсскую	рýсское
	or рýсского		
instr.	рýсским	рýсской (ою)	рýсским
*prep.	о рýсском	о рýсской	о рýсском

Group II (-ж, -ч, -ш, -щ + -ий, -ая, -ее)

	masculine	feminine	neuter
nom.	хорóший	хорóшая	хорóшее
gen.	хорóшего	хорóшей	хорóшего
dat.	хорóшему	хорóшей	хорóшему
acc.	хорóший	хорóшую	хорóшее
	or хорóшего		
instr.	хорóшим	хорóшей (ею)	хорóшим
prep.	о хорóшем	о хорóшей	о хорóшем

unstressed о becomes е

* Note that these cases follow the pattern of Group I of hard adjectives.

→ 272

Group III (-г, -к, -х, -ж, -ч, ш, -щ + -ой, -ая, -ое) *accent on ending!*

	masculine	feminine	neuter
nom.	дорогой	дорогая	дорогое
*gen.	дорогого	дорогой	дорогого
*dat.	дорогому	дорогой	дорогому
*acc.	дорогой *or* дорогого	дорогую	дорогое
instr.	дорогим	дорогой (ою)	дорогим
*prep.	о дорогом	о дорогой	о дорогом

24-2. Declension of the Demonstrative Pronoun этот in the Singular †

	masculine	feminine	neuter
nom.	этот	эта	это
gen.	этого	этой	этого
dat.	этому	этой	этому
acc.	этот *or* этого	эту	это
instr.	этим	этой	этим
prep.	об этом	об этой	об этом

24-3. Declension of Possessive Adjective-Pronouns in the Singular

a. The possessives мой, моя, моё and твой, твоя, твоё are both adjectives and pronouns. When used as adjectives, they precede the noun they modify, and mean *my* and *your*; when used as pronouns, they follow the noun and mean *mine* and *yours*. For example:

Это мой дом.	This is *my* house.
Этот дом мой.	This house is *mine*.
Это твоя комната.	This is *your* room.
Эта комната твоя.	This room is *yours*.
Это моё кресло.	This is *my* armchair.
Это кресло моё.	This armchair is *mine*.

* Note that these cases follow the pattern of Group II of hard adjectives.
† See ¶ 14-1.

	masculine	feminine	neuter
nom.	мой	моя́	моё
gen.	моего́	мое́й	моего́
dat.	моему́	мое́й	моему́
acc.	мой	мою́	моё
	or моего́		
instr.	мои́м	мое́й (е́ю)	мои́м
prep.	о моём	о мое́й	о моём

Note: Except for stress and the accusative endings, both are declined like **после́дний**.

b. The possessives **наш, на́ша, на́ше** and **ваш, ва́ша, ва́ше** are also adjectives or pronouns, depending on whether they precede or follow the noun. When used as adjectives, they mean *our* and *your*; when used as pronouns, they mean *ours* and *yours*. For example:

Э́то **наш** дом.   This is *our* house.
Э́тот дом **наш.**   This house is *ours*.

	masculine	feminine	neuter
nom.	наш	на́ша	на́ше
gen.	на́шего	на́шей	на́шего
dat.	на́шему	на́шей	на́шему
acc.	наш	на́шу	на́ше
	or на́шего		
instr.	на́шим	на́шей (е́ю)	на́шим
prep.	о на́шем	о на́шей	о на́шем

Note: Except for the nominative and accusative endings, **наш, на́ша, на́ше** and **ваш, ва́ша, ва́ше** are declined like **хоро́ший**.

Упражне́ния (Exercises)

A. Decline the following in the singular.

1. э́тот ма́льчик. 2. э́та де́вочка. 3. э́то упражне́ние. 4. ми́лый учи́тель. 5. тру́дная рабо́та. 6. коро́ткое письмо́. 7. пуста́я дере́вня. 8. большо́е кре́сло. 9. после́дний обе́д. 10. си́няя дверь. 11. хоро́ший слова́рь. 12. дорого́й оте́ц.

13. хоро́шее сочине́ние.   14. твой портре́т.   15. твоя́ коро́ва.
16. твоё сча́стье.   17. ваш трамва́й.   18. на́ша семья́.   19. ва́ша
ча́шка.   20. на́ше окно́.

B. In place of the blanks, supply the appropriate case endings.

1. Мы сего́дня идём к наш_____ хоро́ш_____, това́рищу.
2. В наш_____ больш_____ ко́мнате стои́т си́нее кре́сло.   3. Ты
лю́бишь гуля́ть в наш_____ краси́в_____ саду́.   4. Она́ не
объясни́ла после́дн_____ уро́ка по исто́р_____.   5. Он до́лго
разгова́ривал с э́т___м_ молод___ым_ челове́ком.   6. Учи́тельница
всегда́ пи́шет э́т_____ си́н_____ карандашо́м.   7. Она́ ча́сто хо́дит
к тво_____ сестре́ и к тво_____ бра́ту.   8. Мы говори́ли о ваш_____
хоро́ш_____ шко́ле и о ваш_____ прекра́сн_____ учи́теле.   9. Она́
лю́бит е́здить верхо́м на э́т_____ бе́л_____ ло́шади.   10. Я вам
дал после́д___ей_ кни́гу из мо___ей_ библиоте́ки.
          что

C. In the following sentences, supply the appropriate verb forms
in place of the English words and translate at sight.

1. Мы всегда́ встаём в семь часо́в утра́, но сего́дня мы *got up*
в шесть.   2. За́втра мы опя́ть *shall get up* ра́но.   3. Наш оте́ц
всегда́ *used to get up* ра́но.   4. Учи́тель всегда́ прекра́сно
explained матема́тику.   5. Сего́дня учи́тельница хорошо́ *explained* уро́к.   6. Мы с Ива́ном занима́емся вме́сте и он *will
explain* мне но́вый уро́к.   7. Что *will say* мой учи́тель, е́сли он
меня́ *will see* (*notice*) в па́рке?   8. Она́ до́лго говори́ла, но я не
по́мню, что она́ *said*.   9. Почему́ ты всегда́ так мно́го занима́лся,
а тепе́рь совсе́м не *study*?   10. Я тебе́ ничего́ не скажу́, потому́
что ты сейча́с же всё *will forget* (*once*).   11. Пожа́луйста, *tell*;
я ничего́ не *will forget* (*once*).   12. К сожале́нию, она́ *forgot* всё,
что я ей *explained*.

Перево́д (Translation)

A. Omit the words in parentheses and include the words in
brackets.   Translate all possessives.

1. I conversed with my hostess (for) a long time.   2. He explained the lesson (to) my brother.   3. Unfortunately, he forgot
the last Russian word.   4. He had a chat with your younger brother.
5. He is going (walking) to our young teacher (*m.*).   6. We told
our hostess that you (*fam.*) have to study today.   7. I shall have a
chat with your good friend [дру́гом].   8. You forgot this old lady.
9. Fortunately, I noticed him in the theater, and told him that you

were [are] waiting for him.   10. We were talking about our last examination.   11. Did you see our summer house?   12. Do not forget that tomorrow we shall get up early.   13. We prefer to live in your (*fam.*) big house.   14. You did not write your exercise.   15. Arithmetic, algebra, and geometry are easy subjects.

B. Omit the words in parentheses and include the words in brackets.

1. I do not like to get up early, but today I got up at six.   2. I have an examination in geometry tomorrow morning, and shall be studying all day.   3. Our mathematics teacher [**профе́ссор матема́тики**] told me that the examination will be (a) very difficult (one).   4. Unfortunately, he always tells the truth.   5. Our teacher explains the lessons very well.   6. A week ago he explained a difficult lesson and I understood [**по́нял**] everything.   7. But in [**че́рез**] two days I forgot everything.   8. He is the smartest pupil in our class.   9. It is very pleasant to study with such a good pupil.

Вопро́сы (Questions)

1. Когда́ вы обыкнове́нно встаёте?   2. Почему́ вы сего́дня вста́ли в шесть?   3. Когда́ вы вста́нете за́втра?   4. По како́му предме́ту у вас за́втра экза́мен?   5. Матема́тика лёгкий и́ли тру́дный предме́т?   6. Каки́е предме́ты лёгкие?   7. А каки́е са́мые тру́дные?   8. Как ваш учи́тель матема́тики объясня́ет уро́ки?   9. С кем вы занима́етесь?   10. Вам прия́тно с ним (с ней) занима́ться?   Почему́?   11. Вы лю́бите му́зыку?   12. У кого́ вы берёте уро́ки му́зыки?   13. Когда́ вы хо́дите на уро́к к ва́шему учи́телю (к ва́шей учи́тельнице)?   14. Что Фёдор Па́влович сказа́л Ми́ше, как то́лько он его́ уви́дел?   15. Фёдор Па́влович всегда́ говори́т пра́вду?

Pattern Drills

A. 1. Study the Vocabulary in this unit.   Listen to the teacher (or the tape) and repeat the following sentences.   Then supply the *perfective* form in the same person and tense according to the model sentences in the "Student" column.

| *Teacher* | *Student* |
| вставать | встать |

Я всегда вставал очень рано.	Вчера я встал очень рано.
Я буду вставать очень рано.	Завтра я встану очень рано.
Всегда вставай рано.	Завтра встань рано.

| объяснять | объяснить |

Учитель объяснял уроки.	Вчера он объяснил урок.
Учитель будет объяснять уроки.	Завтра он _____ урок.
Объясняйте уроки.	_____ урок.

| забывать | забыть |

| Ты забывал новые слова. | Ты забыл новое слово. |
| Ты будешь забывать _____. | Ты _____ новое слово. |

| видеть | увидеть |

Мы видели озеро.	Мы _____ озеро.
Мы будем видеть _____.	Мы _____.
(no *imper.*)	(no *imper.*)

| говорить | сказать |

Учительница говорила о Маше.	Учительница сказала, что Маша прилежная ученица.
Учительница будет говорить о Маше.	Учительница _____, что Маша прилежная ученица.
Говорите о Маше.	_____, что Маша прилежная ученица.

2. Turn to page 201. Read aloud (or tape-record) exercise C.

B. 1. Turn to ¶24-1. Listen to the teacher (or the tape) and repeat the declensions of (a) hard, (b) soft, and (c) mixed adjectives.

2. Drill similarly on ¶ **24-2** and **24-3.**

3. Turn to page 200 . Read aloud (or tape-record) the declensions of adjectives and nouns in exercise A.

4. Turn to page 201 . Read aloud (or tape-record) exercise B.

UNIT 25

МОЙ ЗАНЯТИЯ И МОЙ УЧИТЕЛЯ (Continued)

Мы с Олéгом тáкже изучáем тепéрь рýсский язы́к, рýсскую литератýру и рýсскую истóрию. Для меня́ эти предмéты сáмые лёгкие и сáмые интерéсные, но для Олéга они́ сáмые трýдные. Поэтому они́ емý не óчень нрáвятся, но он óчень лю́бит Николáя Ивáновича Орлóва, котóрый преподаёт все эти предмéты в нáшей шкóле.

Николáй Ивáнович Орлóв прекрáсный преподавáтель и óчень ми́лый и культýрный человéк. Егó роди́тели бы́ли óчень богáтые лю́ди. У них был большóй дом в Москвé, завóд в Тýле и дáча в Крымý, на берегý Чёрного мóря. Когдá Николáй Ивáнович был мáленьким мáльчиком, у негó былá гувернáнтка, котóрая говори́ла с ним тóлько по-францýзски и́ли по-англи́йски. Поэтому он хорошó знáет англи́йский язы́к.

Господи́н Орлóв учи́лся в Москвé и стал инженéром. Потóм он рабóтал на фáбрике в Крымý. Из Кры́ма он поéхал на Кавкáз и там рабóтал на фéрме. С Кавкáза он поéхал на Украи́ну и там сначáла рабóтал на пóчте, а потóм на вокзáле. Потóм он дóлго жил в Áнглии и во Фрáнции и наконéц уéхал в США.

Словáрь (Vocabulary)

литератýра literature
для (*with gen.*) for
эти (*pl. of* этот) these
поэтому therefore
Орлóв Orlov
преподавáть (**I**); преподаю́, -даёшь, -даю́т; *imper.* преподавáй, - йте
    to teach

преподава́тель (*m.*) teacher
культу́рный, -ая, -ое cultured
бога́тый, -ая, -ое rich
лю́ди (*nom. pl. of* **челове́к**) people, men and women
заво́д plant (industrial)
Ту́ла Tula (an industrial town)
Крым (*prep.* with **в=Крыму́**) Crimea
Чёрное мо́ре Black Sea
гуверна́нтка governess
англи́йский, -ая, -ое English
учи́ться (**II**) *intrans*; **учу́сь, у́чишься, -атся** to study, to attend school
стать (**I**) (*pf. of* **станови́ться**); **ста́ну, ста́нешь, -ут**; *past* **стал, -ла, -ло, -ли**; *imper.* **стань, ста́ньте** to become
инжене́р engineer
фа́брика factory
пое́хать (**I**) (*pf. of* **е́хать**) to go, to set out (by conveyance)
на to, at, in (see **¶25-1**)
с from (see **¶25-1**)
Кавка́з Caucasus
Украи́на Ukraine
по́чта post office
вокза́л railway station
А́нглия England
во in, to, into (see **¶25-1d**)
Фра́нция France
уе́хать (**I**) (*pf. of* **е́хать**) + **в** to leave for, depart for
США (*pr.* **Сэ Ша А**) (**Соединённые Шта́ты Аме́рики**) U.S.A.

Грамма́тика (Grammar)

25-1. Prepositions в — из, на — с, к — от with Verbs of Motion

This paragraph is largely a review of **¶3-3, 11-1,** and **15-5.**

a. **в — из.**

1. We have seen that the preposition **в** + *accusative* indicates motion to the interior of an object having enclosed space (see **¶11-1**), whereas **в** + *prepositional* indicates location within such a space (see **¶3-3**). For example:

Ма́льчик идёт **в** шко́лу.   The boy is going to school (*is going inside*).
        (Answers the question: **Куда́** ма́льчик идёт?)
Ма́льчик **в** шко́ле.   The boy is in school (*inside*).
        (Answers the question: **Где** ма́льчик?)
Ма́льчик рабо́тает **в** па́рке.   The boy is working *in* the park.
        (Answers the question: **Где** ма́льчик рабо́тает?)

Ма́льчик гуля́ет **в** па́рк**е**.   The boy is taking a walk *in* the park.

(Answers the question: **Где** ма́льчик гуля́ет?)

Note: In the second example, **в** + *prepositional* situates an *object* within an enclosed space, while in the third and fourth examples an *action* is situated within such space.

2. **из** + *genitive* indicates motion *from within* an object having enclosed space.   For example:

Ма́льчик идёт **из** шко́л**ы**.   The boy is coming from (*out of the*) school.

Ма́льчик е́дет **из** го́род**а**.   The boy is coming (*by vehicle*) from town.

ШКО́ЛА

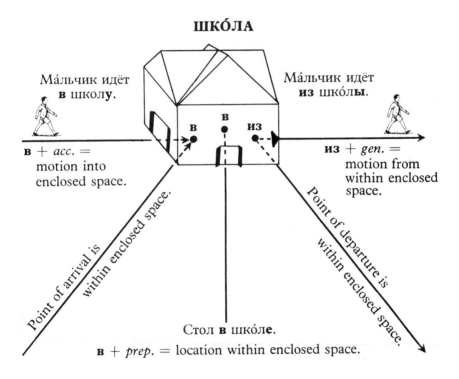

Ма́льчик идёт **в шко́лу.**

в + *acc.* = motion into enclosed space.

Point of arrival is within enclosed space.

Ма́льчик идёт **из шко́лы.**

из + *gen.* = motion from within enclosed space.

Point of departure is within enclosed space.

Стол **в** шко́ле.

в + *prep.* = location within enclosed space.

b. **на — с.**

The preposition **на**, governing the *accusative* or the *prepositional,* and its corresponding preposition **с**, governing the *genitive,* are often used instead of **в** and **из** as follows:

1. With nouns designating *occasions* or *events* (see ¶ **11-1**). For example:

Ма́льчик идёт **на** уро́к, **на** концéрт.	The boy is going *to* the lesson, *to* the concert.
Ма́льчик идёт **с** уро́ка, **с** концéрта.	The boy is coming *from* the lesson, *from* the concert.

Note: With such nouns that designate no specific physical space, the use of **в** and **из** is inconceivable.

2. With nouns designating some specific surface area. Motion then is *to within* or *from within* the area.

Я иду́ **на** пло́щадь, **на** у́лицу. I am going *to* the (interior of the) square, *into* the street.

Я иду́ **с** пло́щади, **с** у́лицы. I am coming *from* (within) the square, *from* the street.

Солда́т éдет **на** фронт, **на** аэродро́м, **на** юг. The soldier is going *to* the front, *to* the airport, south.

Солда́т éдет **с** фро́нта, **с** аэродро́ма, **с** ю́га. The soldier is coming *from* the front, *from* the airport, *from* the south.

ПЛО́ЩАДЬ

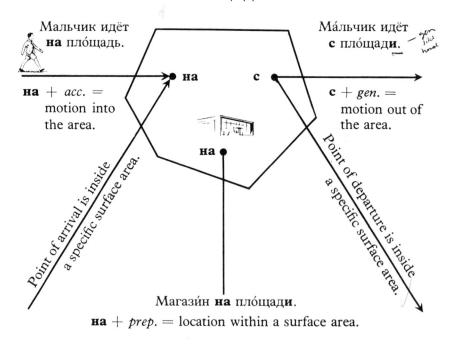

на + *prep.* = location within a surface area.

3. With special nouns, e.g., **Кавка́з, Украи́на, фа́брика, заво́д, по́чта, вокза́л.**

Солда́т е́дет **на** Кавка́з, **на** Украи́ну.	The soldier is going *to* the Caucasus, *to* the Ukraine.
Солда́т живёт **на** Кавка́зе, **на** Украи́не.	The soldier lives *in* the Caucasus, *in* the Ukraine.
Солда́т е́дет **с** Кавка́за, **с** Украи́ны.	The soldier is coming *from* the Caucasus, *from* the Ukraine.
Челове́к идёт **на** фа́брику, **на** заво́д, **на** по́чту, **на** вокза́л.	The man is going *to* the factory, *to* the plant, *to* the post office, *to* the railway station.
Челове́к рабо́тает **на** фа́брике, **на** заво́де, **на** по́чте, **на** вокза́ле.	The man is working *at* the factory, *at* the plant, *at* the post office, *at* the railway station.
Челове́к идёт **с** фа́брики, **с** заво́да, **с** по́чты, **с** вокза́ла.	The man is coming *from* the factory, *from* the plant, *from* the post office, *from* the railway station.

c. **к — от.**

1. We have seen that **к** + *dative* indicates motion toward or up to, but *not inside* an object (see ¶ 15-5). For example:

Я иду́ **к** о́зеру.	I am going to the lake (*not into it*).
Я иду́ **к** бра́ту.	I am going to brother's.

2. **от** + *genitive* indicates motion away from an object. The point of departure is *outside* the object itself. For example:

Я иду́ **от** о́зера.	I am coming from the lake (*was not in it*).
Я иду́ **от** бра́та.	I am coming from brother's

Note: With **к** and **от** the points of arrival and departure are *outside* the object.

ÓЗЕРО

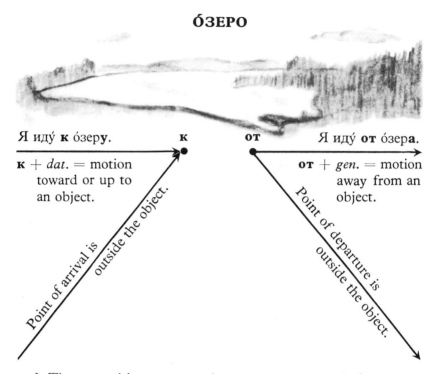

Я иду́ **к** о́зеру.   **к**   **от**   Я иду́ **от** о́зера.

к + *dat.* = motion toward or up to an object.

от + *gen.* = motion away from an object.

Point of arrival is outside the object.

Point of departure is outside the object.

d. The prepositions **в**, **к**, **с** change to **во**, **ко**, **со** before words beginning with certain groups of consonants. For example:

во Фра́нции	in France
во вто́рник	on Tuesday
ко мне	to me
со мно́й	with me

25-2. Predicative Instrumental

a. The instrumental instead of the nominative is usually used in the predicate with forms of **быть** (*infinitive*, *past*, *future*, and *imperative*) to indicate a temporary state or change. For example:

Сестра́ хо́чет **быть** учи́тельни**цей**.	Sister wants *to be* a teacher.
Господи́н Орло́в **был** инжене́р**ом**, пото́м учи́тел**ем**.	Mr. Orlov *was* an engineer, then a teacher.
Э́тот студе́нт **бу́дет** профе́ссо**ром**.	This student *will be* a professor (now he is not).
Будь хоро́ш**им** това́рищ**ем**.	*Be* a good friend!

b. When no change or temporary state is implied, the nominative is used. For example:

Его родители были богатые люди.	His parents *were* rich people (*and remained so*).

c. Certain verbs require the instrumental with all forms (especially verbs of *becoming* and *seeming*).

Он делается большим мальчиком	He *is becoming* a big boy.
Он стал доктором.	He *became* a doctor.
Он кажется старым.	He *seems* old.

25-3. Instrumental Singular of Nouns with Stems in a Sibilant

If the stem of a noun ends in **ж, ч, ш, щ,** or **ц,** it is important to note the stress.

a. When the stress is on the case endings, the instrumental takes the regular endings: **-ой** for the feminine and **-ом** for the masculine and neuter. For example:

Feminine		Masculine		Neuter	
nom.	*instr.*	*nom.*	*instr.*	*nom.*	*instr.*
госпожá	госпожóй	карандáш	карандашóм	плечó (shoulder)	плечóм
овцá (sheep)	овцóй	отéц	отцóм	лицó	лицóм

b. When the stress is on the stem, the letter **о** in the instrumental endings changes to **е,** i.e., **-ой** becomes **-ей** and **-ом** becomes **-ем.** For example:

Feminine		Masculine		Neuter	
nom.	*instr.*	*nom.*	*instr.*	*nom.*	*instr.*
дáча	дáчей	муж	мýжем	сóлнце (sun)	сóлнцем
Мáша	Мáшей	товáрищ	товáрищем	сéрдце (heart)	сéрдцем
птица	птицей	американец	американцем		

Упражнения (Exercises)

A. Give the instrumental of the following:

1. улица.   2. Миша.   3. красавица.   4. Маша.   5. дама.
6. алгебра.   7. девочка.   8. музыка.   9. юноша.   10. Волга.
11. озеро.   12. гараж.   13. борщ.   14. учитель.   15. американец.   16. товарищ.   17. Иванович.   18. инженер.

B. Supply Russian equivalents for the English words and translate.

1. Господин Орлов едет *to Tula*.   2. Госпожа Орлова недавно приехала *from Moscow*.   3. Сегодня вечером мы идём *to the theater*.   4. Они приехали *from New York* в девять часов вечера.   5. Мы долго жили *in France*.   6. *From France* мы поехали *to the U.S.A*.   7. Они два часа гуляли *in the garden*.   8. Она теперь должна идти *to the lesson*.   9. Наш преподаватель только что приехал *from the lesson*.   10. Они стоят *in the street* и ждут трамвая.   11. Он поехал *to the examination*.   12. Она идёт *from work*.   13. Мы с *husband* и его *friend* едем *to the Ukraine*.   14. Мы будем *in the Ukraine* две недели.   15. Наш преподаватель долго преподавал *in the Caucasus*.   16. Ваш инженер приехал *from the Caucasus* год тому назад.   17. Хотите поехать со мной (with me) *to the plant*?   18. *From the factory* мы идём *to town*.   19. Я был *at the post office* сегодня.   20. *From the post office* я поехал *to the railway station*.   21. Вы теперь идёте *to the doctor*?   22. Нет, я теперь иду *from the doctor*.   23. Твой отец уехал *for the U.S.A*.   24. Он часто ездит *to the lake*.   25. Они шли *from the lake*.

C. Supply the proper case endings for the words in parentheses, and translate the sentences into English.

1. Олег хочет стать (инженер).   2. Маша хотела быть (учительница).   3. Я думаю, что Иван будет (хороший доктор).   4. Иван станет (мой хороший товарищ).   5. Она не хочет быть (гувернантка).   6. Мой преподаватель был (культурный человек).   7. Николай Иванович будет (американец).   8. Он учился в Крыму и стал (учитель).   9. Наша белая лошадь стала очень (красивая).   10. Отец Акима был (умный человек).

Перевóд (Translation)

1. Anna Pavlovna Orlova is our Russian teacher. 2. She teaches Russian, Russian literature, and Russian history in our school. 3. She is a very cultured person, and it is always pleasant to converse with her.

4. She speaks French and German excellently, because she had [**у неё бы́ли**] two governesses when she was a little girl [**мáленькой дéвочкой**]. 5. Her father was a very rich man [person]. 6. He had a plant in the Ukraine, a factory in the Caucasus, and a summer house in the Crimea on the shore of the Black Sea.

7. Anna Pavlovna's husband is also a very cultured person. 8. He studied in the Ukraine and became an engineer. 9. From the Ukraine he went [**поéхал**] to the Caucasus, and there worked in a plant (for) two years. 10. From the Caucasus he went to France and studied in a French university. 11. He finally went to the U.S.A.

12. Anna Pavlovna Orlova and Nicholas Ivanovich Orlov are very happy people. 13. They have lovely children—one boy and two (little) girls. 14. In the summer the whole family lives in the country. 15. There they have a beautiful summer house on the sea shore. 16. Oleg and I like to go to their summer home [**к ним на дáчу**]. 17. My sister said yesterday that we like Anna Pavlovna because she prepares for us borshch, cutlets, and Russian dessert. 18. Fortunately, my sister does not always tell the truth.

Вопрóсы (Questions)

1. Какие предмéты Миша и Олéг тепéрь изучáют? 2. Для когó э́ти предмéты сáмые лёгкие? 3. Для когó они́ сáмые трýдные? 4. Почемý они́ не óчень нрáвятся Олéгу? 5. Какие предмéты он лю́бит? 6. Кто преподаёт все э́ти предмéты? 7. Николáй Ивáнович хорóший преподавáтель? 8. Где он жил, когдá он был мáленьким мáльчиком? 9. Где он учи́лся? 10. Кем он стал сначáла, инженéром и́ли преподавáтелем? 11. Где он рабóтал, когдá он был инженéром? 12. Кудá он поéхал из Кры́ма? 13. Где он рабóтал на Кавкáзе? 14. Кудá он поéхал с Кавкáза? 15. Как Николáй Ивáнович говори́т по-англи́йски? 16. Когдá и где он изучáл англи́йский язы́к? 17. А где он изучáл францýзский язы́к, дóма и́ли во Фрáнции?

Pattern Drills

A. Listen to the teacher (or the tape) and repeat the following sentences. Then read aloud each sentence in the "Student" column supplying the noun in the required case according to the model sentence.

1. Study ¶25-1*a*, then do the following drill.

Teacher	*Student*
Учи́тельница идёт **в** класс.	Учи́тель идёт **из** кла́сса.
Учени́цы иду́т **в** парк.	Ученики́ иду́т **из**_____.
Де́вочка идёт **в** библиоте́ку.	Ма́льчик идёт **из** _____.
Роди́тели е́дут **во** Фра́нцию.	Де́ти прие́хали **из** _____.
Спортсме́нки пое́хали **в** Áнглию.	Спортсме́ны прие́хали **из** _____.

2. Study ¶25-1*b*.1, then do the following drill.

Студе́нтки иду́т **на** уро́к.	Студе́нты иду́т **с** уро́ка.
Госпожа́ Орло́ва е́дет **на** рабо́ту.	Господи́н Орло́в е́дет **с** _____.
Де́вушки иду́т **на** экза́мен.	Ма́льчики иду́т **с** _____.
Ма́ша идёт **на** конце́рт.	Ми́ша идёт **с** _____.

3. Study ¶25-1*b*.2, then do the following drill.

На́дя е́дет **на** пло́щадь.	Фе́дя е́дет **с** пло́щади.
Ка́тя идёт **на** у́лицу.	Ва́ня идёт **с** _____.
Солда́ты е́дут **на** фронт.	Инжене́ры е́дут **с** _____.

4. Study ¶25-1*b*.3, then do the following drill.

Хозя́йка была́ **на** фа́брике.	Хозя́ин прие́хал **с** фа́брики.
Óльга рабо́тает **на** по́чте.	Оле́г идёт **с** _____.
Тётя пое́хала **на** вокза́л.	Дя́дя прие́хал **с** _____.
Преподава́тели пое́хали **на** Кавка́з.	Инжене́ры прие́хали **с** _____.
Ба́бушка жила́ **на** Украи́не.	Де́душка прие́хал **с** _____.

5. Study ¶25-1*c*, then do the following drill.

Де́вушка идёт **к** о́зеру.	Ю́ноша идёт **от** о́зера.
Гуверна́нтка идёт **к** бе́регу мо́ря.	Де́ти иду́т **от** _____ мо́ря.
Учи́тельница идёт **к** доске́.	Учени́к идёт **от** _____.
Я е́ду **к** до́ктору.	Ты е́дешь **от** _____.

B. Study ¶25-1. Then turn to page 212. and read aloud (or tape-record) exercise B.

C. Study ¶25-2. Then turn to page 212. and read aloud (or tape-record) exercise C supplying the words in parentheses in the required cases.

D. Study ¶25-3. Then read aloud (or tape-record) the following supplying the instrumental of each noun.

инжене́р	_____	ры́ба	_____
това́рищ	_____	де́вушка	_____
ю́ноша	_____	Ма́ша	_____
преподава́тель	_____	Ми́ша	_____
оте́ц	_____	пти́ца	_____
муж	_____	краса́вица	_____
вокза́л	_____	у́лица	_____
каранда́ш	_____	госпожа́	_____
гара́ж	_____	кре́сло	_____
са́ндвич	_____	письмо́	_____

U N I T 26

ЕВРОПÉЙСКИЕ ТУРÍСТЫ В США

Господи́н Смит встреча́ет парохо́д, на кото́ром прие́хали тури́сты из Евро́пы.

Смит: — Здра́вствуйте. Вы господи́н Никола́ев?

Никола́ев: — Да, я Никола́ев. А вы господи́н Смит, наш гид?

Смит: — Да, моя́ фами́лия Смит. О́чень прия́тно с ва́ми познако́миться.

Никола́ев: — Мне то́же о́чень прия́тно. Как э́то ми́ло, что вы нас встреча́ете!

Смит: — Ско́лько тури́стов в ва́шей гру́ппе?

Никола́ев: — Девятна́дцать челове́к — оди́ннадцать мужчи́н и во́семь же́нщин.

Смит: — Вы все ру́сские?

Никола́ев: — О нет! То́лько госпожа́ Бра́ун и я ру́сские. Мы преподаём ру́сский язы́к в Пари́же.

Смит: — А кто э́ти ю́ноши и де́вушки?

Никола́ев: — Э́то на́ши студе́нты и студе́нтки. Они́ говоря́т друг с дру́гом то́лько по-ру́сски. Им нельзя́ говори́ть ни по-францу́зски, ни по-англи́йски.

Смит: — А! тепе́рь я понима́ю, почему́ вам да́ли ги́да, кото́рый говори́т по-ру́сски. А вам мо́жно говори́ть по-англи́йски?

Никола́ев: — Мне и госпоже́ Бра́ун, коне́чно, мо́жно.

Словарь (Vocabulary)

европейский, -ая, -ое European
турист tourist
Смит Smith
встречать (I); встречаю, -ешь, -ют to meet
пароход steamer
Европа Europe
Николаев Nikolaev
гид guide
фамилия surname
знакомиться (II); знакомлюсь, знакомишься, -ятся; *pf.* **познако-**
  миться (II) to become acquainted
очень приятно с вами познакомиться very pleased to meet you
мило it is nice
сколько (*with gen. pl. of objects that can be counted*) how much, how many
сколько туристов? how many tourists? (**сколько молока?** how much
  milk?)
группа group
девятнадцать nineteen
мужчина (*m.*) man
женщина woman
Браун Brown
Париж Paris
наши (*pl. of* **наш**) our
друг с другом with each other
нельзя (it is) impossible, one may not (see ¶ 16-1)
ни . . . ни neither . . . nor
можно (it is) possible, one may (see ¶ 16-1)

II

ЕВРОПЕЙСКИЕ ТУРИСТЫ В США (Continued)

Смит: — Вы сказали, что госпожа Браун русская?

Николаев: — Да, она русская, но её муж англичанин, поэтому её фамилия Браун. Скажите, пожалуйста, сколько дней
мы будем в Нью-Йорке и сколько в Вашингтоне?

Смит: — Вы будете в Нью-Йорке три дня — в четверг, в
пятницу и в субботу. В воскресенье вы поедете в Вашингтон
и будете там в понедельник и во вторник. В среду вы едете
дальше.

Николаев: — Куда мы поедем из Вашингтона?

Смит: — Из Вашингтона вы поедете на юг, а затем в Кали-
форнию. Что вы хотите видеть в Нью-Йорке?

Никола́ев: — Всё! Никто́ из нас ещё не ви́дел Нью-Йо́рка; мы в США в пе́рвый раз. В журна́лах и газе́тах мы мно́го чита́ли о теа́трах, музе́ях, универма́гах, гости́ницах и рестора́нах Нью-Йо́рка. Наконе́ц, мы всё э́то уви́дим!

Смит: — Вы, коне́чно, не всё уви́дите. По́мните, что вы прие́хали в Нью-Йо́рк то́лько на три дня. Но я покажу́ вам гла́вные музе́и, библиоте́ки, университе́ты, Уо́лл-стрит, Центра́льный вокза́л, Рокфе́ллеровский центр, Эмпа́йр стейт би́лдинг и Ко́ни-А́йленд.

Никола́ев: — Когда́ на́ша пе́рвая экску́рсия?

Смит: — За́втра у́тром. Ита́к, до за́втра!

Никола́ев: — До за́втра, господи́н Смит!

Слова́рь (Vocabulary)

The days of the week are given first. Note that **в** + name of day in the accusative means *on*.

понеде́льник	**в** понеде́льник	*on* Monday
вто́рник	**во** вто́рник	*on* Tuesday
среда́	**в** сре́ду	*on* Wednesday
четве́рг	**в** четве́рг	*on* Thursday
пя́тница	**в** пя́тницу	*on* Friday
суббо́та	**в** суббо́ту	*on* Saturday
воскресе́нье	**в** воскресе́нье	*on* Sunday

англича́нин (*nom. pl.* **англича́не**, *gen. pl.* **англича́н**) Englishman
юг south
зате́м after that, then
Калифо́рния California
никто́ (*pron.*) nobody, no one
никто́ из нас none of us
музе́й (*m.*) museum
универма́г department store
гости́ница hotel
пока́зывать (**I**); **пока́зываю, -ешь, -ют**; *pf.* **показа́ть** (**I**); *fut.* **покажу́, пока́жешь, пока́жут**; *imper.* **покажи́, -и́те** to show
гла́вный, -ая, -ое main, chief
Уо́лл-стрит Wall Street
Центра́льный вокза́л Grand Central Station
Рокфе́ллеровский це́нтр Rockefeller Center
Эмпа́йр стейт би́лдинг Empire State Building
Ко́ни-А́йленд Coney Island
экску́рсия excursion, trip

Грамма́тика (Grammar)

Part I

26-1. Declension of Personal Pronouns in the Plural

For the *singular*, see ¶ 21-2.

Case	Plural: All Genders			
			Third person	
	First person	Second person		With governing prepositions
nom.	мы	вы	они́	
gen.	нас	вас	их	у них
dat.	нам	вам	им	к ним
acc.	нас	вас	их	на них
instr.	на́ми	ва́ми	и́ми	с ни́ми
prep.	о нас	о вас	о них	о них

26-2. Declension of the Demonstratives э́тот, э́та, and э́то in the Plural

For the *singular*, see ¶ 24-2.

PLURAL : ALL GENDERS

nom.	э́ти	*acc.*	э́ти *or* э́тих
gen.	э́тих	*instr.*	э́тими
dat.	э́тим	*prep.*	об э́тих

26-3. First Declension of Nouns in the Plural

For the *singular*, see ¶ 15-7c; for the formation of the *nominative plural*, see ¶ 20-2; for the *accusative plural* of inanimate nouns, see ¶ 20-3; and for plurals ending in -а́ or -я́, see ¶ 23-3.

Case	Hard	Soft		
	-а *(nom. sing.)*	-я *(nom. sing.)*		-ня *(nom. sing.)*
nom.	ка́рты	неде́ли	дя́ди	а́рмии
gen.	карт	неде́ль	дя́дей	а́рмий
dat.	ка́ртам	неде́лям	дя́дям	а́рмиям
acc.	ка́рты	неде́ли	дя́дей	а́рмии
instr.	ка́ртами	неде́лями	дя́дями	а́рмиями
prep.	о ка́ртах	о неде́лях	о дя́дях	об а́рмиях

a. The *accusative* of inanimate nouns is the same as the nominative; the accusative of animate nouns is the same as the genitive. For example:

$$nom.\ \&\ acc. \begin{cases} \text{ка́рты} \\ \text{а́рмии} \end{cases} \qquad gen.\ \&\ acc. \begin{cases} \text{дя́дей} \\ \text{коро́в} \end{cases}$$

b. The genitive.

1. The genitive of nouns in **-a** is their stem, i.e., they lose the ending of the nominative singular. For example: **ка́рта — карт**.

2. The genitive of nouns in **-я** is their stem, but **-ь** is added to retain the softness of the preceding consonant. For example: **неде́ля — неде́ль**.

3. Nouns in **-ия** take **-ий**. For example : **а́рмия — а́рмий**.

4. *Exceptions.* The following nouns thus far studied take **-ей**:

nom.	*gen.*
дя́д**я**	дя́д**ей**
тёт**я**	тёт**ей**
семь**я́**	сем**е́й**
ю́нош**а**	ю́нош**ей**

c. The genitive with fleeting **-o** or **-e**. A number of nouns with stems ending in two consonants insert the letter **o** or **e** before the last consonant to make pronunciation easier.

1. *Hard* nouns usually insert **o** :

nom.	*gen.*
студе́нтка	студе́нт**o**к
доска́	дос**о́**к

2. *Soft* nouns usually insert **e** :

nom.	*gen.*
пе́сня	пе́с**e**н
дере́вня	дере**е́**нь

3. The **e** is also inserted when the consonant next to the last in the stem ending is a sibilant:

nom.	*gen.*
ча́шка	ча́ш**e**к
де́вочка	де́воч**e**к

Part II

26-4. Second Declension of Masculine Nouns in the Plural

For the *singular*, see ¶ 18-4d; for the formation of the *nominative plural*, see ¶ 20-2.

Case	Hard	Soft		
	Consonant (*nom. sing.*)	-ь (*nom. sing.*)		-й (*nom. sing.*)
		Stress on stem	Stress on ending	
nom.	журна́лы	автомоби́ли	дожди́	трамва́и
gen.	журна́лов	автомоби́лей	дожде́й	трамва́ев
dat.	журна́лам	автомоби́лям	дождя́м	трамва́ям
acc.	журна́лы	автомоби́ли	дожди́	трамва́и
instr.	журна́лами	автомоби́лями	дождя́ми	трамва́ями
prep.	о журна́лах	об автомоби́лях	о дождя́х	о трамва́ях

a. The genitive.

1. Nouns in a consonant take **-ов**. For example: журна́л — журна́лов.

2. Nouns in **-ь** take **-ей**. For example: автомоби́ль — автомоби́лей.

3. Nouns in **-й** take **-ев**. For example: трамва́й — трамва́ев. When stressed on the ending, they take **-ёв**: чай — чаёв.

4. Nouns in **-ц** take **-ов** when ending is stressed: отéц — отцóв. When the stem is stressed, they take **-ев**: мéсяц (*month*) — мéсяцев.

5. *Exceptions.*

(a) Nouns in **ж, ч, ш,** or **щ** take **-ей** instead of **-ов**:

гара́ж	гаражéй
каранда́ш	карандашéй
това́рищ	това́рищей

(b) The following nouns are identical in the nominative singular and the genitive plural:

nom. sing.	*gen. pl.*	
глаз	глаз	eye
раз	раз	time (occasion)
солдáт	солдáт	soldier
человéк	человéк*	man, person

b. The *accusative* of inanimate nouns is the same as the nominative; the accusative of animate nouns is the same as the genitive. For example:

nom. & acc. { журнáл**ы**
{ автомобúл**и**

gen. & acc. { студéнт**ов**
{ учител**éй**

Упражнéния (Exercises)

A. Decline the following nouns in singular and plural.

1. пóчта.   2. фáбрика (see ¶ 20-2a).   3. дéдушка.   4. студéнтка.   5. чáшка.   6. гостúница (see ¶ 25-3b).   7. фамúлия.   8. тётя.   9. вокзáл.   10. конéц.   11. универмáг.   12. сáндвич.   13. американец.   14. преподавáтель.   15. музéй.

B. Supply equivalents for the English words and translate. (Memorize ¶ 26-1 and 26-2 before doing this exercise.)

1. Кто *these* турúсты?   2. Я хочý познакóмиться с *these* студéнтами.   3. Как дóлго вы разговáривали с *them*?   4. Мы вчерá говорúли о *them*, а не о *you* (*pl.*).   5. Мы показáли *them* парохóд.   6. Я вúдел *these* жéнщин, когдá мы бы́ли в музéе.   7. Мы *you* (*pl.*) óчень хорошó вúдим, но *them* мы совсéм не вúдим.   8. Нельзя́ разговáривать с *us*, когдá мы занимáемся.   9. Что вы читáли *about these* ю́ношах?   10. Не давáйте ничегó (*to*) *these* дéвочкам.   11. Вы (*to*) *us* дáли óчень интерéсную кнúгу.   12. (*To*) *you* мóжно говорúть по-англúйски на урóке францýзского языкá?

C. Replace all nouns in parentheses with plurals in the required cases.   (Master ¶ 26-3 and 26-4 before doing this exercise.)

1. (Кáрта) (ученúк) лежáт на (стол).   2. Мы девятнáдцать (день) рабóтали в (сад).   3. Господúн Смит дóлго говорúл об (универмáг), (гостúница) и (музéй) США.   4. В нáшем гóроде

---

* This form is used after definite and some indefinite numbers.

нет (трамва́й), но есть мно́го (автомоби́ль). 5. Вы ещё не по-
знако́мились с э́тими (студе́нт) и (студе́нтка). 6. В э́тих
(магази́н) нет ни (кни́га), ни (журна́л), ни (газе́та) и ни (каран-
да́ш). 7. В на́шей шко́ле пятна́дцать (учи́тель) и два́дцать
(учи́тельница). 8. Ско́лько (ю́ноша) и (де́вушка) в ва́шем
кла́ссе? 9. Я не зна́ю (фами́лия) э́тих (тури́ст). 10. Господи́н
Никола́ев лю́бит разгова́ривать с (америка́нец).

Перево́д (Translation)

A. Translate, including words in brackets.

1. Today is Wednesday. 2. On Wednesday I have a music
lesson at five o'clock. 3. Yesterday was Tuesday. 4. On
Tuesday morning I was at the railway station. 5. Tomorrow is
Thursday. 6. On Thursday I go to the post office. 7. On
Friday we dine in a restaurant. 8. On Saturday we shall be in
Washington. 9. On Sunday we usually rest. 10. On Monday
our class is going on [на] an excursion.

B. Omit the words in parentheses and include the words in
brackets.

1. The guide is meeting the tourists who arrived from France.
2. His surname is Smith.   3. He [ему́] is very pleased to become
acquainted with these tourists. 4. Mr. Nikolaev and Mrs. Brown
teach Russian in a French university. 5. Their students speak
only Russian. 6. They may not speak French or English. 7. The
teachers (*use dat.*), of course, may speak French or English. 8. The
French tourists have not yet seen the theaters, museums, libraries,
and hotels of New York. 9. They will be in New York on Sunday,
Monday, and Tuesday. 10. On Wednesday they will leave for
[пое́дут] California.

Вопро́сы (Questions)

1. Како́й сего́дня день, понеде́льник и́ли вто́рник? 2. Како́й
день был вчера́? 3. Како́й день бу́дет за́втра? 4. Что вы
де́лали во вто́рник? 5. Где вы бы́ли в сре́ду? 6. Куда́ вы
пое́дете в суббо́ту? 7. Что вы бу́дете де́лать в четве́рг?
8. Вы всегда́ отдыха́ете в воскресе́нье?

9. Кого́ встреча́ет господи́н Смит? 10. С кем он разгова́ривает? 11. Ско́лько мужчи́н и ско́лько же́нщин в гру́ппе тури́стов? 12. Что господи́н Никола́ев преподаёт в Пари́же? 13. Кому́ нельзя́ говори́ть по-англи́йски? 14. Кому́ мо́жно говори́ть и по-англи́йски и по-францу́зски? 15. Кто муж госпожи́ Бра́ун, ру́сский, англича́нин и́ли америка́нец? 16. Куда́ европе́йские тури́сты пое́дут из Вашингто́на? 17. О чём э́ти тури́сты так мно́го чита́ли в журна́лах и газе́тах? 18. Что господи́н Смит хо́чет показа́ть тури́стам?

Pattern Drills

A. 1. Study ¶26-1. Listen to the teacher (or the tape) and repeat the following questions. Then read each answer aloud supplying the required case of the second person plural of the personal pronoun according to the model sentence in the "Student" column.

Teacher	*Student*
Вы **нас** жда́ли в понеде́льник?	Да, мы **вас** жда́ли в понеде́льник.
Кто прие́хал к **нам** во вто́рник?	Това́рищи прие́хали к _____ во вто́рник.
Кто бу́дет петь с **на́ми** в сре́ду?	Де́ти бу́дут петь с _____ в сре́ду.
Кто о **нас** писа́л в дневнике́?	Ма́ша о _____ писа́ла в дневнике́.

2. Read the questions and answers above substituting the third person plural for the first and second persons; as in the following model sentences.

— Вы **их** жда́ли в понеде́льник? — Да, мы **их** жда́ли в понеде́льник.

B. Study ¶26-1 and 26-3. Listen to the teacher (or the tape) and repeat the following sentences. Then replace the nouns with plural personal pronouns in the required cases.

Teacher	*Student*
Мы е́дем к учи́тельницам.	Мы е́дем к **ним.**
Вот письмо́ от това́рищей.	Вот письмо́ от _____.
Вы говори́ли о де́вушках.	Вы говори́ли о _____.

Они́ ча́сто знако́мились
с ю́ношами.   Они́ ча́сто знако́мились с _____ .

Мы ви́дим студе́нток в
музе́е.   Мы _____ ви́дим в музе́е.

C. Study ¶26-2. Listen to the teacher (or the tape) and repeat the following sentences. Then form similar sentences repeating the same pronouns and supplying the corresponding feminine noun, as in the model sentence.

Teacher	*Student*
Кто э́ти студе́нты?	Кто э́ти студе́нтки?
Мы познако́мились с э́тими мужчи́нами.	Мы познако́мились с _____?
Что вы зна́ете об э́тих ю́ношах?	Что вы зна́ете об_____?
Не дава́йте ничего́ э́тим ма́льчи- кам!	Не дава́йте ничего́ _____!
Вы ви́дите э́тих ученико́в?	Вы ви́дите_____?

D. Study ¶26-1 and 26-2. Turn to page 222. Read aloud (or tape-record) exercise B.

E. Study ¶26-3 and 26-4. Read aloud (or tape-record) exercise C on page 222.

U N I T 27

ИНТЕРВЬЮ́ С ЕВРОПЕ́ЙСКИМИ ТУРИ́СТАМИ

Репортёры студе́нческой газе́ты "На́ше вре́мя" встреча́ют европе́йских тури́стов в гости́нице. Тури́сты всю ночь е́хали по́ездом из Чика́го в Нью-Йо́рк и о́чень уста́ли, но они́ всё-таки ра́ды познако́миться и поговори́ть с америка́нскими студе́нтами.

Молоды́е тури́сты уже́ бы́ли в Вашингто́не, в Но́вом Орлеа́-не, в Лос-А́нжелосе, в Сан-Франци́ско, в Чика́го и в други́х больши́х и интере́сных города́х Соединённых Шта́тов. Всю́ду они́ знако́мились и разгова́ривали с ученика́ми и учени́цами сре́дних школ и с их учителя́ми и учи́тельницами. Они́ та́кже ча́сто бесе́довали с мужчи́нами и же́нщинами, кото́рых встреча́ли в гости́ницах, универма́гах, теа́трах и́ли в поезда́х и трамва́ях. Они́ прекра́сно провели́ вре́мя и Соединённые Шта́ты им о́чень нра́вятся.

Молоды́е америка́нские репортёры никогда́ ещё не́ были в Евро́пе и им интере́сно поговори́ть о шко́лах, университе́тах, и о жи́зни ученико́в в ра́зных европе́йских стра́нах. Среди́ тури́стов есть францу́зы, англича́не, испа́нцы и не́мцы, а господи́н Никола́ев и госпожа́ Бра́ун, их учителя́, ру́сские.

Слова́рь (Vocabulary)

интервью́ (*n.*; *not decl.*; *pr.* **интэрвью́**) interview
репортёр reporter
студе́нческий, -ая, -ое student (*adj.*)
вре́мя (*n.*) (*gen.* **вре́мени**) time

ночь (*f.*) night
по́езд (*pl.* **поезда́**) train
е́хать по́ездом to go by train
уста́л, уста́ла, -ло, -ли tired
всё-таки all the same
ра́ды (*pl. of* **рад**) glad
Но́вый Орлеа́н New Orleans
Лос-А́нжелос Los Angeles
Сан-Франци́ско (*not decl.*) San Francisco
соединённый, -ая, -ое united
штат state
всю́ду (*adv.*) everywhere
сре́дний, -яя, -ее middle (*adj.*)
сре́дняя шко́ла high school
бесе́довать (I); **бесе́дую, бесе́дуешь, -ют** to chat, to talk; *pf.* **побесе́довать** (I) to have a talk
проводи́ть (II); **провожу́, прово́дишь, -ят**; *pf.* **провести́** (I); *fut.* **проведу́, -ёшь, -у́т**; *past* **провёл, провела́, -ло́, -ли́** to spend (time)
они́ прекра́сно провели́ вре́мя they had a wonderful time
о about, concerning
жизнь (*f.*) life
ра́зный, -ая, -ое various
страна́ (*pl.* **стра́ны**) country
среди́ (*with gen.*) among
францу́з Frenchman
испа́нец^{*fl*} (pl. **испа́нцы**) Spaniard
не́мец^{*fl*} (*pl.* **не́мцы**) German

II

ИНТЕРВЬЮ́ С ЕВРОПЕ́ЙСКИМИ ТУРИ́СТАМИ
(Continued)*

Пе́рвый репортёр: — Мы зна́ем, что вы час тому́ наза́д прие́хали из Чика́го и о́чень уста́ли.

Господи́н Го́фман: — Мы уста́ли, но нам всё-таки о́чень прия́тно с ва́ми побесе́довать.

Второ́й репортёр: — Нам то́же о́чень прия́тно. Скажи́те, пожа́луйста, как ва́ша фами́лия?

Г-н. Го́фман: — Я не́мец. Моя́ фами́лия Го́фман. А как ва́ша?

Вт. реп.: — Моя́ фами́лия Го́пкинс, а фами́лия моего́ това́рища — Уа́йт.

Пер. реп.: — Ско́лько студе́нтов в ва́шей гру́ппе?

Г-н. Шаро́н: — Нас бы́ло семна́дцать, но тепе́рь нас то́лько шестна́дцать, потому́ что одна́ из на́ших тури́сток уже́ уе́хала.

* This material may be used for dramatization in class.

Вт. реп.: — Вы о́чень хорошо́ говори́те по-англи́йски.

Г-н. Шаро́н: — О, нет! У меня́ плохо́е произноше́ние. Я изуча́л англи́йский язы́к без учи́теля. По-ру́сски я говорю́ лу́чше, чем по-англи́йски. Мы все лу́чше говори́м по-ру́сски.

Пер. реп.: — Как э́то мо́жет быть?

Госпожа́ Го́мес: — Мы мно́го занима́емся и всё вре́мя говори́м друг с дру́гом то́лько по-ру́сски. Ка́ждый день мы пи́шем ру́сские упражне́ния и́ли сочине́ния.

Г-жа. Фо́стер: — У меня́ уже́ есть восемна́дцать тетра́дей с ру́сскими упражне́ниями и сочине́ниями.

Г-жа. Бра́ун: — Мы ещё не рассказа́ли репортёрам о на́шей пое́здке по Соединённым Шта́там.

Вт. реп.: — Ва́ша пое́здка нас о́чень интересу́ет. Пожа́луйста, расскажи́те, где вы бы́ли, что вы де́лали, и как вам нра́вится на́ша страна́?

Г-н. Шаро́н: — Мне о́чень нра́вится Вашингто́н с его́ краси́выми у́лицами, прекра́сными зда́ниями и па́рками.

Г-жа. Го́мес: — А я люблю́ Нью-Йо́рк! Нигде́ я ещё не ви́дела таки́х больши́х магази́нов и замеча́тельных зда́ний и гости́ниц.

Г-жа. Фо́стер: — А мне бо́льше нра́вится Ло́ндон. Вы ещё не́ были в Ло́ндоне, госпожа́ Го́мес. Как жаль!

Г-н. Го́фман: — А я полюби́л Калифо́рнию. Каки́е краси́вые па́рки, у́лицы, дома́ и сады́ в Лос-А́нжелосе и в Сан-Франци́ско! И како́й там кли́мат! — всегда́ светло́ и тепло́, и не́бо всегда́ я́сное.

Пер. реп.: — Ну, в Сан-Франци́ско иногда́ о́чень хо́лодно, и ча́сто идёт дождь.

Вт. реп.: — Мы о́чень ра́ды, что вы так хорошо́ провели́ вре́мя в США, и что всё вам так нра́вится. Ита́к, до свида́ния, и большо́е спаси́бо за прия́тный и интере́сный разгово́р.

Слова́рь (Vocabulary)

Го́фман Hoffmann
второ́й, -а́я, -о́е second
как ва́ша фами́лия? what is your last name?
Го́пкинс Hopkins
Уа́йт White (*surname*)

семна́дцать seventeen
Шаро́н Charon
нас бы́ло семна́дцать there were seventeen of us
шестна́дцать sixteen
тури́стка (*gen. pl.* **тури́сток**) tourist (*f.*)
произноше́ние pronunciation
без (*with gen.*) without
чем (*conj.*) than
как э́то мо́жет быть? how is this possible?
Го́мес (*foreign names of women not decl.*) Gomez
Фо́стер (*foreign names of women not decl.*) Foster
восемна́дцать eighteen
рассказа́ть (**I**) (*pf. of* **расска́зывать**); *fut.* **расскажу́, расска́жешь, -ут**
    to relate, to tell
пое́здка (*gen. pl.* **пое́здок**) trip
зда́ние building
бо́льше (*adv.*) more
Ло́ндон London
полюби́ть (**II**) (*pf. of* **люби́ть**) to fall in love, to become fond of
кли́мат climate
отдохну́ть (**I**) (*pf. of* **отдыха́ть**); *fut.* **отдохну́, отдохнёшь, -у́т**; *imper.*
    отдохни́, -и́те to rest
разгово́р conversation

Грамма́тика (Grammar)

Part I

27-1. Second Declension of Neuter Nouns in the Plural

For the *singular*, see ¶18-4e; for the formation of the *nominative plural*, see ¶20-2; for the *accusative plural* of inanimate nouns, see ¶20-3.

| Case | Hard | Soft | |
	-о (*nom. sing.*)	**-е** (*nom. sing.*)	**-ие** (*nom. sing.*)
nom.	слова́	моря́	сочине́ния
gen.	слов	море́й	сочине́ний
dat.	слова́м	моря́м	сочине́ниям
acc.	слова́	моря́	сочине́ния
instr.	слова́ми	моря́ми	сочине́ниями
prep.	о слова́х	о моря́х	о сочине́ниях

a. The genitive (note resemblances to First Declension):

1. The genitive of nouns in -o is their stem; e.g., сло́во — слов.
2. Nouns in -e take -ей; e.g., мо́ре — море́й.
3. Nouns in -ие take -ий; e.g., сочине́ние — сочине́ний.

b. The genitive with fleeting -o and -e. A number of neuter nouns with stems ending in two consonants insert an **o** or **e** before the last consonant.

nom. sing.	*gen. pl.*
окно́	о́кон
кре́сло	кре́сел
письмо́	пи́сем (e replaces ь)

27-2. Third Declension in the Plural

For the *singular,* see ¶ 19-2; for the formation of the *nominative plural,* see ¶ 20-2.

Case	Stress on oblique case endings		Stress on stem
	-ь (*nom. sing.*)	Sibilant (ж, ч, ш, щ) + -ь (*nom. sing.*)	-ь (*nom. sing.*)
nom.	ло́шади	но́чи	тетра́ди
gen.	лошаде́й	ноче́й	тетра́дей
dat.	лошадя́м	ноча́м	тетра́дям
acc.	лошаде́й	но́чи	тетра́ди
instr.	лошадя́ми *or* лошадьми́	ноча́ми	тетра́дями
prep.	о лошадя́х	о ноча́х	о тетра́дях

a. The *accusative* of inanimate nouns is the same as the nominative; the accusative of animate nouns is the same as the genitive. For example: *gen.* and *acc.* **лошаде́й.**

b. Nouns with stems in **ж, ч, ш,** or **щ** have hard endings in the *dative, instrumental,* and *prepositional,* as in **ночь.**

Part II

27-3. Full Declension of Adjectives in the Plural

For the *singular,* see ¶ 24-1.

Note: The accusative of adjectives modifying inanimate nouns is

the same as the nominative; that of adjectives modifying animate
nouns is the same as the genitive.

ALL GENDERS

a. Hard:

	Group I (-ый, -ая, -ое)	*Group II* (-ой, -áя, -ое)
nom.	нóвые	молодьíе
gen.	нóвых	молодьíх
dat.	нóвым	молодьíм
acc.	нóвые *or* нóвых	молодьíе *or* молодьíх
instr.	нóвыми	молодьíми
prep.	о нóвых	о молодьíх

b. Soft (-н + ий, -н + яя, -н + ее):   *Compare with Pers.*
Pron. Pl. (¶26-1)

nom.	послéдние	онú
gen.	послéдних	их
dat.	послéдним	им
acc.	послéдние *or* послéдних	их
instr.	послéдними	úми
prep.	о послéдних	о них

c. Mixed:

	Group I (-г, -к, -х + -ий, -ая, -ое)	*Group II* (-ж, -ч, -ш, -щ + -ий, -ая, -ее)	*Group III* (-г, -к, -х, -ж, -ч, -ш, -щ + -ой, -áя, -ое)
nom.	рýсские	хорóшие	дорогúе
gen.	рýсских	хорóших	дорогúх
dat.	рýсским	хорóшим	дорогúм
acc.	рýсские *or* рýсских	хорóшие *or* хорóших	дорогúе *or* дорогúх
instr.	рýсскими	хорóшими	дорогúми
prep.	о рýсских	о хорóших	о дорогúх

27-4. Possessive Adjective-Pronouns in the Plural

For the *singular*, see ¶24-3.

мой, *m.*; моя́, *f.*;	наш, *m.*; на́ша, *f.*;
моё, *n.*	на́ше, *n.*

nom.	мой	на́ши
gen.	мои́х	на́ших
dat.	мои́м	на́шим
acc.	мой *or* мои́х	на́ши *or* на́ших
instr.	мои́ми	на́шими
prep.	о мои́х	о на́ших

Note: The possessives **твой, твоя́, твоё** and **ваш, ва́ша, ва́ше** are declined respectively like **мой, моя́, моё** and **наш, на́ша, на́ше**.

27-5. Cardinal Numerals 1 through 20

a. Formation of 11 to 20.

Note how these numerals are formed: **-на-** (meaning *plus*) and **дцать** (a contraction of **де́сять**) are added to the numerals **оди́н** through **де́вять**. Thus, **оди́ннадцать**, for example, is composed of **оди́н** + **-на-** + **дцать** (pr. **ццать**), and literally means *one above* (*plus*) *ten*. On the other hand, **два́дцать** is composed of **два** + **дцать**, and means *two tens*.

1. оди́н (*m.*)	+ на + дцать =	оди́ннадцать	= 11
2. две (*f.*)	+ на́ + дцать =	двена́дцать	= 12
3. три	+ на́ + дцать =	трина́дцать	= 13
4. четы́р(е)	+ на + дцать =	четы́рнадцать	= 14
5. пят(ь)	+ на́ + дцать =	пятна́дцать	= 15
6. шест(ь)	+ на́ + дцать =	шестна́дцать	= 16
7. сем(ь)	+ на́ + дцать =	семна́дцать	= 17
8. во́сем(ь)	+ на́ + дцать =	восемна́дцать	= 18
9. де́вят(ь)	+ на́ + дцать =	девятна́дцать	= 19
два	+ дцать =	два́дцать	= 20

b. Agreement with adjectives and nouns.

Два, три, and **четы́ре** require the adjective in the *genitive plural* and the noun in the *genitive singular*. The numbers **пять** through **два́дцать** require both the adjective and the noun in the *genitive plural*. (See ¶9-3 and 20-8.)

For example:

два ру́сских журна́ла; две ру́сских ка́рты; два но́вых слова́; пять ру́сских журна́лов; двена́дцать ру́сских карт; два́дцать но́вых слов.

Упражне́ния (Exercises)

A. Decline the following nouns in the plural. (Master ¶27-1 first.)

1. лицо́. 2. окно́. 3. кре́сло. 4. письмо́. 5. зда́ние.
6. произноше́ние. 7. о́зеро (*nom. pl.* озёра).

B. Decline the following adjectives in all genders, singular and plural. (Master ¶27-3 first.)

1. ра́зный. 2. сре́дний. 3. пусто́й. 4. плохо́й. 5. америка́нский.

C. Decline the following adjectives and nouns in the singular and plural. (Master ¶27-2 and 27-4 first.)

1. хоро́ший това́рищ. 2. большо́е зда́ние. 3. твоя́ ло́шадь.
4. ва́ша тетра́дь. 5. сре́дняя шко́ла.

D. Count from 1 through 20 with each of the following adjectives and nouns. (Master ¶27-5 first.) For example:
одна́ молода́я тури́стка, две молоды́х тури́стки . . . пять молоды́х тури́сток, etc.

1. хоро́ший това́рищ. 2. лёгкое сло́во. 3. пусто́е зда́ние.
4. прекра́сный день. 5. бе́лая ло́шадь. 6. дли́нная ночь.
7. сре́дняя шко́ла. 8. коро́ткое письмо́. 9. гла́вный музе́й.
10. интере́сная экску́рсия.

E. In place of the blanks supply the appropriate case endings in the plural, and translate.

1. В гости́ниц_____ Нью-Йо́рка мно́го тури́ст_____ и тури́ст_____ (*f.*). 2. Европе́йск_____ студе́нт_____ хоте́ли побесе́довать с америка́нск_____ репортёр_____. 3. Мы ещё никогда́ не ви́дели таки́х больш_____ и краси́в_____ зда́н_____. 4. Ва́ш_____ това́рищ_____ неда́вно познако́мились с учени́к_____ и учени́ц_____ сре́дн_____ школ. 5. Всю́ду мы встреча́ли счастли́в_____ и весёл_____ ма́льчик_____ и

де́воч_____. 6. Вы сказа́ли, что ваш_____ роди́тели изуча́ют иностра́нн_____ язык_____ без учител_____, без книг и без словар_____. Как э́то мо́жет быть? 7. В наш_____ теа́тр _____, музе́_____ и библиоте́к_____ нельзя́ кури́ть (smoke). 8. Мы ещё никогда́ не ви́дели таки́х больш_____ и хорош _____ трамва́_____. 9. Среди́ тури́ст_____ бы́ло мно́го доктор_____, профессор_____ и инжене́р_____. 10. В одну́ неде́лю мой приле́жн_____ учени́к_____ написа́ли двена́дцать упражне́н_____ и шесть сочине́н_____. 11. Репортёры разгова́ривали с европе́йск_____ ю́нош_____ об их заня́т_____, преподава́тел_____, и о ра́зн_____ предме́т _____, кото́р_____ они́ тепе́рь изуча́ют в сре́дн_____ шко́л _____. 12. Америка́нск_____ тури́стки полюби́ли Пари́ж с его́ краси́в_____ у́лиц_____, хоро́ш_____ теа́тр_____ и замеча́тельн_____ универма́г_____ и музе́_____.

Перево́д (Translation)

Include the words in brackets and omit the words in parentheses.

An Interview with American Tourists

1. The reporters of the French magazine *Our Life* are meeting American tourists who just arrived from England. 2. The Americans are very tired [**о́чень уста́ли**] but are glad to become acquainted and to have a talk with the French reporters. 3. The tourists had a wonderful time in England. 4. Everywhere they were making the acquaintance of [**знако́мились с**] pupils and teachers. 5. They also often chatted with men and women whom they met in theaters, restaurants, museums, libraries, and [at] railway stations. 6. They like Europe very much. 7. Mr. White has fallen in love with London, and Mr. Hopkins with Paris. 8. They all [**Все**] think that Paris is a remarkable city. 9. They have never seen such beautiful streets, buildings, and parks, and have never dined in such excellent restaurants. 10. They also like the climate of France. 11. It is always warm and bright, and the sky is clear. 12. They will be in Paris sixteen days. 13. The tourists prefer to speak French, but the reporters want to speak English. 14. Unfortunately, both the Americans and the Frenchmen have a very bad pronunciation. 15. Therefore, they often do not understand each other. 16. But all the same, the conversation is very pleasant and interesting.

Вопро́сы (Questions)

1. Кто встреча́ет европе́йских тури́стов? 2. Где репортёры их встреча́ют? 3. Как до́лго тури́сты е́хали по́ездом из Чика́го в Нью-Йо́рк? 4. Каки́е америка́нские города́ они́ уже́ ви́дели? 5. С кем они́ всю́ду знако́мились и разгова́ривали? 6. С кем они́ разгова́ривали в поезда́х и в трамва́ях? 7. Как они́ провели́ вре́мя в Соединённых Шта́тах? 8. Соединённые Шта́ты нра́вятся европе́йским тури́стам? 9. Репортёры студе́нческой газе́ты уже́ бы́ли в Евро́пе? 10. О чём им интере́сно поговори́ть с европе́йскими тури́стами? 11. Как фами́лия ру́сского учи́теля? 12. Почему́ фами́лия ру́сской учи́тельницы "Бра́ун"? 13. Как фами́лия не́мца? Францу́за? Пе́рвого репортёра? Второ́го репортёра? 14. Ско́лько челове́к в гру́ппе тури́стов? 15. Ско́лько студе́нтов в э́той гру́ппе? 16. Почему́ господи́н Шаро́н лу́чше говори́т по-ру́сски, чем по-англи́йски? 17. Почему́ господи́ну Шаро́ну так нра́вится Вашингто́н? 18. Почему́ госпожа́ Го́мес лю́бит Нью-Йо́рк? 19. Почему́ господи́н Го́фман полюби́л Калифо́рнию? 20. Пого́да всегда́ хоро́шая в Лос-А́нжелосе? 21. А в Сан-Франци́ско не́бо всегда́ я́сное?

Pattern Drills

A. 1. Study ¶27-1 and 27-2. Drill aloud on the declensions, then tape-record them without looking in the book. Check with the text for accuracy.

2. Study ¶27-3. Drill aloud on the full declension of adjectives in the plural, then tape-record it without looking in the book. Check with the text for accuracy.

B. Study ¶27-4. Listen to the teacher (or the tape) and repeat the declension of **твои́ пи́сьма**. Then decline **ва́ши кре́сла** aloud.

	Teacher	Student
nom.	твои́ пи́сьма	ва́ши кре́сла
gen.	твои́х пи́сем	ва́ших _____
dat.	твои́м пи́сьмам	_____
acc.	твои́ пи́сьма	_____
instr.	твои́ми пи́сьмами	_____
prep.	о твои́х пи́сьмах	_____

C. Study ¶**27-5a** and **27-5b**.   Listen to the teacher (or the tape) and repeat the following phrases with each numeral in the "Student" column.   Make the necessary changes in number and case, as in the model sentences.

Teacher	*Student*
Оди́н си́ний каранда́ш.	Два си́них карандаша́.
	Три_____.
	Пять си́них карандаше́й.
Два хоро́ших учи́теля.	3, 4, 5, 10, 12.
Три молоды́х де́вушки.	1, 2, 7, 8, 11.
Четы́ре но́вых сло́ва.	1, 2, 13, 17, 20.
Пять бе́лых лошаде́й.	2, 9, 14, 15, 18.
Шесть дли́нных ноче́й.	3, 4, 9, 16, 19.
Семь сре́дних школ.	1, 2, 4, 11, 20.
Во́семь интере́сных музе́ев.	2, 3, 12, 17, 18.
Де́вять больши́х зда́ний.	1, 2, 5, 6, 7.
Де́сять францу́зских тури́сток.	1, 4, 8, 9, 10.
Оди́ннадцатъ прекра́сныхъ экску́рсий.	1, 3, 6, 12, 17.
Двена́дцать пусты́х гараже́й.	1, 2, 5, 13, 18.
Четы́рнадцать ми́лых ю́ношей.	1, 2, 4, 19, 20.
Пятна́дцать плохи́х сочине́ний.	1, 3, 5, 13, 18.
Два́дцать дороги́х автомоби́лей.	1, 3, 4, 16, 17.

D. Turn to page 233 .   Read aloud (or tape-record) exercise E.

UNIT 28

REVIEW LESSON

Grammar Review

A. Conjugate the following verbs in full, in the *imperfective* (present, past, compound future, and imperative) and *perfective* (past, future, and imperative) aspects.

1. писа́ть — написа́ть. 2. объясня́ть — объясни́ть. 3. рисова́ть — нарисова́ть. 4. встава́ть — встать. 5. люби́ть — полюби́ть. 6. забыва́ть — забы́ть. 7. бесе́довать — побесе́довать. 8. проводи́ть — провести́. 9. говори́ть — сказа́ть. 10. пока́зывать — показа́ть.

B. Conjugate the following verbs in the present, past, and compound future.

1. смея́ться. 2. занима́ться. 3. знако́миться.

C. Decline the following adjectives and nouns in the plural.

1. лёгкий уро́к. 2. большо́й гара́ж. 3. хоро́ший инжене́р. 4. ти́хая у́лица. 5. бога́тая же́нщина. 6. си́нее кре́сло. 7. дли́нное упражне́ние. 8. прия́тная экску́рсия. 9. ста́рый трамва́й. 10. молодо́й не́мец.

D. Supply the nominative plural of the following.

1. пусто́й дом. 2. друго́й бе́рег. 3. культу́рный учи́тель. 4. прия́тный ве́чер. 5. большо́й лес. 6. си́ний глаз. 7. хоро́ший до́ктор. 8. стра́нный го́лос. 9. ру́сский го́род. 10. европе́йский профе́ссор.

E. Count from 1 through 20 with each of the following adjectives and nouns.

1. но́вая ка́рта.   2. си́ний дива́н.   3. ру́сское сло́во.   4. хоро́ший преподава́тель.   5. тру́дное сочине́ние.

Reading and Comprehension Drill

A. Read the following sentences aloud and translate them orally into idiomatic English.

1. Сего́дня моя́ сестра́ в пе́рвый раз написа́ла хоро́шее сочине́ние.   2. Мы сде́лали все уро́ки, пообе́дали и пото́м пое́хали к на́шим това́рищам.   3. Éсли хоти́те, мы снача́ла поу́жинаем, а пото́м поговори́м о на́шей экску́рсии.   4. Посиди́те немно́го в э́том кре́сле и отдохни́те, а пото́м пое́дем на рабо́ту.   5. Все вдруг заговори́ли об испа́нских тури́стках.   6. Когда́ на́ша учи́тельница объясня́ет геоме́трию в кла́ссе, я всё понима́ю.   К сожале́нию, че́рез де́сять мину́т я забыва́ю всё, что она́ объясни́ла.   7. К сча́стью, мы с Ири́ной занима́емся вме́сте, и она́ объясни́т мне уро́к по геоме́трии.   8. Я вам ничего́ не скажу́, потому́ что вы сейча́с же всё забу́дете.   9. За́втра у нас экза́мен по исто́рии Соединённых Шта́тов Аме́рики.   10. Вы всегда́ встаёте в де́вять часо́в утра́.   Почему́ вы сего́дня вста́ли в семь?

B. Supply the endings or Russian equivalents of English words; then read aloud and translate.

1. Америка́нские тури́ст_____ и европе́йск_____ репортёр_____ о́чень полюби́ли друг дру́г_____.   2. Мои́ роди́тели бы́ли о́чень бога́т_____ и культу́рн_____ (people).   3. Когда́ мы бы́ли ма́леньк_____ де́вочк_____, у нас бы́ли гуверна́нтк_____, кото́р_____ говори́ли (with us) то́лько по-францу́зски.   4. С Кавка́з_____ мы пое́хали на Украи́н_____ и там рабо́тали на фа́брик_____ не́сколько (weeks).   5. Мы с му́ж_____ ча́сто е́здим (by train) в Калифо́рн_____.   6. О́чень прия́тно с (you) познако́миться.   7. Как фами́лия ва́шего англи́йск_____ преподава́тел_____?   8. Мы говори́м друг с дру́г_____ то́лько (Spanish).   9. В журна́лах и кни́г _____ мы мно́го чита́ли о больши́х универма́г_____, библиоте́к_____ и музе́_____ Ло́ндона.   10. Среди́ тури́ст_____ есть мно́го францу́з_____, испа́нц_____, не́мц_____ и ру́сск_____.

Перево́д (Translation)

Include the words in brackets and omit the words in parentheses.

1. The American reporters arrived from California. 2. Our friends are going to the Ukraine. 3. Tomorrow my sister and I are going to the factory. 4. From the post office, the tourists (*f.*) went (by vehicle) to the railway station. 5. I am now coming from the doctor. 6. Our students will become good engineers. 7. Masha always wanted to be a teacher. 8. One may not converse with us when we are studying. 9. What did you read about these little girls? 10. Your pupils' books were lying on the floor. 11. The European tourists conversed for a long time with the Americans about the big buildings, the excellent hotels, and remarkable museums of Paris. 12. In this store there are neither books, newspapers, pencils, nor notebooks. 13. In our class there are seventeen girls and eighteen boys. 14. We do not know the surnames of these ladies. 15. On Monday, [on] Tuesday, and [on] Wednesday I work in Washington. 16. On Thursday, [on] Friday, and [on] Saturday I work in New York. On Sunday I rest. 17. The pupils of our high school wanted to have a chat with the European boys and girls. 18. The American tourists (*f.*) fell in love with London—with its beautiful streets, big department stores, and remarkable museums. 19. We are very glad that you had such a good time in the country. 20. You are very tired and have to have a rest.

Вопро́сы (Questions)

1. Как ва́ша фами́лия? 2. Где живёт ва́ша семья́? 3. А где вы живёте? 4. Где вы у́читесь? 5. Вы мно́го занима́етесь? 6. Ско́лько часо́в в день (a day) вы занима́етесь? 7. Вы хоро́ший учени́к? (Вы хоро́шая учени́ца?) 8. Когда́ вы вста́ли сего́дня у́тром? 9. Когда́ вы обыкнове́нно встаёте? 10. Вы уже́ поза́втракали? 11. Куда́ вы вчера́ пое́хали по́сле за́втрака? 12. Куда́ вы за́втра пое́дете по́сле у́жина? 13. Како́й сего́дня день, среда́ и́ли четве́рг? 14. Что вы обыкнове́нно де́лаете в сре́ду? 15. У кого́ вы берёте уро́ки му́зыки? 16. Каки́е предме́ты вы изуча́ете в шко́ле? 17. Каки́е предме́ты вас о́чень интересу́ют? 18. Каки́е иностра́нные языки́ вы уже́ зна́ете дово́льно хорошо́? 19. Как вы обыкнове́нно прово́дите вре́мя в суббо́ту ве́чером? 20. Вы

любите танцовать? 21. С кем вы предпочитаете танцовать? Почему? 22. Какие большие города Соединённых Штатов вы уже видели? 23. Вы уже были в Европе? 24. Какие европейские города нравятся американским туристам? 25. Как им нравится климат Англии?

APPENDIX

EVERYDAY EXPRESSIONS

The following expressions deal with everyday situations and provide material for oral drill and conversation.

A. In the Classroom

1. Откройте, пожалуйста, дверь.
2. Закройте, пожалуйста, окно.
3. Откройте, пожалуйста, книгу.
4. Читайте, пожалуйста.
5. Переведите с русского на английский.
6. Идите к доске.
7. Пишите перевод на доске.
8. Пишите упражнение в тетради.
9. Напишите короткое сочинение на завтра.
10. Приготовьте урок на завтра.
11. Отвечайте на все вопросы по-русски.
12. Пожалуйста, повторите ответ ещё раз.
13. Слушайте внимательно.
14. Читайте медленнее, пожалуйста.
15. Пишите быстрее.
16. Говорите громче.
17. Читайте тише.
18. Будем читать все вместе.
19. Это правильно.
20. Это неправильно. Вот ошибка.

1. Open the door, please.
2. Please close the window.
3. Please open the book.
4. Please read.
5. Translate from Russian into English.
6. Go to the blackboard.
7. Write the translation on the blackboard.
8. Write the exercise in the notebook.
9. Write a short composition for tomorrow.
10. Prepare the lesson for tomorrow.
11. Answer all the questions in Russian.
12. Please repeat the answer again.
13. Listen attentively.
14. Please read more slowly.
15. Write faster.
16. Speak louder.
17. Read more quietly.
18. Let us all read together.
19. This is correct.
20. This is incorrect. Here is a mistake.

B. Greetings and Good Wishes

1. Здра́вствуйте.	1. Hello. How do you do?
2. До́брое у́тро.	2. Good morning.
3. До́брый день.	3. Good day.
4. До́брый ве́чер.	4. Good evening.
5. О́чень рад вас ви́деть.	5. I am very glad to see you.
6. Как вы пожива́ете?	6. How are you?
7. Спаси́бо, о́чень хорошо́. А вы?	7. Very well, thank you. And you?
8. Та́к себе.	8. So so.
9. Сади́тесь, пожа́луйста.	9. Please have a seat.
10. Бу́дьте как до́ма.	10. Make yourself at home.
11. Что у вас но́вого?	11. What's new with you?
12. До свида́ния.	12. Goodbye.
13. Споко́йной но́чи.	13. Good night.
14. До за́втра.	14. See you tomorrow (*lit.* until tomorrow)
15. Всего́ хоро́шего.	15. Good luck (*lit.* the best of everything).
16. Счастли́вого пути́.	16. Happy journey.
17. Жела́ю вам успе́ха.	17. I wish you success.
18. С днём рожде́ния!	18. Happy birthday!
19. С Рождество́м Христо́вым!	19. Merry Christmas!
20. С Но́вым Го́дом!	20. Happy New Year!

C. Politeness

1. Спаси́бо!	1. Thank you!
2. Большо́е спаси́бо!	2. Many thanks!
3. Не́ за что!	3. Don't mention it! That's nothing!
4. Извини́те, пожа́луйста.	4. Pardon me, please.
5. Бу́дьте добры́.	5. Be so kind!
6. Переда́йте, пожа́луйста, соль.	6. Please pass the salt.

D. Introductions

1. Позвóльте вам
   предстáвить Вéру
   Ивáновну.
2. Как вáше и́мя?
3. Как вáша фами́лия?
4. Как вáше и́мя и
   óтчество?
5. Óчень прия́тно
   познакóмиться.

1. Permit me to introduce to
   you Vera Ivanovna.
2. What is your name?
3. What is your last name?
4. What is your first name
   and patronymic?
5. I am very pleased to meet
   you.

E. Health

1. Как вáше здорóвье?
2. Спаси́бо. Я здорóв.
3. Я бóлен.
4. У меня́ головá боли́т.
5. У меня́ нáсморк.

6. Сегóдня мне лýчше.
7. Вчерá мне бы́ло хýже.

1. How is your health?
2. Thank you.   I am well.
3. I am ill.
4. I have a headache.
5. I have a cold (in the
   head).
6. Today I feel better.
7. Yesterday I felt worse.

F. Time

1. Котóрый тепéрь час?
2. Тепéрь пять часóв.
3. В котóром часý вы
   бýдете дóма?
4. Я бýду дóма в два часá.

1. What time is it now?
2. It is now five o'clock.
3. At what time will you be
   home?
4. I shall be home at two
   o'clock.

G. Weather

1. Какáя сегóдня погóда?
2. Сегóдня óчень хорóшая
   погóда.
3. Вчерá былá плохáя
   погóда.
4. Хóлодно сегóдня.
5. Вчерá бы́ло óчень теплó.
6. Сегóдня идёт снег.
7. Вчерá шёл дождь.

1. How is the weather today?
2. The weather is very fine
   today.
3. The weather was bad
   yesterday.
4. It is cold today.
5. It was very warm yesterday.
6. It is snowing today.
7. It rained yesterday.

МАТЕРИА́Л ДЛЯ ЧТЕ́НИЯ

The following short selections are offered as additional reading material and are intended to increase the students' passive vocabulary. Hence, no grammatical explanations or questions in Russian accompany the text.

The selections have been taken from readers published in Russia for Russian pupils, but are here retold in simpler language and with the introduction of few new words. Unfamiliar words and expressions are translated in the footnotes.

I

Чле́ны[1] челове́ческого[2] те́ла[3]

Одна́жды[4] чле́ны челове́ческого те́ла поссо́рились[5] и не хоте́ли служи́ть[6] друг дру́гу.[7]

— Не хоти́м ходи́ть, говоря́т но́ги;[8] ходи́те са́ми![9]

— Не хоти́м рабо́тать для вас, говоря́т ру́ки;[10] рабо́тайте са́ми!

— Не хочу́ корми́ть[11] вас, кричи́т рот.[12]

— Не хоти́м смотре́ть! крича́т глаза́.

Так как[13] рот не корми́л те́ло, ру́ки не рабо́тали, но́ги не ходи́ли, а глаза́ не смотре́ли, то[14] все чле́ны ста́ли о́чень сла́быми.[15] Наконе́ц, все по́няли,[16] что нельзя́ ссо́риться,[17] а что ну́жно помога́ть[18] друг дру́гу. Ско́ро по́сле э́того всё те́ло ста́ло здоро́вым[19] и кре́пким.[20, 21]

Слова́рь (Vocabulary)

1. **член** member
2. **челове́ческий** human
3. **те́ло** body
4. **одна́жды** once
5. **поссо́риться (II)** *pf.* to have a quarrel
6. **служи́ть (II)** to serve
7. **друг дру́гу** (*dat.*) each other
8. **нога́** foot, leg
9. **сам** (*pron.*) myself, yourself, himself, *etc.*
10. **рука́** hand
11. **корми́ть (II)** to feed
12. **рот** mouth

13. **так как**   since, as
14. **то**   then, so
15. **сла́бый**   weak
16. **поня́ть (I)** *pf.*   to understand, to grasp
17. **ссо́риться (II)**   to quarrel
18. **помога́ть (I)**   to help
19. **здоро́вый**   healthy
20. **кре́пкий**   strong
21. **ста́ло здоро́вым и кре́пким** (*pred. instr.* is used with **стать**)   became healthy and strong.

II

Бога́ч[1] и портно́й[2]

В го́роде в одно́м[3] до́ме жи́ли бога́тый купе́ц[4] и бе́дный[5] портно́й — купе́ц наверху́,[6] а портно́й внизу́.[7] Портно́й всегда́ рабо́тал о́чень по́здно и за рабо́той[8] пел[9] пе́сни. У портно́го был хоро́ший го́лос и он обыкнове́нно пел о́чень весёлые пе́сни. Э́ти пе́сни нра́вились купцу́. К несча́стью,[10] портно́й ча́сто пел так гро́мко, что купе́ц не мог спать.

Одна́жды[11] купе́ц дал портно́му мно́го де́нег.[12] Бе́дный портно́й тепе́рь стал богачо́м и переста́л[13] рабо́тать. Он та́кже переста́л[13] петь, потому́ что он всё[14] вре́мя боя́лся,[15] что украду́т[16] у него́ де́ньги. Он ма́ло спал но́чью, а иногда́ всю ночь совсе́м не спал.

Наконе́ц портно́й по́нял,[17] что он несча́стен,[18] потому́ что бога́т. Тогда́ он верну́л[19] де́ньги купцу́, и сказа́л: "Я лу́чше бу́ду рабо́тать и пе́сни петь."

Слова́рь (Vocabulary)

1. **бога́ч**   rich man
2. **портно́й**   tailor
3. **оди́н**   one
4. **купе́ц**   merchant
5. **бе́дный**   poor
6. **наверху́**   upstairs
7. **внизу́**   downstairs
8. **за рабо́той**   at work
9. **петь (I)**   to sing
10. **к несча́стью**   unfortunately
11. **одна́жды**   once
12. **де́ньги** (*pl. only*)   money
13. **переста́ть (I)** *pf.*   to cease, to stop
14. **всё вре́мя**   all the time

15. **бо́яться (II)** to fear
16. **укра́сть (I)** *pf.* to steal
      что украду́т that one will steal
17. **поня́ть (I)** *pf.* to understand
18. **несча́стен** (*m.*) unhappy
19. **верну́ть (I)** *pf.* to return, to give back

III

Москва́

Москва́ — столи́ца[1] СССР. Э́то полити́ческий,[2] экономи́ческий[3] и культу́рный центр[4] страны́.

В це́нтре Москвы́ нахо́дится Кремль,[5] а о́коло Кремля́ — Кра́сная[6] пло́щадь.[7] На Кра́сной пло́щади нахо́дятся Храм Васи́лия Блаже́нного[8] — замеча́тельный па́мятник[9] ру́сской архитекту́ры,[10] мавзоле́й Ле́нина и Ста́лина,[11] огро́мный[12] универма́г ГУМ,[13] гости́ница "Москва́" и други́е больши́е зда́ния.

В Москве́ мно́го библиоте́к, музе́ев, теа́тров и карти́нных галере́й.[14] Библиоте́ка и́мени Ле́нина[15] в Москве́ — са́мая больша́я библиоте́ка СССР. В Москве́ та́кже нахо́дится Всесою́зная Акаде́мия нау́к,[16] Консервато́рия[17] и Моско́вский университе́т — са́мый ста́рый университе́т в стране́.

Слова́рь (Vocabulary)

1. **столи́ца** capital
2. **полити́ческий** political
3. **экономи́ческий** economic
4. **центр** center
5. **Кремль** the Kremlin
6. **Кра́сная** red
7. **пло́щадь** square
8. **Храм Васи́лия Блаже́нного** Saint Basil's Cathedral
9. **па́мятник** monument
10. **архитекту́ра** architecture
11. **мавзоле́й Ле́нина и Ста́лина** the Lenin and Stalin Mausoleum
12. **огро́мный** huge
13. **Госуда́рственный универса́льный магази́н** State Department Store
14. **карти́нная галере́я** picture gallery
15. **Библиоте́ка и́мени Ле́нина** the Lenin Library
16. **Всесою́зная Акаде́мия нау́к** the All-Union Academy of Sciences
17. **Консервато́рия** the Conservatory

IV

Перча́тки *

Потеря́ли котя́тки
На доро́ге перча́тки
И в слеза́х прибежа́ли домо́й.
— Ма́ма, ма́ма, прости́,
Мы не мо́жем найти́
Перча́тки!

— Потеря́ли перча́тки?
Вот дурны́е котя́тки!
Я вам ны́нче не дам пирога́.
Мя́у-мя́у, не дам
Мя́у-мя́у, не дам
Я вам ны́нче не дам пирога́!

Побежа́ли котя́тки,
Отыска́ли перча́тки
И смея́сь, прибежа́ли домо́й.
— Ма́ма, ма́ма, не злись,
Потому́ что нашли́сь,
Потому́ что нашли́сь
Перча́тки!

— Отыска́ли перча́тки?
Вот спаси́бо, котя́тки!
Я за э́то вам дам пирога́.
Мур-мур-мур, пирога́,
Мур-мур-мур, пирога́,
Я за э́то вам дам пирога́!

* From **Плывёт, плывёт кора́блик** by С. Марша́к—his version of *Three Little Kittens.* An English translation appears on page 250.

Three Little Kittens

The three little kittens
They lost their mittens,
And they began to cry,
Oh! mommy dear,
We sadly fear,
Our mittens we have lost.

What! lost your mittens?
You naughty kittens,
Then you shall have no pie.
Mi-ew, mi-ew, mi-ew, mi-ew,
Then you shall have no pie.

The three little kittens
They found their mittens,
And they began to cry,
Oh! mommy dear,
See here, see here,
Our mittens we have found.

What! found your mittens?
You darling kittens,
Then you shall have some pie.
Mi-ew, mi-ew, mi-ew, mi-ew,
Then you shall have some pie.

ПОСЛÓВИЦЫ (Proverbs)

1. **В гостя́х хорошó, а дóма ещё лу́чше.**
   There's no place like home.

2. **Век живи́ — век учи́сь.**
   Live and learn.

3. **Куй желéзо покá горячó.**
   Strike while the iron's hot.

4. **Лу́чше пóздно, чем никогдá.**
   Better late than never.

5. **Не всё то зóлото, что блести́т.**
   All is not gold that glitters.

6. **Не отклáдывай на зáвтра, то что мóжно сдéлать сегóдня.**
   Never put off till tomorrow what can be done today.

7. **Повторéнье — мать учéнья.**
   Practice makes perfect.

8. **Прáвда дорóже зóлота.**
   Truth is dearer than gold.

9. **Рукá ру́ку мóет.**
   One hand washes the other.

10. **Слóво — серебрó, молчáние — зóлото.**
    Speech is silver, but silence is golden.

11. **Ти́ше éдешь — дáльше бу́дешь.**
    Haste makes waste.

12. **Что посéешь, то и пожнёшь.**
    As ye sow, so shall ye reap.

ЗАГА́ДКИ (Riddles)

1. Что э́то ?*

Нет ног,[1] а хожу́
рта нет,[2] а скажу́:
когда́ спать,
когда́ встава́ть,
когда́ рабо́ту начина́ть.

[1] I have no feet   [2] I have no mouth

2. Что э́то ?*

В огне́[1] не гори́т,[2] в воде́[3] не то́нет.[4]

[1] In fire   [2] does not burn   [3] in water   [4] does not sink

3. Что э́то ?*

Ска́терть[1] бе́ла,[2] всё по́ле[3] оде́ла.[4]

[1] tablecloth   [2] white   [3] field   [4] dressed, covered

4. Что э́то ?*

Овсо́м[1] не ко́рмят,[2]
кнуто́м[3] не го́нят,[4]
а как па́шет,[5] —
семь плуго́в[6] та́щит.[7]

[1] with oats   [2] they do not feed   [3] with a whip   [4] they do not drive
[5] plows   [6] seven plows   [7] pulls, drags

* For answer, see p. 254.

5. Что э́то ?*

Два бра́та спе́реди[1] бегу́т,[2] два бра́та сза́ди[3] догоня́ют.[4]

[1] in front   [2] are running   [3] behind   [4] are catching up, are chasing

6. Что э́то ?*

Без рук,[1] без ног,[2] а дом сторожи́т.[3]

[1] without hands   [2] without feet   [3] guards, watches over

7. Что э́то ?*

Тóнкая[1] девчóнка,[2]
Бéлая юбчóнка,[3]
Крáсный[4] нос.[5]

Чем длинне́е[6] нóчи
Тем онá корóче[7]
От[8] горю́чих слёз.[9]

[1] thin   [2] little girl   [3] little skirt   [4] red   [5] nose   [6] the longer   [7] the shorter she is   [8] from   [9] scalding tears

* For answer, see p. 254.

Answers to Загáдки (Riddles)

1. **Часы́** — clock.

2. **Лёд** — ice.

3. **Снег** — snow.

4. **Трáктор** — tractor.

5. **Четы́ре колесá** — four wheels.

6. **Замóк** — lock.

7. **Свечá** — candle.

РУ́ССКИЕ ПЕ́СНИ

Брат Ива́н (Кано́н)

(Printed by arrangement with the Thrift Press, Ithaca, New York)

Брат И - ван, Брат И - ван,

спишь - ли ты, спишь-ли ты?

Звони в коло - ко - ла, звони в коло - ко - ла,

Динь, динь, динь, динь, динь, динь!

255

Харитóша

(Printed by arrangement with Leeds Music Corporation)

Е - ду, е - ду, е - ду, е - ду, е - ду,

пись-ма раз-да - ю... Не схо-дя с ве-ло-си-

пе-да,   я с у-лыб-кой всем по - ю: Не ску-

чай-те,   по-лу-чай-те, кто за-ждал-ся, кто влюб-

лен.   Пись-ма неж-ны-е, род - ны-е,   де-ло-

вы-е,   за-каз-ны-е —Всем вру-ча-ет Ха-ри-

то - ша,   ак-ку-рат-ный поч-та - льон.

1. Еду, еду, еду, еду,
   Еду, письма раздаю . . .
   Не сходя с велосипеда,
   Я с улыбкой всем пою:

2. Я везу любовь и радость
   И дыхание весны
   Из Москвы и Ленинграда
   И со всех концов страны.

3. Здесь конверты разной масти
   И газетные листы . . .
   В этой сумке смех и счастье
   И надежды и мечты.

4. Я берусь письмо доставить,
   Чтобы в срок оно пришло.
   Я хочу собой прославить
   Почтальона ремесло.

   Припев:
   Не скучайте, получайте,
   Кто заждался, кто влюблен.
   Письма нежные, родные,
   Деловые, заказные —
   Всем вручает Харитоша,
   Аккуратный почтальон.

Катю́ша

(Printed by arrangement with Leeds Music Corporation)

Рас - цве - та - ли   я - бло - ни и

гру - ши,   по - плы - ли   ту - ма - ны над ре -

кой.   Вы - хо - ди - ла

на бе - рег Ка - тю - ша,   на вы -

со - кий бе - рег на кру - той.

1. Расцветали яблони и груши,
   Поплыли туманы над рекой.
   Выходила на берег Катюша,
   На высокий берег на крутой.

2. Выходила, песню заводила
   Про степного сизого орла,
   Про того, которого любила,
   Про того, чьи письма берегла.

3. Ой ты, песня, песенка девичья,
   Ты лети за ясным солнцем вслед
   И бойцу на дали пограничной
   От Катюши передай привет.

4. Пусть он вспомнит девушку простую,
   Пусть услышит, как она поёт,
   Пусть он землю бережёт родную,
   А любовь Катюша сбережёт.

Во ку́знице

(Printed by arrangement with Leeds Music Corporation)

Во ку . . . во куз - ни - це. Во
ку . . . во куз - ни - це. Во куз-
ни - це мо - ло - ды - е куз-не - цы, во куз-
ни - це мо - ло - ды - е куз-не - цы.

Во ку . . . во кузнице,
Во кузнице молодые кузнецы.
Они, они куют,
Они куют, приговаривают:
"Пойдём, пойдём, Дуня,
Пойдём Дуня, в огород, в огород.
Сорвём, сорвём Дуне,
Сорвём Дуне лопушок, лопушок,
Сошьём, сошьём Дуне,
Сошьём Дуне сарафан, сарафан.
Носи, носи, Дуня,
Носи Дуня, не марай, не марай.
По пра . . . по праздничкам,
По праздничкам надевай, надевай.

Each line is repeated twice.

Вечéрний звон

(Printed by arrangement with the Thrift Press, Ithaca, New York)

Вечерний звон, вечерний звон,
Как много дум наводит он!

О юных днях в краю родном,
Где я любил, где отчий дом!

И как я с ним навек простясь
Там слышал звон в последний раз.

Вечерний звон, вечерний звон,
Как много дум наводит он!

Эй у́хнем

(Printed by arrangement with the Thrift Press, Ithaca, New York)

Эй   ухнем!   Эй   ухнем!

Ещё   ра - зик,   е - щё   раз!

Ра - зовьём   мы   бе - ре - зу,

ра - зовьём мы кудря - ву.

Ай да, да, ай да, ай да, да ай да,

ра - зовьём кудря-ву - ю!

Эй ухнем, эй ухнем!

Колоко́льчик

(Printed by arrangement with Leeds Music Corporation)

1. Од - но - звуч-но гре-мит ко - ло -
2. Столь - ко чувс-тва в той пе - сне у -
3. И при - пом-нил я в но - чи дру -

- коль - чик, И до - ро - га пы -
- ны - лой, Столь-ко чувс - тва в на -
- ги - е И род - ны - е по -

- лит-ся слег-ка,_____ И у-ны-ло по ро - вно-му
- пе-ве род-ном,_____ Что в гру-ди мо-ей хлад-ной, ос -
- ля и ле - са _____ И на о-чи, дав-но уж су-

по - лю За-ли - ва-ет-ся песнь ям - щи - ка.
- ты - лой Раз-го - ре-ло-ся сер - дце ог - нём.
- хи - е На-бе - жа-ла, как ис - кра, сле - за.

4. Однозвучно гремит колокольчик
   И дорога пылится слегка
   И замолк мой ямщик, а дорога,
   Предо мной далека, далека.

Вниз по ма́тушке по Во́лге

(Printed by arrangement with Leeds Music Corporation)

1. Вниз по ма - туш - ке по Во-лге по
2. По ши-ро - ко - му раз-до-лью раз-
3. Ни - че-го вввол-нах не ви-дно не

Во - - - лге по ши -
до - - - лью под - ни -
ви - - - дно, о - дна

- ро - ко-му раз-до - - - лью.
- ма - ла-ся по - го - - - да.
ло - до-чка чер-не - - - ет.

PRONUNCIATION CHARTS

The charts on pages 269–272 represent only an approximation of Russian sounds, as it is impossible to give exact English equivalents. Therefore, when consulting the charts, refer to the more detailed rules on pronunciation.

Chart 1.   Hard and Soft Vowels (See ¶1-A)

hard: **а э о у ы**

soft: **я е ё ю и**

The first four *soft* vowels represent a combination of the *y* sound in *yes* and the corresponding *hard* vowels; thus:

$$y + \text{а} = \text{я}$$
$$y + \text{э} = \text{е}$$
$$y + \text{о} = \text{ё}$$
$$y + \text{у} = \text{ю}$$

Chart 2.   Voiced and Voiceless Consonants (See ¶9-A)

Voiced:	**б**	**в**	**г**	**д**	**ж**	**з**
Voiceless:	**п**	**ф**	**к**	**т**	**ш**	**с**

The consonants **л, м, н** and **р** are always voiced.

The consonants **ц, ч,** and **щ** are always voiceless.

Chart 3. Pronunciation of Vowels

For the pronunciation of **a**, see **¶2-A**; for **я**, **¶10-A**; for **e**, **¶4-A**; for **o**, **¶3-A**; for **ë**, *The Written Alphabet* (p. 8) and **¶8-D**; after sibilants, **¶8-C**.

Vowel	Stressed	Unstressed	After some letters (unstressed)	In connected speech
А а	As *a* in c*a*r: Ива́н она́	As *a* in ciga-rette: сады́ Ве́ра	After **ч** or **щ**, like *e* in cheroot: часы́ пло́щадь	
Я я	As *ya* in *ya*rd: моя́, я	As *ye* in *ye*ar: язы́к, янва́рь	тся = ца ться = ца	
Э э	As *e* in *e*gg: э́та дуэ́т	As *e* in *e*vict: эта́ж экра́н		
Е е	As *ye* in *ye*s (when initial or after a vowel): е́сли уе́хал	As *e* in *e*vent: сестра́ стена́	After **ж**, **ш**, and **щ**, like *i* in b*i*t: то́же пи́шет	
Ы ы	As *y* in s*y*l-lable: ты, вы забы́ть	Same as stressed		
И и	As *e* in *e*vil: пить Йда	Same as stressed	After **ж**, **ш**, and **ц**, like **ы**: жить маши́на	As **ы** (when pre-ceded by hard con-sonant): брат **и** я бу́дем игра́ть
О о	As *o* in sp*o*rt: заво́д стол	As *o* in c*o*me: когда́ Москва́		
Ё ё	As *yo* in *yo*lk: её, ёлка своё	Always stressed		
У у	As *oo* in b*oo*ty: у́тро	Same as stressed		
Ю ю	As *u* in *u*se: ю́мор, юг, даю́	Same as stressed		
Й й	This letter always stands after a vowel, and forms the second part of a diphthong. Compare with *y* in boy.			

Chart 4. Pronunciation of Consonants

For final в, see ¶4-B; for final д, see ¶3-B. For hard and soft consonants, see ¶8-B. For voiced and voiceless consonants, see ¶9-A. For ъ and ь, see ¶10-B.

Con-so-nant	Hard	Soft	Voiced	Voiceless
Б б	As *b* in *b*ook: брат бума́га соба́ка	As *b* in *b*eauty: библиоте́ка бе́лый		In final position or before voiceless consonant, like *p* in *p*art: хле*б*, клу*б*, тру́*б*ка
В в	As *v* in *v*ote: Во́лга ва́за	As *v* in *v*iew: ви́деть Ве́ра		In final position or before voiceless consonant, like *f* in *f*our: Ивано́*в*, студе́н-то*в*, вчера́, *в* час
Г г	As *g* in *g*lad: го́лос го́род	As *g* in *g*eese: гид	As *v* in *v*ote: in genitive case ending его́, о́го	In final position or before voiceless consonant, like *k* in *k*eep: дру*г* As *ch* in lo*ch* before к: ле*г*ко́, мя́*г*ко
Д д	As *d* in *d*o: да	As *d* in *d*ew: дя́дя		In final position or before voiceless consonant, like *t* in *t*ake: ви*д*, са*д*
Ж ж	As *s* in plea*s*ure: журна́л	Always hard		In final position or before voiceless consonant, like *sh* in *sh*ip: му*ж*, му*ж*ско́й
З з	As *z* in *z*one: заво́д ва́за	As *z* in cra*z*ier: зима́ взять		In final position or before voiceless consonant, like *s* in *s*alt: ра*з*, гла*з* бе*з* карт
К к	As *k* in *k*ing: как ко́фе	As *c* in *c*ue: уро́ки кем	Before voiced consonant, like *g* in *g*ood: *к* дя́де та*к* же	

Chart 4 (continued).

Con-so-nant	Hard	Soft	Voiced	Voiceless
Л л	As *ll* in we*ll:* ла́мпа Ло́ндон	As *ll* in mi*ll*ion лицо́ люби́ть		
М м	As *m* in *m*y: Москва́ ма́ленький	As *m* in *m*usic: мя́со мел		
Н н	As *n* in *n*o: на, наш ночь	As *n* in ge*n*ial: нет, не́бо		
П п	As *p* in *p*ark: парк по́чта	As *p* in *p*ew: пить, пе́сня пять		
Р р	As *r* in *r*ose: рад ра́дио, ру́сский	As *r* in seri-ously: ряд, река́ орёл		
С с	As *s* in *s*top: солда́т Сталингра́д	As *s* in *s*eek: си́ний всё	Before voiced consonant, like *z* in *z*one: сде́лать сдава́ть: про́сьба	
Т т	As *t* in *t*ip: там, то́лько тут	As *t* in s*t*eel: ти́хо тётя		
Ф ф	As *f* in *f*our: фами́лия фронт, факт	As *f* in *f*ew: Фе́дя		
Х х	As *ch* in lo*ch* (Scotch): хорошо́ са́хар	As *h* in *h*uge (with strong breath): хи́мия		
Ц ц	As *ts* in boo*ts:* центр цвет	Always hard		
Ч ч	Always soft	As *ch* in *ch*eck: час, чем чита́ть		
Ш ш	As *sh* in *sh*ip: шко́ла штат	Always hard		
Щ щ	Always soft	As *shch* in fresh *ch*eese: ещё, борщ		

Chart 5. Vowel Changes

The replacement of one vowel by another when preceded by certain consonants often occurs in Russian. The chart below summarizes the most important rules governing such changes, and should prove valuable in explaining many irregularities in the inflection of nouns, adjectives, pronouns, and verbs. Remember this chart and refer to it frequently.

The sign > stands for *is replaced by*.

After gutturals г, к, х	After sibilants ж, ч, ш, щ	After ц
ь can never stand		и > ы (except in words of foreign origin)
ы > и ю > у я > а	ы > и ю > у я > а	ы (remains) ю > у я > а
	unstressed о > е	unstressed о > е

For **ы > и**, see ¶7-A and ¶7-B.   For **ю > у**, see ¶5-A.

TABLES

Declension of Nouns

Table 1. First Declension

SINGULAR*

Case	Hard	Soft		
	-а	**-я**		**-ия**
nom.	ка́рта	неде́ля	дя́дя	а́рмия
gen.	ка́рты	неде́ли	дя́ди	а́рмии
dat.	ка́рте	неде́ле	дя́де	а́рмии
acc.	ка́рту	неде́лю	дя́дю	а́рмию
instr.	ка́ртой (**-ою**)	неде́лей (**-ею**)	дя́дей (**-ею**)	а́рмией (**-ею**)
prep.	о ка́рте	о неде́ле	о дя́де	об а́рмии

PLURAL†

Case	Hard	Soft		
	-а (*nom. sing.*)	**-я** (*nom. sing.*)		**-ия** (*nom. sing.*)
nom.	ка́рты	неде́ли	дя́ди	а́рмии
gen.	карт	неде́ль	дя́дей	а́рмий
dat.	ка́ртам	неде́лям	дя́дям	а́рмиям
acc.	ка́рты	неде́ли	дя́дей	а́рмии
instr.	ка́ртами	неде́лями	дя́дями	а́рмиями
prep.	о ка́ртах	о неде́лях	о дя́дях	об а́рмиях

* For membership, see ¶15-7a. For classification into *hard* and *soft*, see ¶15-7b. For the *accusative* of animate objects, see ¶15-7 c-2. For irregularities in declension, see ¶25-3b.

† For formation of the *nominative plural*, see ¶20-2a, b. For the *accusative plural* of animate and inanimate nouns, see ¶26-3a. For the *genitive plural*, see ¶26-3b. For the *genitive plural* with fleeting **-o** or **-e**, see ¶26-3c.

273

Table 2.   Second Declension

MASCULINE SINGULAR *

Case	Hard	Soft		
	Consonant	-ь		-й
		Stress on stem	Stress on ending	
nom.	журна́л	автомоби́ль	дождь	трамва́й
gen.	журна́ла	автомоби́ля	дождя́	трамва́я
dat.	журна́лу	автомоби́лю	дождю́	трамва́ю
acc.	журна́л	автомоби́ль	дождь	трамва́й
instr.	журна́лом	автомоби́лем	дождём	трамва́ем
prep.	о журна́ле	об автомоби́ле	о дожде́	о трамва́е

MASCULINE PLURAL †

Case	Hard	Soft		
	Consonant (*nom. sing.*)	-ь (*nom. sing.*)		-й (*nom. sing.*)
		Stress on stem	Stress on ending	
nom.	журна́лы	автомоби́ли	дожди́	трамва́и
gen.	журна́лов	автомоби́лей	дожде́й	трамва́ев
dat.	журна́лам	автомоби́лям	дождя́м	трамва́ям
acc.	журна́лы	автомоби́ли	дожди́	трамва́и
instr.	журна́лами	автомоби́лями	дождя́ми	трамва́ями
prep.	о журна́лах	об автомоби́лях	о дождя́х	о трамва́ях

* † See notes at the end of this table on p. 275.

Table 2. Second Declension (Continued)

NEUTER SINGULAR*

Case	Hard		Soft
	-o	-e	-ие
nom.	сло́во	мо́ре	сочине́ние
gen.	сло́ва	мо́ря	сочине́ния
dat.	сло́ву	мо́рю	сочине́нию
acc.	сло́во	мо́ре	сочине́ние
instr.	сло́вом	мо́рем	сочине́нием
prep.	о сло́ве	о мо́ре	о сочине́нии

NEUTER PLURAL †

Case	Hard		Soft
	-o (*nom. sing.*)	-e (*nom. sing.*)	-ие (*nom. sing.*)
nom.	слова́	моря́	сочине́ния
gen.	слов	море́й	сочине́ний
dat.	слова́м	моря́м	сочине́ниям
acc.	слова́	моря́	сочине́ния
instr.	слова́ми	моря́ми	сочине́ниями
prep.	о слова́х	о моря́х	о сочине́ниях

* For membership, see ¶ 18-4a. For classification into *hard* and *soft*, see ¶ 18-4b. For the *accusative* of animate objects, see ¶ 18-4 d-2.

† For formation of the *nominative plural*, see ¶ 20-2. For the *accusative plural* of animate and inanimate nouns, see ¶ 26-4b. For formation of the *genitive plural* of masculine nouns, see ¶ 26-4a; for neuter nouns, see ¶ 27-1a. For the *genitive plural* of neuter nouns with fleeting -o or -e, see ¶ 27-1b.

Table 3.   Third Declension

SINGULAR *

Case	-ь	Sibilant (ж, ч, ш, щ) + -ь	-ь
nom.	ло́шадь	ночь	тетра́дь
gen.	ло́шади	но́чи	тетра́ди
dat.	ло́шади	но́чи	тетра́ди
acc.	ло́шадь	ночь	тетра́дь
instr.	ло́шадью	но́чью	тетра́дью
prep.	о ло́шади	о но́чи	о тетра́ди

PLURAL †

Case	Stress on oblique case endings		Stress on stem
	-ь (nom. sing.)	Sibilant (ж, ч, ш, щ) + -ь (nom. sing.)	-ь (nom. sing.)
nom.	ло́шади	но́чи	тетра́ди
gen.	лошаде́й	ноче́й	тетра́дей
dat.	лошадя́м	ноча́м	тетра́дям
acc.	лошаде́й	но́чи	тетра́ди
instr.	лошадя́ми or лошадьми́	ноча́ми	тетра́дями
prep.	о лошадя́х	о ноча́х	о тетра́дях

* For membership, see ¶ 19-2a.   For the *accusative* of animate objects, see ¶ 19-2b.

† For formation of the *nominative plural*, see ¶ 20-2b.   For the *accusative plural* of animate and inanimate nouns, see ¶ 27-2a.   For nouns with stems in ж, ч, ш, or щ, see ¶ 27-2b.

Declension of Adjectives

For classification of adjectives, see ¶ 14-2a, b.   For agreement of adjectives in the *accusative singular* with nouns, see ¶ 14-1 *note*. For formation of the *nominative plural*, see ¶ 20-4.   For agreement of adjectives in the *accusative plural* with nouns, see ¶ 27-3.

Table 4. Hard Declension

GROUP I (-ый, -ая, -ое)

Case	Singular			Plural for all genders
	m.	*f.*	*n.*	
nom.	но́вый	но́вая	но́вое	но́вые
gen.	но́вого	но́вой	но́вого	но́вых
dat.	но́вому	но́вой	но́вому	но́вым
acc.	но́вый *or* но́вого	но́вую	но́вое	но́вые *or* но́вых
instr.	но́вым	но́вой (ою)	но́вым	но́выми
prep.	о но́вом	о но́вой	о но́вом	о но́вых

GROUP II (-о́й, -а́я, -о́е)

Case	Singular			Plural for all genders
	m.	*f.*	*n.*	
nom.	молодо́й	молода́я	молодо́е	молоды́е
gen.	молодо́го	молодо́й	молодо́го	молоды́х
dat.	молодо́му	молодо́й	молодо́му	молоды́м
acc.	молодо́й *or* молодо́го	молоду́ю	молодо́е	молоды́е *or* молоды́х
instr.	молоды́м	молодо́й (о́ю)	молоды́м	молоды́ми
prep.	о молодо́м	о молодо́й	о молодо́м	о молоды́х

Table 5.   Soft Declension

(-н + -ий; -н + -яя; -н + -ее)

Case	Singular			Plural for all genders
	m.	*f.*	*n.*	
nom.	последний	последняя	последнее	последние
gen.	последнего	последней	последнего	последних
dat.	последнему	последней	последнему	последним
acc.	последний *or* последнего	последнюю	последнее	последние *or* последних
instr.	последним	последней (ею)	последним	последними
prep.	о последнем	о последней	о последнем	о последних

Table 6. Mixed Declension

GROUP I (-г, -к, -х + -ий, -ая, -ое)

Case	Singular			Plural for all genders
	m.	*f.*	*n.*	
nom.	ру́сский	ру́сская	ру́сское	ру́сские
gen.	ру́сского	ру́сской	ру́сского	ру́сских
dat.	ру́сскому	ру́сской	ру́сскому	ру́сским
acc.	ру́сский *or* ру́сского	ру́сскую	ру́сское	ру́сские *or* ру́сских
instr.	ру́сским	ру́сской (ою)	ру́сским	ру́сскими
prep.	о ру́сском	о ру́сской	о ру́сском	о ру́сских

GROUP II (-ж, -ч, -ш, -щ + -ий, -ая, -ее)

Case	Singular			Plural for all genders
	m.	*f.*	*n.*	
nom.	хоро́ший	хоро́шая	хоро́шее	хоро́шие
gen.	хоро́шего	хоро́шей	хоро́шего	хоро́ших
dat.	хоро́шему	хоро́шей	хоро́шему	хоро́шим
acc.	хоро́ший *or* хоро́шего	хоро́шую	хоро́шее	хоро́шие *or* хоро́ших
instr.	хоро́шим	хоро́шей (ею)	хоро́шим	хоро́шими
prep.	о хоро́шем	о хоро́шей	о хоро́шем	о хоро́ших

GROUP III (-г, -к, -х; -ж, -ч, -ш, -щ; + -о́й, -а́я, -о́е)

Case	Singular			Plural for all genders
	m.	*f.*	*n.*	
nom.	дорого́й	дорога́я	дорого́е	дороги́е
gen.	дорого́го	дорого́й	дорого́го	дороги́х
dat.	дорого́му	дорого́й	дорого́му	дороги́м
acc.	дорого́й *or* дорого́го	дорогу́ю	дорого́е	дороги́е *or* дороги́х
instr.	дороги́м	дорого́й (о́ю)	дороги́м	дороги́ми
prep.	о дорого́м	о дорого́й	о дорого́м	о дороги́х

Declension of Adjective-Pronouns

Table 7. Possessive

The possessives **eró**, **eë**, and **их**, are not declined.

Case	Singulars (modifying singulars)			Singulars (modifying plurals, all genders)
	m.	*f.*	*n.*	
nom.	мой	моя́	моё	мои́
gen.	моего́	мое́й	моего́	мои́х
dat.	моему́	мое́й	моему́	мои́м
acc.	мой *or* моего́	мою́	моё	мои́ *or* мои́х
instr.	мои́м	мое́й (е́ю)	мои́м	мои́ми
prep.	о моём	о мое́й	о моём	о мои́х

твой is declined like **мой**.

Case	Plurals (modifying singulars)			Plurals (modifying plurals, all genders)
	m.	*f.*	*n.*	
nom.	наш	на́ша	на́ше	на́ши
gen.	на́шего	на́шей	на́шего	на́ших
dat.	на́шему	на́шей	на́шему	на́шим
acc.	наш *or* на́шего	на́шу	на́ше	на́ши *or* на́ших
instr.	на́шим	на́шей (ею)	на́шим	на́шими
prep.	о на́шем	о на́шей	о на́шем	о на́ших

ваш is declined like **наш**.

Declension of Pronouns

Table 8. Personal Pronouns

SINGULAR

Case	First person (m., f., & n.)	Second person (m., f., & n.)
nom.	я	ты
gen.	меня	тебя
dat.	мне	тебе
acc.	меня	тебя
instr.	мной (мною)	тобой (тобою)
prep.	обо мне	о тебе

Case	Third person* (m. & n.)	With governing prepositions	Third person * (f.)	With governing prepositions
nom.	он оно́		она́	
gen.	его́	у него́	её	у неё
dat.	ему́	к нему́	ей	к ней
acc.	его́	на него́	её	на неё
instr.	им	с ним	ей, е́ю	с ней, с не́ю
prep.	о нём	о нём	о ней	о ней

* Pronouns of the third person take the prefix **н-** when they are governed by a preposition.

Table 8 is continued on the next page.

Table 8.   Personal Pronouns (Continued)

PLURAL

Case	All genders			
	First person	Second person	Third person*	
				With governing prepositions
nom.	мы	вы	они́	
gen.	нас	вас	их	у них
dat.	нам	вам	им	к ним
acc.	нас	вас	их	на них
instr.	на́ми	ва́ми	и́ми	с ни́ми
prep.	о нас	о вас	о них	о них

* Pronouns of the third person take the prefix **н-** when they are governed by a preposition.

Table 9. Relative and Interrogative Pronouns *

nom.	кто	что
gen.	кого́	чего́
dat.	кому́	чему́
acc.	кого́	что
instr.	кем	чем
prep.	о ком	о чём

* See ¶ 12-2, 21-1.

Table 10. Demonstrative *

Case	Singular			Plural for all genders
	m.	*f.*	*n.*	
nom.	э́тот	э́та	э́то	э́ти
gen.	э́того	э́той	э́того	э́тих
dat.	э́тому	э́той	э́тому	э́тим
acc.	э́тот *or* э́того	э́ту	э́то	э́ти *or* э́тих
instr.	э́тим	э́той (ою)	э́тим	э́тими
prep.	об э́том	об э́той	об э́том	об э́тих

* For agreement of the masculine э́тот in the *accusative singular with nouns,* see ¶ 14-1. For agreement of the *accusative plural* of э́ти with nouns, see ¶ 27-3.

Table 11. Reflexive Pronoun Singular and Plural (All Genders and Persons) *

nom.	none
gen.	себя́
dat.	себе́
acc.	себя́
instr.	собо́й (ою)
prep.	о себе́

* See ¶ 19-1.

Numerals

Table 12.   Cardinal Numerals 1 through 20 *

1. оди́н, одна́, одно́	11. оди́ннадцать
2. два (*m. and n.*), две (*f.*)	12. двена́дцать
3. три	13. трина́дцать
4. четы́ре	14. четы́рнадцать
5. пять	15. пятна́дцать
6. шесть	16. шестна́дцать
7. семь	17. семна́дцать
8. во́семь	18. восемна́дцать
9. де́вять	19 девятна́дцать
10. де́сять	20. два́дцать

* For formation of 11 through 20, see ¶ **27-5a**. For nouns and adjectives governed by cardinal numerals, see ¶ **9-3**. **20-8**. and **27-5b**.

Table 13.   Time of Day—On the Hour

P.M.	A.M.
1:00 час дня	час но́чи
2:00 два часа́ дня	два часа́ но́чи
3:00 три часа́ дня	три часа́ но́чи
4:00 четы́ре часа́ дня	четы́ре часа́ утра́
5:00 пять часо́в дня	пять часо́в утра́
6:00 шесть часо́в ве́чера	шесть часо́в утра́
7:00 семь часо́в ве́чера	семь часо́в утра́
8:00 во́семь часо́в ве́чера	во́семь часо́в утра́
9:00 де́вять часо́в ве́чера	де́вять часо́в утра́
10:00 де́сять часо́в ве́чера	де́сять часо́в утра́
11:00 оди́ннадцать часо́в ве́чера	оди́ннадцать часо́в утра́
12:00 двена́дцать часо́в но́чи	двена́дцать часо́в дня

The afternoon hours 1:00–5:00 are regarded as hours of the *day* = **дня**; 6:00–11:00 p.m. as hours of the *evening* = **ве́чера**; 12:00 midnight–3:00 a.m. as hours of the *night* = **но́чи**; and 4:00–11:00 a.m. as hours of the *morning* = **утра́**. Twelve noon is considered an hour of the *day* = **дня**.

Verbs

Forms of verbs deviating from the regular conjugations are given in the *Russian-English Vocabulary*, pages 253-271.

For *classification* of verbs, see ¶**4-2**, **7-1**, and **7-2**.

For the *habitual* and *actual* forms of verbs, see ¶**13-3**.

For details on the *perfective* and *imperfective aspects*, see ¶**23-1** and **23-2**.

For *reflexive* verbs, see ¶**16-6**.

For formation of *present* tense, see ¶**4-2** and **7-1**; of *past* tense, see ¶**10-8** and **23-2**; for *compound future*, see ¶**11-3**; for *perfective future*, see ¶**23-2**; for *imperative*, see ¶**11-5**, **20-10**, and **23-2e**.

Table 14.   Conjugation of Быть (to be)

Singular   Plural

PRESENT

я (есмь)⎫ *obsolete*   мы (éсмы)⎫ *obsolete*
ты (есй) ⎭   вы (éсте) ⎭
он есть   онй суть   *seldom used*

PAST

я, ты, он был   мы ⎫
я, ты, онá былá   вы ⎬ бы́ли
онó бы́ло   онй ⎭

FUTURE

я бýду   мы бýдем
ты бýдешь   вы бýдете
он бýдет   онй бýдут

IMPERATIVE

будь   бýдьте

Table 15. Regular Conjugations

CONJUGATION I   CONJUGATION II

INFINITIVE

чита́ть *to read*   **говори́ть** *to speak*

PRESENT TENSE

я чита́ю	я говорю́
ты чита́ешь	ты говори́шь
он чита́ет	он говори́т
мы чита́ем	мы говори́м
вы чита́ете	вы говори́те
они́ чита́ют	они́ говоря́т

PAST TENSE

я, ты, он чита́л	я, ты, он говори́л
я, ты, она́ чита́ла	я, ты, она́ говори́ла
оно́ чита́ло	оно́ говори́ло
мы, вы, они́ чита́ли	мы, вы, они́ говори́ли

COMPOUND FUTURE TENSE

я бу́ду	я бу́ду
ты бу́дешь	ты бу́дешь
он бу́дет	он бу́дет
мы бу́дем **чита́ть**	мы бу́дем **говори́ть**
вы бу́дете	вы бу́дете
они́ бу́дут	они́ бу́дут

IMPERATIVE

чита́й	говори́
чита́йте	говори́те

Table 16.   Reflexive Verbs

INFINITIVE

купа́ться   *to bathe (oneself)*

PRESENT TENSE

я купа́ю**сь**
ты купа́ешь**ся**   (*pr.* купа́ешь**са**)
он, она́, оно́ купа́ет**ся**   (*pr.* купа́е**ца**)
мы купа́ем**ся**   (*pr.* купа́ем**са**)
вы купа́ете**сь**
они́ купа́ют**ся**   (*pr.* купа́ю**ца**)

PAST TENSE

я, ты, он купа́л**ся**   мы ⎫
я, ты, она́ купа́ла**сь**   вы ⎬ купа́ли**сь**
оно́ купа́ло**сь**   они́ ⎭

COMPOUND FUTURE TENSE

я бу́ду купа́ть**ся**, *etc.*

IMPERATIVE

купа́й**ся**   купа́йте**сь**

Table 17. Impersonal Expressions *

PRESENT TENSE

Affirmative	хо́лодно it *is* cold	мне тебе́ ему́ ей } хо́лодно	I am you are he is she is } cold
		нам вам им } хо́лодно	we are you are they are } cold
Negative	**не** хо́лодно it *is not* cold	мне **не** хо́лодно	I am not cold, *etc.*

PAST TENSE

Affirmative	бы́ло хо́лодно it *was* cold	мне тебе́ ему́ ей { бы́ло хо́лодно	I was you were he was she was } cold
		нам вам им { бы́ло хо́лодно	we were you were they were } cold
Negative	**не́** было хо́лодно it *was not* cold	мне **не́** было хо́лодно	I was not cold, *etc.*

FUTURE TENSE

Affirmative	бу́дет хо́лодно it *will be* cold	мне тебе́ ему́ ей { бу́дет хо́лодно	I shall be you will be he will be she will be } cold
		нам вам им } бу́дет хо́лодно	we shall be you will be they will be } cold
Negative	**не** бу́дет хо́лодно it *will not* be cold	мне **не** бу́дет хо́лодно	I shall not be cold, *etc.*

---

* See ¶ **10-5**, **16-1**, and **16-5**.

VOCABULARIES

The following abbreviations are used throughout the text and in the vocabularies. Ordinarily, an italicized word in parentheses applies to the Russian word it follows; for example, **автомобиль** (*m.*) means that **автомобиль** is a masculine noun. Parts of speech are indicated only when confusion might arise; gender only when it is not obvious from the ending. Important grammatical references are also included.

Abbreviations

acc.	accusative	*irr.*	irregular
act.	actual verb	*lit.*	literally
adj.	adjective	*m.*	masculine
adv.	adverb	*n.*	neuter
colloq.	colloquial	*nom.*	nominative
comp.	comparative	*not decl.*	not declined
conj.	conjugation	*pers.*	personal
dat.	dative	*pf.*	perfective
decl.	declension,	*pl.*	plural
	declined	*pol.*	polite
dim.	diminutive	*pred.*	predicative
f.	feminine	*prep.*	prepositional
fam.	familiar	*pr.*	pronounced
fut.	future	*pron.*	pronoun
gen.	genitive	*reflex.*	reflexive
hab.	habitual	*rel. pron.*	relative pronoun
imper.	imperative	*sing.*	singular
imp.	imperfective	*v.*	verb
instr.	instrumental	*fl*	fleeting **o** or **e**
interr.	interrogative	I	First Conjugation
intrans.	intransitive	II	Second Conjugation

RUSSIAN-ENGLISH VOCABULARY

See this vocabulary for references to rules on grammar and pronunciation; for verb forms, especially irregular ones; and for all irregularities in the declensions of nouns, adjectives, and pronouns.

This vocabulary also includes both the imperfective and perfective aspects if both have been used in this book. Therefore, if only the imperfective aspect is known, consult the vocabulary to find the perfective, and vice versa.

А

а and, but; ah
автомоби́ль (*m.*) automobile
Аки́м Joachim
а́лгебра algebra
алло́ hello (in answering a telephone)
Аме́рика America (*colloq.* the U.S.A.)
америка́нецᴬ (*noun, m.*) (*gen.* **америка́нца**) American
америка́нский, -ая, -ое American (*adj.*)
англи́йский, -ая, -ое English (*adj.*)
англича́нин (*nom. pl.* **англича́не**; *gen. pl.* **англича́н**) Englishman
А́нглия England
А́нна Anne
аппети́т (*only in sing.*) appetite
арифме́тика arithmetic
ах! oh!

Б

ба́бушка grandmother
баскетбо́л basketball
без (*with gen.*) without
бейзбо́л baseball
бе́лый, -ая, -ое white
бе́рег (*prep.* **берегу́**, see ¶20-6; *pl.* **берега́**) shore
   на берегу́ on the shore
бесе́довать (**I**); **бесе́дую, бесе́дуешь, -ют**; *imper.* **бесе́дуй, -йте** to chat, to talk
   pf. **побесе́довать** (**I**) to have a talk
библиоте́ка library
бли́зко (*adv. with* **от**) near
бога́тый, -ая, -ое rich
бо́лен (*m.*), **больна́** (*f.*), **больны́** (*pl.*) sick

боли́т aches (*v.*)

   у него́ боли́т голова́ his head aches

бо́льше (*adv.*) more

большо́й, -а́я, -о́е ; *pl.* **-и́е** big

   большо́е спаси́бо many thanks

Бори́с Boris

борщ (*gen.* **борща́,** *pl.* **борщи́**) borshch (beet soup)

брат brother

брать (**I**); **беру́, берёшь, беру́т;** *past* **брал, -ла́, -ло, -ли;** *imper.* **бери́, -и́те** to take

Бра́ун Brown (surname)

бу́дет will be (see ¶ **11-2**)

бу́ду I shall be

бума́га paper

бы́стро (*adv.*) rapidly

быть (*irr.*); **бу́ду, -ешь, -ут;** *past* **был, -ла́, -ло, -ли** (see *Unit* 11); *imper.* **будь, бу́дьте** to be

   не мо́жет быть (it is) impossible

В

в (во) (*with acc.*) to, into (direction); (*with acc.*) at, per (time); (*with prep.*) in, at (location)

ва́за vase

Ва́ня Vanya

Ва́ся Basil

ваш, ва́ша, ва́ше; *pl.* **ва́ши** your, yours

Вашингто́н Washington

вдруг suddenly

Ве́ра Vera

верхо́м (*adv.*) astride (a horse); *see* **е́здить верхо́м**

ве́село it is cheerful, gay; cheerfully, gaily

весёлый, -ая, -ое cheerful, gay

весно́й (*adv.*) in the spring

весь, вся, всё (*pron. & adj.*) entire, whole

   все (*pl.*) all, everybody

ве́чер (*pl.* **вечера́**) evening

   ве́чером in the evening

   до́брый ве́чер good evening

   сего́дня ве́чером this evening, tonight

ви́деть (**II**) (*pf.* **уви́деть,** **II**); **ви́жу, ви́дишь, ви́дят;** (*no imper.*) to see

вме́сте (*adv.*) together

внима́тельно carefully, attentively

во (*see* **в**) in, to (see ¶ **25-1d**)

вода́ water

война́ (*pl.* **во́йны**) war

вокза́л railway station (see ¶ **25-1 b-3**)

вокру́г (*with gen.*) around

волейбо́л volleyball

Во́лга Volga (*river in the U.S.S.R.*)

вопро́с question
восемна́дцать eighteen
во́семь eight
воскресе́нье Sunday
　　в воскресе́нье on Sunday
вот here is, here are (see ¶ 4-1)
вре́мя (*n.*) (*gen.* **вре́мени**) time
　　проводи́ть вре́мя to spend time
все (*pl. of* весь, вся, всё) all, everybody
　　всё э́то all this
　　всё-таки all the same
всегда́ always
встава́ть (I) (*pf.* **встать,** I); встаю́, встаёшь, встаю́т　to get up, to rise
встать (I) (*pf. of* встава́ть, I); *fut.* вста́ну, вста́нешь, -ут; *imper.*
　　встань, вста́ньте to get up, to rise
встреча́ть (I); встреча́ю, -ешь, -ют　to meet
всю́ду (*adv.*) everywhere
вто́рник Tuesday
　　во вто́рник on Tuesday (see ¶ 25-1d)
второ́й, -а́я, -о́е second
входи́ть (II); вхожу́, вхо́дишь, вхо́дят　to go in, to enter
вчера́ yesterday
вы you (*pl. & polite sing.*)

Г

газе́та newspaper
гара́ж (*gen.* **гаража́**) garage
где where
геоме́трия geometry
гид guide
гла́вный, -ая, -ое main, chief
глаз (*gen.* **гла́за,** *pl.* **глаза́,** *gen. pl.* **глаз**) eye
глу́пый, -ая, -ое stupid
говори́ть (II); говорю́, -и́шь, -я́т　to speak, to say, to talk
　　pf. **сказа́ть** (I); *fut.* скажу́, ска́жешь, -ут; *imper.* скажи́, -и́те　to
　　say, to tell (once)
говоря́т one says, people say
год year
голова́ head
го́лос (*pl.* **голоса́**) voice
Го́мес Gomez
Го́пкинс Hopkins
го́род (*pl.* **города́,** see ¶ 23-3) town
господи́н Mister, gentleman
госпожа́ Mrs., Miss
гости́ница hotel
Го́фман Hoffman
грамма́тика grammar
гро́мко loudly
гру́ппа group
гуверна́нтка (*gen. pl.* **гуверна́нток**) governess
гуля́ть (I) (*pf.* **погуля́ть,** I) to walk (for pleasure), to take a walk

Д

да yes

дава́ть (I); даю́, даёшь, даю́т; *past* дава́л, -ла, -ло, -ли   to give

да́же even

дал (*past of pf.* дать) gave

далеко́ (*adv.*) far

да́льше (*adv.*) further

да́ма lady

да́ча summer house

    на да́че at a summer house

два (*m. & n.*); две (*f.*)   two

два́дцать twenty

две (*f.*) two

двена́дцать twelve

дверь (*f.*) door

де́вочка (*gen. pl.* де́вочек)   little girl

де́вушка (*gen. pl.* де́вушек)   girl

девятна́дцать nineteen

де́вять nine

де́душка (*gen. pl.* де́душек)   grandfather

де́лать (I)   to do

    pf. сде́лать (I)   to have done

день^л (*m.*) (*gen.* дня, *pl.* дни)   day

    до́брый день   good afternoon

    хоро́ший день   beautiful day

дере́вня village, country

десе́рт dessert

    на десе́рт   for dessert

де́сять ten

де́ти (*pl. of* дитя́) children

дива́н divan

дли́нный, -ая, -ое long

дневни́к (*gen.* дневника́) diary

днём in the daytime

до (*with gen.*) to, up to, until; before

до свида́ния goodbye

до́брый good, kind

    до́брый день   good afternoon

    до́брое у́тро   good morning

дово́льно (*adv.*) quite, rather

дождь (*m.*) (*pl.* дожди́) rain

    идёт дождь   it is raining

    шёл дождь   it was raining

до́ктор (*pl.* доктора́, see ¶23-3) doctor

до́лго (*adv.*) for a long time

до́лжен, должна́, -о́ obliged to, have to, must

    я до́лжен был   I had to

дом (*nom. pl.* дома́, see ¶23-3) house

до́ма (*adv.*) at home (location)

домо́й (*adv.*) home, homeward (direction) (see ¶10-6)

дорого́й, -а́я, -о́е; *pl.* -и́е dear
доска́ (*pl.* до́ски, *gen. pl.* досо́к) blackboard
друг friend
    друг дру́га each other
    друг с дру́гом with each other
друго́й, -а́я, -о́е; *pl.* други́е (*adj. & pron.*) other, another
ду́мать (**I**) (*pf.* поду́мать, **I**); ду́маю, -ешь, -ют to think
дя́дя (*m.*) (*gen. pl.* дя́дей) uncle

<h1 style="text-align:center">Е</h1>

Евро́па Europe
европе́йский, -ая, -ое European
его́ his, him
    его́ ещё нет he is not here yet (see ¶16-3)
её her
е́здить (**II**) *hab.*; е́зжу, е́здишь, -ят to go (by conveyance) (see ¶13-3)
    е́здить верхо́м ⎫
    е́здить верхо́м на ло́шади ⎬ to ride horseback
    е́здить на ло́шади ⎭
    е́здить на автомоби́ле to go by automobile
    е́здить на трамва́е to go by streetcar
ей (*dat. of* она́) to her
е́сли if (*never means* whether)
есть there is
есть (*irr.*); ем, ешь, ест, еди́м, еди́те, едя́т to eat (see ¶15-2)
е́хать (**I**) *act.*; е́ду, е́дешь, -ут to go (by conveyance) (see ¶11-4 & 13-3)
    pf. пое́хать (**I**) to go, to set out (by conveyance)
ещё more, still
    что ещё? what else?

<h1 style="text-align:center">Ж</h1>

жаль it is a pity
    о́чень жаль it is a great pity, it is too bad
    как жаль! what a pity!
ждать (**I**); жду, ждёшь, ждут; *past* ждал, -ла́, -ло, -ли to wait (see ¶16-4)
же then, but (*emphatic*), however
    что же what then
жена́ (*pl.* жёны) wife
же́нщина woman
жизнь (*f.*) life
жить (**I**); живу́, живёшь, -у́т; *past* жил, жила́, жи́ло, -ли to live
журна́л magazine

<h1 style="text-align:center">З</h1>

за (*with acc.*) for
забыва́ть (**I**) (*pf.* забы́ть, **I**); забыва́ю, -ешь, -ют to forget

забы́ть (I) (*pf. of* **забыва́ть**, I); *fut.* забу́ду, -ешь, -ут; *imper.* забу́дь, забу́дьте   to forget

заво́д   plant (industrial)

за́втра   tomorrow

   за́втра у́тром   tomorrow morning

за́втрак   breakfast

за́втракать (I) (*pf.* **поза́втракать**, I); за́втракаю, -ешь, -ют   to have breakfast, to have lunch (noon)

заговори́ть (II) (*pf. of* **говори́ть**, II); *fut.* заговорю́, -и́шь, -я́т; *imper.* заговори́, -и́те   to begin to talk

закрича́ть (II) (*pf. of* **крича́ть**, II); *fut.* закричу́, -и́шь, -а́т; *imper.* закричи́, -и́те   to begin shouting

замеча́тельный, -ая, -ое   remarkable

занима́ться (I) *intrans.*; занима́юсь, -ешься, -ются   to study, to busy oneself with

заня́тия (*n. pl.*)   studies

запе́ть (I) (*pf. of* **петь**, I); *fut.* запою́, -ёшь, -ю́т; *imper.* запо́й, запо́йте   to begin singing

запла́кать (I) (*pf. of* **пла́кать**, I); *fut.* запла́чу, -ешь, -ут; *imper.* запла́чь, запла́чьте   to burst out crying, to begin weeping

засмея́ться (I) (*pf. of* **смея́ться**, I); *fut.* засмею́сь, -ёшься, -ю́тся; *imper.* засме́йся, засме́йтесь   to burst into laughter

зате́м   after that, then

заче́м   why, wherefore

зда́ние   building

здесь   here

здоро́в (*m.*)   well (*adj.*)

здоро́ва (*f.*)   well (*adj.*)

здра́вствуйте   how do you do? hello

зимо́й (*adv.*)   in the winter

знако́миться (II) (*pf.* **познако́миться**, II); знако́млюсь, знако́мишься, -ятся; *imper.* знако́мься, знако́мьтесь   to become acquainted

знать (I)   to know

зна́чит   (that) means

И

и   and, even

и . . . и . . .   both . . . and . . .

Ива́н   Ivan

Ивано́ва   Ivanova

Ива́нович   Ivanovich (see ¶ 15-1)

игра́ть (I)   to play

   pf. **поигра́ть** (I)   to play awhile

   игра́ть в те́ннис   to play tennis (see ¶ 16-2)

   игра́ть на роя́ле   to play the piano (see ¶ 16-2)

идти́ (I); *act.* иду́, идёшь, -у́т; *past* шёл, шла, шло, шли   to go, to walk (see ¶ 10-7)

   идём   let's go

из (*with gen.*)   from, out of

изуча́ть (I)   to study (see ¶ 10-1)

и́ли   or

инженéр engineer
иногдá sometimes
инострáнный, -ая, -ое   foreign
интервью́ (*n.*; *not decl.*; *pr.* интэрвью́) interview
интерéсно it is interesting
интерéсный, -ая, -ое   interesting; attractive (of a person)
интересовáть (I); интересу́ю, -ешь, -ют   to interest
Ири́на Irene
испáнец^{fl} (*pl.* испáнцы) Spaniard
испáнский, -ая, -ое; *pl.* -ие Spanish
истóрия history
итáк well then

К

к (*with dat.*)   to, towards (see ¶ 15-5)
Кавкáз Caucasus
кáждый, -ая, -ое   every, each
как   how
    как вы поживáете?   how are you?
    как дóлго?   how long?
какóй, -áя, -óе; *pl.* -и́е   what a, what kind of
Калифóрния California
карандáш pencil
кáрта map
карти́на picture
Кáтя (*f.*) Katya
кинó (*n.*;*not decl.*)   movies, movie theater
класс class
класть (I); кладу́, -ёшь, -у́т   to put
кли́мат climate
кни́га book
когдá when
кóмната room
компóт stewed fruit
конéц^{fl} (*pl.* концы́)   end
конéчно (*pr.* конéшно)   of course, certainly
Кóни-Áйленд Coney Island
контóра office
кончáть (I); кончáю, -ешь, -ют   to finish
кончáться (I) (*intrans., used mostly in the third person*); кончáется, кон-
    чáются   to end, to come to an end
корóва cow
корóткий, -ая, -ое; *pl.* -ие   short
котлéты (*pl. of* котлéта)   cutlets, Russian meat balls
котóрый, -ая, -ое (*rel. & interr. pron.*)   which, who (see ¶ 18-2)
кóфе (*m.*; *not decl.*) coffee
кóшка (*gen. pl.* кóшек) cat
красáвица beauty, a beautiful woman
краси́вый, -ая, -ое   pretty
крéсло (*gen. pl.* крéсел) armchair

крича́ть (II) (*pf.* закрича́ть, II); кричу́, -и́шь, -а́т   to shout, to scream
Крым   Crimea
   в Крыму́   in the Crimea
кто   who (see ¶ 12-2)
   кто э́то?   who is this?
   кто у телефо́на?   who is on the phone?
куда́   where to, whither
культу́рный, -ая, -ое   cultured
купа́ться (I) (*pr.* купа́ца); купа́юсь, -ешься (*pr.* купа́ешьса), купа́ют-
   ся (*pr.* купа́юца)   to bathe (oneself)   (see ¶ 16-6)
купи́л   bought
ку́шать (I); ку́шаю, -ешь, -ют   to eat (see ¶ 15-6)

Л

ла́мпа   lamp
лежа́ть (II) (*pf.* полежа́ть, II); лежу́, -и́шь, -а́т   to lie, to lie awhile
лёгкий, -ая, -ое; *pl.* -не (*pr.* лёхкий)   easy
лес (*pl.* леса́, see ¶ 23-3)   forest
   в лесу́ (*prep. with* в)   in the forest (see ¶ 20-6)
ле́том (*adv.*)   in the summer
литерату́ра   literature
лицо́ (*pl.* ли́ца)   face
Ло́ндон   London
Лос-А́нжелос   Los Angeles
ло́шадь (*f.*)   horse
лу́чше (*adv.*; *comp. of* хорошо́)   better
   мне лу́чше   I feel better
люби́ть (II); люблю́, лю́бишь, -ят   to love, to like
   pf. полюби́ть (II)   to fall in love, to become very fond of
   не люби́ть   to dislike
лю́ди (*nom. pl. of* челове́к)   people, men and women

М

магази́н   store
Макси́м   Maxim
ма́ленький, -ая, -ое; *pl.* -не (*adj.*)   small, little
ма́ло (*adv.*)   little (not much)
ма́льчик   boy
ма́ма   mama
ма́сло   butter
матема́тика (*sing. in Russian*)   mathematics
мать   mother
Ма́ша   Masha, Mary
ме́дленно (*adv.*)   slowly
мел   chalk
ми́ло   it is nice
ми́лый, -ая, -ое   nice, dear, lovely
   он тако́й ми́лый   he is such a dear
мину́та   minute

мир peace
Ми́ша (*m.*) Misha
мла́дший, -ая, -ее; *pl.* **-ие** younger, junior
мне (*dat. of* **я**) to me
мно́го (*adv.*) much
мо́жет быть perhaps
    не мо́жет быть (it is) impossible
мо́жно it is possible, one may (see **¶ 16-1b**)
мой, моя́, моё; *pl.* **мои́** (*adj. & pron.*) my, mine
молодо́й, -а́я, -о́е young
молоко́ milk
мо́ре (*n.*) (*pl.* **моря́**) sea
Москва́ Moscow
мочь (**I**); **могу́, мо́жешь, мо́гут;** *past* **мог, могла́, могло́, могли́;** (*no fut. & no imper.*) to be able to, to be in a position to (see **¶ 9-6 & 19-3**)
муж husband
мужчи́на (*m.*) man
музе́й (*m.*) museum
му́зыка music
мы we

Н

на (*with acc.*) to (direction); (*with prep.*) on, at (location); (see **¶ 25-1b**)
наве́рно surely, most likely
На́дя (*f.*) Nadya
наконе́ц at last
на́ми *instr. of* **мы**
наприме́р for instance
    как наприме́р as for instance
написа́ть (**I**) (*pf. of* **писа́ть,** **I**); *fut.* **напишу́, напи́шешь, -ут;** *imper.*
    напиши́, -йте to have written
нарисова́ть (**I**) (*pf. of* **рисова́ть,** **I**); *fut.* **нарису́ю, -ешь, -ют;** *imper.*
    нарису́й, -йте to have drawn
нас *gen. & acc. of* **мы**
    нас бы́ло семна́дцать there were seventeen of us
нахо́дится is situated
начина́ть (**I**); **начина́ю, -ешь, -ют** to begin
наш, -а, -е; *pl.* **на́ши** (*adj. & pron.*) our, ours
не not
не́бо sky
неда́вно recently
недалеко́ not far
неде́ля (*f.*) week
    це́лую неде́лю a whole week (see **¶ 15-3 & 15-4**)
некраси́вый, -ая, -ое unattractive, ugly
нельзя́ (it is) impossible, one may not (see **¶ 16-1**)
не́мец[1] (*pl.* **не́мцы**) German (*noun*)
неме́цкий, -ая, -ое; *pl.* **-ие** German (*adj.*)
немно́го a little
непра́вда untruth, falsehood

не́сколько (*indef. numeral with gen. pl.*)   several, a few
нет   no
ни...ни...   neither ... nor ...
нигде́   nowhere
никогда́   never
Никола́ев   Nikolaev
Никола́евна   Nikolaevna (see ¶15-1)
Никола́й   Nicholas
никто́ (*pron.*)   nobody, no one
ничего́   nothing
но   but
но́вый, -ая, -ое   new
Но́вый Орлеа́н   New Orleans
ночь (*f.*)   night (see ¶27-2)
  но́чью   at night
нра́виться (II); **нра́влюсь, нра́вишься, нра́вятся**   to like, to please (see
      ¶13-5, 14-4, & 18-1)
ну   well
ну́жен, нужна́, -о   necessary (see ¶13-6)
  ну́жно бы́ло   it was necessary (see ¶16-5)
Нью-Йо́рк   New York

О

о   oh!; about
обе́д   dinner
обе́дать (I); **обе́даю, -ешь, -ют**   to dine, to have dinner
  pf. **пообе́дать** (I)   to have dined
объясни́ть (II) (*pf. of* объясня́ть, I); *fut.* **объясню́, -и́шь, -я́т** to explain
      (see ¶10-B)
объясня́ть (I) (*pf.* объясни́ть, II); **объясня́ю, -ешь, -ют**   to explain (see
      ¶10-B)
обыкнове́нно   usually
одева́ться (I); **одева́юсь, -ешься, -ются**   to dress oneself
оди́н, одна́, одно́   one
оди́ннадцать   eleven
о́зеро (*pl.* озёра)   lake
  на о́зере   at the lake
окно́ (*pl.* о́кна, *gen. pl.* о́кон)   window
о́коло (*with gen.*)   near
Оле́г   Oleg
О́льга   Olga
он   he
она́   she
они́   they
оно́   it
опя́ть   again
Орло́в   Orlov
о́сенью (*adv.*)   in the fall
от (*with gen.*)   from
отве́т   answer
  что э́то за отве́т?   what kind of an answer is that?

отвечать (I); отвечаю, -ешь, -ют   to answer
отдохнуть (I) (*pf. of* отдыхать, I); *fut.* отдохну, отдохнёшь, -ут; *imper.*
    отдохни, -йте   to rest
отдыхать (I) (*pf.* отдохнуть, I)   to rest
отец*fl* (*gen.* отца)   father (see **¶9-5**)
очень   very

П

Павел*fl* (*gen.* Павла)   Paul
Павлович   Pavlovich
Павловна   Pavlovna
папа (*m.*)   papa
пароход   steamer
Париж   Paris
парк   park
первый, -ая, -ое   first
    в первый раз   for the first time
перо   pen
песня   song
Пётр*fl* (*gen.* Петра)   Peter
Петров   Petrov
петь (I); пою, поёшь, поют; *imper.* пой, пойте   to sing
    pf. запеть (I)   to begin to sing
Петя (*m.*)   Petya
пешком (*adv.*)   on foot
    ходить пешком   to go on foot
писать (I) (*pf.* написать, I); пишу, пишешь, -ут   to write
письмо (*pl.* письма, *gen. pl.* писем)   letter
пить (I); пью, пьёшь, пьют; *past* пил, -ла, -ло, -ли; *imper.* пей, пейте
    to drink
плавать (I) *hab.*   to swim
плакать (I); плачу, -ешь, -ут; *imper.* плачь, плачьте   to weep
    pf. заплакать (I)   to burst out crying
плохо (*adv.*)   poorly, badly
плохой, -ая, -ое; *pl.* -ие   bad, poor
по (*with dat.*)   on, in
по-английски (*adv.*)   English, in English
побеседовать (I) (*pf. of* беседовать, I); *fut.* побеседую, -ешь, -ют;
    imper. побеседуй, -йте   to have a talk
поговорить (II) (*pf. of* говорить, II)   to have a chat
погода   weather
погулять (I) (*pf. of* гулять, I)   to walk awhile
подумать (I) (*pf. of* думать, I)   to think awhile
поезд (*pl.* поезда)   train
    ехать поездом   to go by train
поездка (*gen. pl.* поездок)   trip
поехать (I) (*pf. of* ехать, I)   to go, to set out (by conveyance)
пожалуйста   please
поживать (I); поживаю, -ешь, -ют   to get on
    как вы поживаете?   how are you?
позавтракать (I) (*pf. of* завтракать, I)   to have had breakfast

по́здно (*adv.*) late

познако́миться (**II**) (*pf. of* знако́миться, **II**); *fut.* познако́м
-ишься, -ятся; *imper.* познако́мься, познако́мьтесь to b
acquainted

поигра́ть (**I**) (*pf. of* игра́ть, **I**) to play awhile

по-испа́нски (*adv.*) Spanish, in Spanish

пока́ for the time being

пока́ ещё as yet, still

показа́ть (**I**) (*pf. of* пока́зывать, **I**); *fut.* покажу́, пока́жешь, -ут;
imper. покажи́, -йте to show

пока́зывать (**I**) (*pf.* показа́ть, **I**); пока́зываю, -ешь, -ют to show

пол (*pl.* полы́) floor

на полу́ (*prep. with* на) on the floor

полежа́ть (**II**) (*pf. of* лежа́ть, **II**) to lie awhile

полюби́ть (**II**) (*pf. of* люби́ть, **II**); *fut.* полюблю́, полю́бишь, -ят; *imper.*
полюби́, -йте to fall in love, to become fond of

по́мнить (**II**); по́мню, -ишь, -ят to remember

понеде́льник Monday

в понеде́льник on Monday

по-неме́цки (*adv.*) German, in German

понима́ть (**I**); понима́ю, -ешь, -ют to understand

пообе́дать (**I**) (*pf. of* обе́дать, **I**) to have dined

порабо́тать (**I**) (*pf. of* рабо́тать, **I**) to work awhile

портре́т portrait

по-ру́сски (*adv.*) Russian, in Russian

посиде́ть (**II**) (*pf. of* сиде́ть, **II**); *fut.* посижу́, посиди́шь, -ят; *imper.*
посиди́, -йте to sit awhile

по́сле (*with gen.*) after

после́дний, -яя, -ее last, final

послу́шать (**I**) (*pf. of* слу́шать, **I**) to listen awhile

поспа́ть (**II**) (*pf. of* спать, **II**); *fut.* посплю́, поспи́шь, -ят; *imper.* поспи́,
-йте to sleep a little, to take a nap

постоя́ть (**II**) (*pf. of* стоя́ть, **II**) to stand awhile

потоло́кᶠˡ (*gen.* потолка́, *pl.* потолки́) ceiling

пото́м then, afterwards

потому́ что because

поу́жинать (**I**) (*pf. of* у́жинать, **I**) to have had supper

по-францу́зски (*adv.*) French, in French

почему́ why

по́чта post office

почти́ almost

поэ́тому therefore

пра́вда truth

э́то не пра́вда this is not true

предме́т subject (of study)

предпочита́ть (**I**); предпочита́ю, -ешь, -ют to prefer

прекра́сно very well, excellently

прекра́сный, -ая, -ое excellent

преподава́тель (*m.*) teacher

преподава́ть (**I**); преподаю́, -ёшь, -ю́т; *imper.* преподава́й, -йте to
teach

приготовля́ть (**I**); приготовля́ю, -ешь, -ют to prepare

ал (*past of pf.* **приéхать**)   arrived

кный, -ая, -ое   diligent

но (*adv.*)   it is pleasant

ный, -ая, -ое   pleasant

сти́ (I) (*pf. of* **проводи́ть**, II); *fut.* **проведу́, -ёшь, -у́т**; *past* **провёл, провела́, -ло́, -ли́**   to spend (time)

проводи́ть (II) (*pf.* **провести́**, I); **провожу́, прово́дишь, -ят**   to spend (time)

продолжа́ть (I); **продолжа́ю, -ешь, -ют**   to continue

произноше́ние   pronunciation

éссор (*pl.* **профессора́**, see ¶ 23-3)   professor

чта́ть (I) (*pf. of* **чита́ть**, I)   to have read

а   bird

го́й, -а́я, -о́е   empty, desolate

пя́тница   Friday

в пя́тницу   on Friday

пятна́дцать   fifteen

пять   five

Р

рабо́та   work

рабо́тать (I) (*pf.* **порабо́тать**, I); **рабо́таю, -ешь, -ют**   to work

рад, -а, -о; *pl.* **ра́ды**   glad

ра́дио (*not decl.*)   radio

раз   time (occasion)

в пе́рвый раз   for the first time

ещё раз   once again

оди́н раз   once

разгова́ривать (I); **разгова́риваю, -ешь, -ют**   to converse

разгово́р   conversation

ра́зный, -ая, -ое   various

ра́но (*adv.*)   early

рассказа́ть (I) (*pf. of* **расска́зывать**, I); *fut.* **расскажу́, расска́жешь, -ут**; *imper.* **расскажи́, -йте**   to relate, to tell

ре́дко (*adv.*)   seldom, rarely

репортёр   reporter

рестора́н   restaurant

рисова́ть (I) (*pf.* **нарисова́ть**, I); **рису́ю, -ешь, -ют**   to draw

роди́тели (*m., pl.*)   parents (father and mother)

Рокфе́ллеровский центр   Rockefeller Center

рома́н   novel

роя́ль (*m.*)   piano

игра́ть на роя́ле   to play the piano (see ¶ 16-2)

ру́сский (*noun & adj.*)   Russian

ру́сский язы́к   Russian (language) (see ¶ 10-2)

ры́ба   fish

С

с (*with instr.*)   with; (*with gen.*)   from (see ¶ 25-1b)

сад   garden

в саду́ (*prep. with* в)   in the garden (see ¶ 20-6)

сала́т   salad

самова́р samovar
са́мый, -ая, -ое (*used with adj. to form superlative*)   the most
Сан-Франци́ско (*not decl.*)   San Francisco
са́ндвич sandwich
са́хар sugar
светло́ (*adv.*) it is bright
сде́лать (**I**) (*pf. of* **де́лать, I**)   to have done
себя́ (*reflex. pron.*) self, oneself (see ¶ 19-1)
   у себя́ at one's (own) . . .
сего́дня (*pr.* **сево́дня**) today
   сего́дня ве́чером tonight, this evening
сейча́с now, presently
   сейча́с же immediately, at once
секре́т secret
семна́дцать seventeen
семь seven
семья́ family (see ¶ 10-В)
серьёзно seriously
серьёзный, -ая, -ое serious
се́рый, -ая, -ое gray
сестра́ sister
сиде́ть (**II**) (*pf.* **посиде́ть, II**); **сижу́, сиди́шь, сидя́т**   to sit
   сиде́ть до́ма to stay home
си́него цве́та (of) blue (color)
си́ний, -яя, -ее blue
сказа́ть (**I**) (*pf. of* **говори́ть, II**); *fut.* **скажу́, ска́жешь, -ут;** *imper.*
   скажи́, -и́те to say, to tell (once)
ско́лько (*used with gen. pl. of objects that can be counted*) how much, how
   many
ско́ро soon
ску́чно (**мне ску́чно**) I am bored (see ¶ 16-1)
сла́ва Бо́гу! thank goodness!
сли́шком (*adv.*) too (much)
слова́рь (*m.*) (*gen.,* **словаря́,** *pl.* **словари́**) dictionary
сло́во (*pl.* **слова́**) word
слу́шать (**I**) (*pf.* **послу́шать, I**); **слу́шаю, -ешь, -ют**   to listen to
слы́шать (**II**); **слы́шу, слы́шишь, слы́шат**   to hear
смешно́ it is funny
смея́ться (**I**); **смею́сь, смеёшься, смею́тся;** *imper.* **сме́йся, сме́йтесь**
   to laugh (see ¶ 18-1)
   pf. **засмея́ться** (**I**) to burst into laughter
Смирно́в Smirnov
Смит Smith
смотре́ть (**II**); **смотрю́, смо́тришь, смо́трят**   to look
   смотре́ть на (*with acc.*) to look at
   смотре́ть телеви́зор to look at television
снача́ла (*adv.*) at first
соба́ка dog
совсе́м (*adv.*) entirely
   совсе́м не not at all, not in the least
сожале́ние regret
   к сожале́нию unfortunately

соединённый, -ая, -ое united
Соединённые Штáты United States
сочинéние (*n.*) composition
спасúбо thanks, thank you
   большóе спасúбо many thanks
спать (II) (*pf.* поспáть, II); сплю, спишь, спят; *past* спал, спалá, -ло,
   -ли to sleep
специалúст specialist
спокóйной нóчи good night
спорт sport
спортсмéн sportsman
спортсмéнка sportswoman
спрáшивать (I) to ask (questions)
средá Wednesday
   в срéду on Wednesday
средú (*with gen.*) among
срéдний, -яя, -ее middle
   срéдняя шкóла high school, secondary school
СССР U.S.S.R.
стакáн glass
Сталингрáд Stalingrad
стáрый, -ая, -ое old
стать (I) (*pf. of* становúться); *fut.* стáну, -ешь, -ут; *past* стал, -ла, -ло,
   -ли; *imper.* стань, стáньте to become
стенá (*pl.* стéны) wall
стол (*gen.* столá, *pl.* столы́) table
столóвая (*noun, f.*; see ¶20-9) dining room
стоя́ть (*pf.* постоя́ть, II); стою́, -úшь, -я́т; *imper.* стой, -йте to stand
странá (*pl.* стрáны) country
стрáнный, -ая, -ое strange, odd
студéнт student (*m.*)
студéнтка (*gen. pl.* студéнток) student (*f.*)
студéнческий, -ая, -ое; *pl.* -ие student (*adj.*)
стул chair
суббóта Saturday
   в суббóту on Saturday
суп (*pl.* супы́, -óв) soup
счастлúвый, -ая, -ое (*pr.* щастлúвый) happy
счáстье (*pr.* щáстье) luck, happiness
   к счáстью fortunately
США (*pr.* Сэ Ша А) (Соединённые Штáты Амéрики) U.S.A.
сюрпрúз surprise

Т

так (*adv.*) so
тáкже also, in addition, likewise
такóй, -áя, -óе; *pl.* -úе such a
там there
танцовáть (I); танцýю, -ешь, -ют to dance
Тáня (*f.*) Tanya
твой, твоя́, твоё; *pl.* твои́ (*adj. & pron.*) your, yours (*fam. sing.*)
теáтр theater

телеви́зор television set

    смотре́ть телеви́зор to look at television

телефо́н telephone

    кто у телефо́на ? who is on the phone?

темно́ it is dark (see ¶16-1)

тепе́рь now

те́ннис tennis

    игра́ть в те́ннис to play tennis (see ¶16-2)

тепло́ it is warm (see ¶16-1)

тетра́дь (*f.*) notebook

тётя (*gen. pl.* **тётей**) aunt

ти́хо (*adv.*) quiet, quietly

това́рищ (*instr.* **това́рищем**, see ¶25-3b) comrade, friend

тогда́ then, at that time (see ¶21-5)

то́же also

то́лько only

    то́лько что just now

    как то́лько as soon as

тому́ наза́д ago

траге́дия tragedy

трамва́й (*m.*) streetcar

    éхать на трамва́е to go by streetcar

три three

трина́дцать thirteen

тру́дный, -ая, -ое difficult

Ту́ла Tula (*an industrial town*)

тури́ст tourist

тури́стка (*gen. pl.* **тури́сток**) tourist (*f.*)

тут here

ты you (*fam. sing.*)

У

у (*with gen.*) by, at

    у меня́ нет I do not have (see ¶13-1)

    у себя́ at one's (own) . . .

Уа́йт White (*surname*)

уви́деть (**II**) (*pf. of* **ви́деть, II**); *fut.* **уви́жу, уви́дишь, -ят**; (*no imper.*) to notice

уе́хать (**I**) (*pf. of* **éхать, I**) to leave, to depart

    уе́хать в to leave for, to depart for

уже́ already

у́жин supper

у́жинать (**I**) (*pf.* **поу́жинать, I**); **у́жинаю, -ешь, -ют** to have supper

Украи́на Ukraine

у́лица (*instr.* **у́лицей**, see ¶25-3b) street

уме́ть (**I**); **уме́ю, -ешь, -ют** to know how (see ¶19-3)

у́мный, -ая, -ое clever, smart

    како́й он у́мный how clever he is

умыва́ться (**I**); **умыва́юсь, -ешься, -ются** to wash oneself

универма́г department store
университе́т university
упражне́ние exercise
Уо́лл-стрит Wall Street
ура́ hurrah
уро́к lesson
уста́л, -ла, -ло, -ли tired
у́тро morning
   до́брое у́тро good morning
у́тром in the morning
учени́к (*gen.* **ученика́**) pupil (*m.*)
учени́ца pupil (*f.*)
учи́тель (*m.*) (*pl.* **учителя́**, see ¶ 23-3) teacher
учи́тельница teacher (*f.*)
учи́ться (**II**) *intrans.*; **учу́сь, у́чишься, -атся** to study, to attend school
ушёл, ушла́, ушло́, ушли́ (*past of pf.* **уйти́**) went away (once)

Ф

фа́брика factory
фами́лия surname
   как ва́ша фами́лия? what is your last name?
Фёдор (*dim.* **Фе́дя**) Theodore
Фе́дя (*dim. of* **Фёдор**) Fedya, Teddy
фе́рма farm
   на фе́рме at the farm
Фо́стер Foster
Фра́нция France
францу́з Frenchman
францу́зский, -ая, -ое; *pl.* **-не** French

Х

хлеб bread
ходи́ть (**II**) *hab.*; **хожу́, хо́дишь, -ят** to walk (see ¶ 13-2 & 13-3)
   ходи́ть пешко́м to go on foot
хозя́йка owner, mistress, hostess, housekeeper
   хозя́йка до́ма owner of the house, hostess
хозя́ин master, owner, host
хо́лодно it is cold (see ¶ 16-1)
холо́дный, -ая, -ое cold
хоро́ший, -ая, -ее; *pl.* **-не** good
   хоро́ший день beautiful day
хорошо́ well, good, O.K., all right
хоте́ть (*irr.*); **хочу́, хо́чешь, хо́чет, хоти́м, -йте, -я́т;** *past* **хоте́л, -ла, -ло, -ли;** (*no imper.*) to want, to wish
ху́же worse
   мне ху́же I feel worse.

Ц

цвет color
целова́ть (**I**); **целу́ю, -ешь, -ют** to kiss (see ¶ 21-7)

це́лый, -ая, -ое whole (integral, complete)
    це́лую мину́ту a whole minute
    це́лую неде́лю a whole week (see ¶ 15-3 & 15-4)
Центра́льный вокза́л Grand Central Station

Ч

чай (*m.*) (*pl.* **чай**) tea
час (*pl.* **часы́**) hour
ча́сто often
ча́шка (*gen. pl.* **ча́шек**) cup
ча́ще oftener, more frequently
челове́к man, person
чем (*instr. of* **что**) with what; (*conj.*) than
че́рез (*with acc.*) in (*lit.*, after the lapse of)
Чёрное мо́ре Black Sea
чёрный, -ая, -ое black
четве́рг Thursday
    в четве́рг on Thursday
четы́ре four
    на четы́ре дня for four days
четы́рнадцать fourteen
Чика́го (*not decl.*) Chicago
чита́ть (I) (*pf.* **прочита́ть,** I); **чита́ю, -ешь, -ют** to read
что what, that (see ¶ 21-1)
    что ещё what else
    что же what then
    что с тобо́й? what's the matter with you?
    что э́то за what kind of
что́бы in order to

Ш

шестна́дцать sixteen
шесть six
шко́ла school
шокола́д chocolate
штат state

Э

экза́мен examination
экску́рсия excursion, trip
Эмпайр стейт би́лдинг Empire State Building
эне́ргия (*pr.* **энэ́ргия**) energy
э́то this is, that is
    э́то всё that is all
э́тот, э́та, э́то; *pl.* э́ти (*adj. & pron.*) this (see ¶ 14-1)

Ю

юг south
ю́ноша (*m.*) youth, young man

Я

я I
язы́к language
яйцо́ (*pl.* **я́йца**) egg
я́сный, -ая, -ое clear

ENGLISH-RUSSIAN VOCABULARY

See the *Russian–English Vocabulary* for references to rules on grammar and pronunciation; for verb forms, especially irregular ones; and for all irregularities in the declensions of nouns, adjectives, and pronouns.

The *Russian–English Vocabulary* also includes the imperfective and perfective aspects if both have been used in this book. In this case, the two aspects are always given together. Therefore, if only the imperfective aspect is known, consult the *Russian–English Vocabulary* to find the perfective, and vice versa.

A

able, to be **мочь (I)**
aches (*v.*) **болит**
    his head aches **у него болит голова**
acquainted, to become **знакомиться (II)**; *pf.* **познакомиться (II)**
addition, in . . . **также**
after **после** (*with gen.*)
after that **затем**
afterwards **потом**
again **опять**
    once again **ещё раз**
ago **тому назад**
algebra **áлгебра**
all **все**
    all this **всё это**
    that is all **это всё**
all right **хорошо**
all the same **всё-таки**
almost **почти**
already **ужé**
also **также, тоже**
always **всегда**
America **Амéрика**
American (*noun, m.*) **Американец**[fl]; (*adj.*) **американский, -ая, -ое;**
    pl. **-ие**
among **среди** (*with gen.*)
and **и, а**
Anne **Áнна**
another **другой, -áя, -óе;** *pl.* **-ие** (*adj. & pron.*)
answer (*noun*) **ответ**
answer, to **отвечать (I)**

311

appetite аппетит
arithmetic арифме́тика
armchair кре́сло
around вокру́г (*with gen.*)
arrived прие́хал
ask (questions), to спра́шивать (**I**)
astride (a horse) верхо́м (*adv.*)
at у (*with gen.*)
at last наконе́ц
attentively внима́тельно
attractive (of a person) интере́сный, -ая, -ое
aunt тётя
automobile автомоби́ль (*m.*)

B

bad (*adj.*) плохо́й
    it is too bad о́чень жаль
badly (*adv.*) пло́хо
baseball бейзбо́л
Basil Ва́ся
basketball баскетбо́л
bathe (oneself), to купа́ться (**I**)
be, to быть (*irr.*)
    will be бу́дет (see ¶ 11-2)
beautiful day хоро́ший день
beautiful girl краса́вица
beauty (person) краса́вица
because потому́ что
become, to стать (**I**) *pf.*
beet soup борщ
before до (*with gen.*)
begin, to начина́ть (**I**)
better (*adv.*) лу́чше
    I feel better мне лу́чше
big большо́й, -а́я, -о́е; *pl.* -и́е
bird пти́ца
black чёрный, -ая, -ое
Black Sea Чёрное мо́ре
blackboard доска́
blue си́ний, -яя, -ее
    (of) blue (color) си́него цве́та
book кни́га
Boris Бори́с
borshch борщ
both . . . and . . . и . . . и . . .
bought купи́л
boy ма́льчик
bread хлеб
breakfast (*noun*) за́втрак
    to have breakfast за́втракать (**I**); *pf.* поза́втракать (**I**)

bright, it is **светло́**
brother **брат**
Brown **Бра́ун** (*surname*)
building **зда́ние**
but **а, но**
butter **ма́сло**
by **у** (*with gen.*)

C

California **Калифо́рния**
carefully **внима́тельно**
cat **ко́шка**
Caucasus **Кавка́з**
ceiling **потоло́к**
certainly **коне́чно**
chair **стул**
chalk **мел**
chat, to have a **поговори́ть** (II) *pf.*; **побесе́довать** (I) *pf.*
cheerful **весёлый, -ая, -ое**
    it is cheerful **ве́село**
cheerfully **ве́село**
Chicago **Чика́го** (*not decl.*)
chief (*adj.*) **гла́вный, -ая, -ое**
children **де́ти**
chocolate **шокола́д**
city **го́род**
class **класс**
clear **я́сный, -ая, -ое**
clever **у́мный, -ая, -ое**
    how clever he is **како́й он у́мный**
climate **кли́мат**
coffee **ко́фе** (*m.; not decl.*)
cold **холо́дный, -ая, -ое**
    it is cold **хо́лодно** (see ¶ **16-1**)
color **цвет**
composition **сочине́ние** (*n.*)
comrade **това́рищ**
Coney Island **Ко́ни-А́йленд**
continue, to **продолжа́ть** (I)
converse, to **разгова́ривать** (I)
country **дере́вня, страна́** (*land*)
course, of . . . **коне́чно**
cow **коро́ва**
Crimea **Крым**
    in the Crimea **в Крыму́**
cry, to **пла́кать** (I)
    to begin to cry **запла́кать** (I) *pf.*
cultured **культу́рный, -ая, -ое**
cutlets **котле́ты**

D

dance, to **танцова́ть (I)**
dark, it is **темно́** (see **¶ 16-1**)
day **день** *f*
 beautiful day **хоро́ший день**
 good day **до́брый день**
daytime, in the . . . **днём**
dear **ми́лый, -ая, -ое; дорого́й, -а́я, -о́е;** *pl.* **-и́е**
depart for, to **уе́хать (I)** *pf.* **+ в**
department store **универма́г**
deserted **пусто́й, -а́я, -о́е**
dessert **десе́рт**
 for dessert **на десе́рт**
diary **дневни́к**
dictionary **слова́рь**
difficult **тру́дный, -ая, -ое**
diligent **приле́жный, -ая, -ое**
dine, to **обе́дать (I)**
 to have dined **пообе́дать (I)** *pf.*
dining room **столо́вая** (see **¶ 20-9**)
dinner **обе́д**
 to have dinner **обе́дать (I)**
 to have had dinner **пообе́дать (I)** *pf.*
dislike **не люби́ть**
divan **дива́н**
do, to **де́лать (I)**
 to have done **сде́лать (I)** *pf.*
doctor **до́ктор**
dog **соба́ка**
door **дверь** (*f.*)
draw **рисова́ть (I)**
 to have drawn **нарисова́ть (I)** *pf.*
dress oneself, to **одева́ться (I)**
drink, to **пить (I)**

E

each **ка́ждый, -ая, -ое**
 each other **друг дру́га**
 with each other **друг с дру́гом**
early (*adv.*) **ра́но**
easy **лёгкий, -ая, -ое;** *pl.* **-ие**
eat **есть** (*irr.*) (see **¶ 15-2**); **ку́шать (I)** (see **¶ 15-6**)
egg **яйцо́** (*pl.* **я́йца**)
eight **во́семь**
eighteen **восемна́дцать**
eleven **оди́ннадцать**
Empire State Building **Э́мпайр стейт би́лдинг**
empty **пусто́й, -а́я, -о́е**
end (*noun*) **коне́ц** *f*
end, to **конча́ться (I)**

energy **энéргия**
engineer **инженéр**
England **Áнглия**
English **англи́йский, -ая, -ое;** *pl.* **-ие**
    in English **по-англи́йски**
Englishman **англичáнин**
enter, to **входи́ть (II)**
entire **весь, вся, всё**
entirely **совсéм**
Europe **Еврóпа**
European **европéйский, -ая, -ое;** *pl.* **-ие**
even **дáже**
evening **вéчер** (*pl.* **вечерá**)
    good evening **дóбрый вéчер**
    in the evening **вéчером**
every **кáждый, -ая, -ое**
everybody **все**
everywhere **всю́ду** (*adv.*)
examination **экзáмен**
excellent **прекрáсный, -ая, -ое**
excellently **прекрáсно**
exclaim, to **закричáть (II)** *pf.*
excursion **экскýрсия**
exercise **упражнéние**
explain, to **объясня́ть (I);** *pf.* **объясни́ть (II)**
eye **глаз** (*gen.* **глáза,** *pl.* **глазá,** *gen. pl.* **глаз**)

F

face **лицó** (*pl.* **ли́ца**)
factory **фáбрика**
fall, in the . . . **óсенью** (*adv.*)
family **семья́**
far (*adv.*) **далекó**
    not far **недалекó**
farm **фéрма**
    at the farm **на фéрме**
fast (*adv.*) **бы́стро**
father **отéц**ᶠˡ (*gen.* **отцá**) (see **¶9-5**)
Fedya **Фéдя** (*dim. of* **Фёдор**) Teddy
feel, to
    I feel better **мне лýчше**
    I feel worse **мне хýже**
few, a **нéсколько**
fifteen **пятнáдцать**
final **послéдний, -яя, -ее**
finish, to **кончáть (I)**
first **пéрвый, -ая, -ое**
    at first **сначáла** (*adv.*)
    for the first time **в пéрвый раз**
fish **ры́ба**

five **пять**
floor **пол**
fond, to become . . . of **полюбить (II)** *pf.*
foot, on . . . **пешком**
    to go on foot **ходить пешком**
for **за** (*with acc.*); **для** (*with gen.*)
foreign **иностранный, -ая, -ое**
forest **лес** (*pl.* **леса**)
forget, to **забывать (I); забыть (II)** *pf.*
fortunately **к счастью**
Foster **Фостер** (*surname*)
four **четыре**
fourteen **четырнадцать**
France **Франция**
French (*adj.*) **французский, -ая, -ое; *pl.* -ие**
    in French **по-французски**
Frenchman **француз**
frequently **часто**
    more frequently **чаще**
Friday **пятница**
    on Friday **в пятницу**
friend **друг, товарищ**
from **от** (*with gen.*); **из** (*with gen.*); **с** (*with gen.*); (see ¶ **25-1**)
fruit, stewed . . . **компот**
funny, it is . . . **смешно**
further **дальше** (*adv.*)

G

gaily **весело**
garage **гараж**
garden **сад**
gay **весёлый, -ая, -ое**
    it is gay **весело**
gentleman **господин**
geometry **геометрия**
German (*noun*) **немец**ᵃ; (*adj.*) **немецкий, -ая, -ое; *pl.* -ие**
    in German **по-немецки** (*adv.*)
get on, to **поживать (I)**
get up, to **вставать (I); встать (I)** *pf.*
girl **девушка**
    little girl **девочка**
give, to **давать (I)**
glad **рад, -а, -о; *pl.* -ы**
glass **стакан**
go (by conveyance), to **ездить (II)** *hab.*; **ехать (I)** *act.*; (see ¶ **13-3**)
go (on foot), to **ходить (II)** *hab.*; **идти (II)** *act.*; (see ¶ **13-2 & 13-3**)
go (set out), to **поехать (I)** *pf.*
go in, to **входить (II)**
Gomez **Гомес**
good (*adj.*) **хороший, -ая, -ее; *pl.* -ие**; (*adv.*) **хорошо**

good afternoon **добрый день**
good morning **доброе утро**
good night **спокойной ночи**
goodbye **до свидания**
governess **гувернантка**
grammar **грамматика**
Grand Central Station **Центральный вокзал**
grandfather **дедушка**
grandmother **бабушка**
gray **серый, -ая, -ое**
group **группа**
guide **гид**

H

happy **счастливый, -ая, -ое**
hate to, to **очень не хотеть**
have to, to **должен, должна, -о**
he **он**
head **голова** (*pl.* **головы**)
headache *see* aches
healthy **здоров** (*m.*), **здорова** (*f.*)
hear, to **слышать** (**II**)
hello **здравствуйте, алло**
her **её**
here **тут, здесь**
here is, here are **вот**
high school **средняя школа**
his **его**
history **история**
Hoffmann **Гофман**
home (homewards) **домой** (see ¶ 10-6)
    at home **дома**
    to stay home **сидеть дома**
Hopkins **Гопкинс**
horse **лошадь** (*f.*)
horseback, to ride ... **ездить верхом, ездить на лошади, ездить верхом на лошади**
host **хозяин**
hostess **хозяйка**
hotel **гостиница**
hour **час**
house **дом** (*pl.* **дома**)
    summer house **дача**
housekeeper **хозяйка**
how **как**
    how are you? **как вы поживаете?**
    how do you do! **здравствуйте!**
    how long? **как долго?**
however **же**
hurrah **ура**
husband **муж**

I

I   **я**
if   **éсли**
immediately   **сейчác же**
impossible, it is . . .   **не мóжет быть; нельзя́** (see ¶ 16-1b)
in   **в, во** (*with prep.*); **чéрез** (*with acc.*) (*lit.*, after the lapse of); **по** (*with dat.*)
instance, for . . .   **напримéр**
    as for instance   **как напримéр**
interest, to   **интересовáть (I)**
interesting   **интерéсный, -ая, -ое**
    it is interesting   **интерéсно**
interview   **интервью́** (*n.*; *not decl.*)
into   **в** (*with acc.*)
Irene   **Ири́на**
is, there . . .   **есть**
Ivan   **Ивáн**
Ivanova   **Ивáнова**
Ivanovich   **Ивáнович**

J

Joachim   **Аки́м**
junior   **млáдший, -ая, -ее;** *pl.* **-ие**
just now   **тóлько что**

K

Katya   **Кáтя**
kind, what . . . of   **какóй, -áя, -óе;** *pl.* **-и́е**
kiss, to   **целовáть (I)** (see ¶ 21-7)
know, to   **знать (I)**
know how, to   **умéть (I)** (see ¶ 19-3)

L

lady   **дáма**
lake   **óзеро** (*pl.* **озёра**)
lamp   **лáмпа**
language   **язы́к**
last   **послéдний, -яя, -ее**
    at last   **наконéц**
late (*adv.*)   **пóздно**
laugh   **смея́ться (I)**
    to burst into laughter   **засмея́ться (I)** *pf.*
leave for, to   **уéхать (I)** *pf.* **+ в**
lesson   **урóк**
letter   **письмó** (*pl.* **пи́сьма**)
library   **библиотéка**
lie, to   **лежáть (II); полежáть (II)** *pf.*
life   **жизнь** (*f.*)
like, to   **люби́ть (II), нрáвиться (II);** (see ¶ 13-5, 14-4, & 18-1)

likely **наве́рно**
likewise **та́кже**
listen to, to **слу́шать (I)**; **послу́шать (I)** *pf.*
literature **литерату́ра**
little (*adj.*) **ма́ленький, -ая, -ое**; *pl.* **-ие**
little (*adv.*) **ма́ло**
    a little **немно́го**
live, to **жить (I)**
London **Ло́ндон**
long **дли́нный, -ая, -ое**
    for a long time **до́лго** (*adv.*)
    how long **как до́лго**
look, to **смотре́ть (II)**
    to look at **смотре́ть на** + *acc.*
    to look at television **смотре́ть телеви́зор**
Los Angeles **Лос-А́нжелос**
loudly **гро́мко**
love, to **люби́ть (II)**
    to fall in love **полюби́ть (II)** *pf.*
lovely **ми́лый, -ая, -ое**
lunch, to have . . . **за́втракать (I)**

M

magazine **журна́л**
main (*adj.*) **гла́вный, -ая, -ое**
mama **ма́ма**
man **мужчи́на** (*m.*); **челове́к** (person); *pl.* **лю́ди** (people)
many, how . . . **ско́лько**
many thanks **большо́е спаси́бо**
map **ка́рта**
Mary **Ма́ша**
Masha **Ма́ша**
master **хозя́ин**
mathematics **матема́тика** (*sing. in Russian*)
Maxim **Макси́м**
may, one . . . **мо́жно** (see ¶ 16-1b)
    one may not **нельзя́** (see ¶ 16-1b)
me, to . . . **мне** (*dat.*)
means (*v.*) **зна́чит**
meatballs (Russian) **котле́ты**
meet, to **встреча́ть (I)**
middle (*adj.*) **сре́дний, -яя, -ее**
milk **молоко́**
minute **мину́та**
Miss **госпожа́**
Misha **Ми́ша** (*m.*)
Mister **господи́н**
mistress **хозя́йка**
Mrs. **госпожа́**

Monday **понеде́льник**
    on Monday **в понеде́льник**
more **ещё, бо́льше**
morning **у́тро**
    good morning **до́брое у́тро**
    in the morning **у́тром**
Moscow **Москва́**
most **са́мый, -ая, -ое**
mother **мать**
movies **кино́** (*not decl.*)
much **мно́го**
    how much **ско́лько**
    too much **сли́шком**
museum **музе́й** (*m.*)
music **му́зыка**
must **до́лжен, должна́, -о́**
my **мой, моя́, моё;** *pl.* **мои́**

N

Nadya **На́дя**
nap, to take a . . . **поспа́ть** (**II**) *pf.*
near **о́коло; бли́зко** (*with* **от**); (*both with gen.*)
necessary **ну́жен**
    it was necessary **ну́жно бы́ло**
need, to **ну́жен** (*with dat.*) (see ¶ **13-6**)
neither . . . nor . . . **ни . . . ни . . .**
never **никогда́**
new **но́вый, -ая, -ое**
New Orleans **Но́вый Орлеа́н**
New York **Нью-Йо́рк**
newspaper **газе́та**
nice **ми́лый, -ая, -ое**
    it is nice **ми́ло**
Nicholas **Никола́й**
night **ночь** (see ¶ **27-2**)
    at night **но́чью**
Nikolaev **Никола́ев**
Nikolaevna **Никола́евна**
nine **де́вять**
nineteen **девятна́дцать**
no **нет**
no one **никто́** (*pron.*)
nobody **никто́** (*pron.*)
not **не**
notebook **тетра́дь** (*f.*)
nothing **ничего́**
notice, to **уви́деть** (**II**) *pf.*
novel **рома́н**
now **тепе́рь, сейча́с**
    just now **то́лько что**
nowhere **нигде́**

O

obliged to **до́лжен, должна́, -о́**
occasion (time) **раз**
odd **стра́нный, -ая, -ое**
office **конто́ра**
often **ча́сто**
oftener **ча́ще**
oh **о, ах**
O.K. **хорошо́**
old **ста́рый, -ая, -ое**
Oleg **Оле́г**
Olga **О́льга**
on **на** (*with prep.*); **по** (*with dat.*)
once **оди́н раз**
    at once **сейча́с же**
    once again **ещё раз**
one **оди́н, одна́, одно́**
oneself **себя́** (*reflex. pron.*) (see ¶ 19-1)
only **то́лько**
or **и́ли**
order, in ... to **что́бы**
Orlov **Орло́в**
other **друго́й, -а́я, -о́е; -и́е**
our **наш, на́ша, на́ше;** *pl.* **на́ши** (*adj. & pron.*)
out of **из** (*with gen.*)
owner **хозя́ин** (*m.*), **хозя́йка** (*f.*)

P

papa **па́па** (*m.*)
paper **бума́га**
parents **роди́тели** (*m. pl.*)
Paris **Пари́ж**
park **парк**
Paul **Па́вел**ᶠˡ
Pavlovich **Па́влович**
Pavlovna **Па́вловна**
peace **мир**
pen **перо́**
pencil **каранда́ш**
people **лю́ди**
perhaps **мо́жет быть**
person **челове́к**
Peter **Пётр**
Petya **Пе́тя**
Petrov **Петро́в**
piano **роя́ль** (*m.*)
    to play the piano **игра́ть на роя́ле** (see ¶ 16-2)
picture **карти́на**
pity, it is a ... **жаль**
    it is a great pity **о́чень жаль**
    what a pity **как жаль**

plant (industrial) **заво́д**
play **игра́ть (I); поигра́ть (I)** *pf.*
 to play tennis **игра́ть в те́ннис** (see ⁋ 16-2)
 to play the piano **игра́ть на роя́ле** (see ⁋ 16-2)
pleasant **прия́тный, -ая, -ое**
 it is pleasant **прия́тно**
please **пожа́луйста**
 to please **нра́виться (II)**
pleasing, to be **нра́виться (II)**
poorly **пло́хо**
portrait **портре́т**
position, to be in a . . . to **мочь (I)**
possible, it is . . . **мо́жно** (see ⁋ 16-1b)
 how is this possible? **как э́то мо́жет быть?**
post office **по́чта**
prefer, to **предпочита́ть (I)**
prepare, to **приготовля́ть (I)**
presently **сейча́с**
pretty **краси́вый, -ая, -ое**
professor **профе́ссор** (*pl.* **профессора́**)
pronunciation **произноше́ние**
pupil **учени́к** (*m.*), **учени́ца** (*f.*)
put, to **класть (I)**

Q

question **вопро́с**
quiet (*adv.*) **ти́хо**
quietly **ти́хо**
quite **дово́льно**

R

radio **ра́дио** (*not decl.*)
railway station **вокза́л**
rain **дождь** (*m.*)
 it is raining **идёт дождь**
 it was raining **шёл дождь**
rapidly **бы́стро**
rarely **ре́дко** (*adv.*)
rather **дово́льно**
read, to **чита́ть (I); прочита́ть (I)** *pf.*
recently **неда́вно**
regret **сожале́ние**
relate (once), to **рассказа́ть (I)** *pf.*
remarkable **замеча́тельный, -ая, -ое**
remember, to **по́мнить (II)**
reporter **репортёр**
rest, to **отдыха́ть (I); отдохну́ть (I)** *pf.*
restaurant **рестора́н**
rich **бога́тый, -ая, -ое**

ride, to **е́здить (II)** *hab.*; **е́хать (I)** *act.*
    to ride horseback **е́здить верхо́м, е́здить верхо́м на ло́шади, е́здить на ло́шади**
right, all . . . **хорошо́**
rise, to· **встава́ть (I)**; **встать (I)** *pf.*
Rockefeller Center **Рокфе́ллеровский це́нтр**
room **ко́мната**
Russian (*noun*) **ру́сский, -ая**; (*adj.*) **ру́сский, -ая, -ое**
    in Russian **по-ру́сски** (*adv.*)
    Russian language **ру́сский язы́к** (see ¶ 10-2)

S

salad **сала́т**
same, all the . . . **всё-таки**
samovar **самова́р**
San Francisco **Сан-Франци́ско** (*not decl.*)
sandwich **са́ндвич**
Saturday **суббо́та**
    on Saturday **в суббо́ту**
say, to **говори́ть (II)**; **сказа́ть (I)** *pf.*
school **шко́ла**
    high school **сре́дняя шко́ла**
scream, to **крича́ть (II)**; **закрича́ть (II)** *pf.*
sea **мо́ре**
second (*adj.*) **второ́й, -а́я, -о́е**
secret **секре́т**
see, to **ви́деть (II)**; **уви́деть (II)** *pf.*
seldom **ре́дко** (*adv.*)
self **себя́** (*reflex. pron.*) (see ¶ 19-1)
serious **серьёзный, -ая, -ое**
seriously **серьёзно**
seven **семь**
seventeen **семна́дцать**
several **не́сколько** (*adv. with gen. pl.*)
she **она́**
shore **бе́рег** (*pl.* **берега́**)
    on the shore **на берегу́**
short **коро́ткий, -ая, -ое**; *pl.* **-ие**
shout, to **крича́ть (II)**; **закрича́ть (II)** *pf.*
show, to **пока́зывать (I)**; **показа́ть (I)** *pf.*
sick **бо́лен, больна́**
sing, to **петь (I)**; **запе́ть (I)** *pf.*
sister **сестра́**
sit, to **сиде́ть (II)**; **посиде́ть (II)** *pf.*
situated, is . . . **нахо́дится**
six **шесть**
sixteen **шестна́дцать**
sky **не́бо**
sleep, to **спать (II)**; **поспа́ть (II)** *pf.*

slowly ме́дленно
small ма́ленький, -ая, -ое; *pl.* -ие
smart у́мный, -ая, -ое
Smirnov Смирно́в
Smith Смит
so (*adv.*) так
sometimes иногда́
song пе́сня
soon ско́ро
    as soon as как то́лько
soup суп
    beet soup борщ
south юг
Spaniard испа́нец *fl*
Spanish испа́нский, -ая, -ое; *pl.* -ие
    in Spanish по-испа́нски
speak, to говори́ть (**II**)
specialist специали́ст
sport спорт
sportsman спортсме́н
sportswoman спортсме́нка
spring, in the . . . весно́й (*adv.*)
Stalingrad Сталингра́д
stand, to стоя́ть (**II**); постоя́ть (**II**) *pf.*
state штат
station (railway) вокза́л
stay home, to сиде́ть до́ма
steamer парохо́д
stewed fruit компо́т
still еще́, пока́ еще́
store магази́н
strange стра́нный, -ая, -ое
street у́лица
streetcar трамва́й
    to go by streetcar е́хать на трамва́е
student (*noun*) студе́нт (*m.*), студе́нтка (*f.*); (*adj.*) студе́нческий, -ая,
    -ое; *pl.* -ие
studies заня́тия (*n. pl.*)
study, to изуча́ть (**I**) (see ¶ 10-1); занима́ться (**I**) *intrans.*; учи́ться (**II**)
    intrans.
stupid глу́пый, -ая, -ое
subject (of study) предме́т
such a тако́й, -а́я, -о́е; *pl.* -и́е
suddenly вдруг
sugar са́хар
summer, in the . . . ле́том (*adv.*)
Sunday воскресе́нье
    on Sunday в воскресе́нье
supper у́жин
    to have supper у́жинать (**I**); поу́жинать (**I**) *pf.*

surely **навéрно**
surname **фамѝлия**
  what is your surname? **как вáша фамѝлия ?**
surprise **сюрпрѝз**
swim, to **плáвать (I)** *hab.*

T

table **стол**
take, to **брать (I)**
talk, to **говорѝть (II); поговорѝть (II)** *pf.* ; **заговорѝть (II)** *pf.*; **бесéдо-
      вать (I)**
  to have a talk **побесéдовать (I)** *pf.*
Tanya **Тáня**
tea **чай** (*m.*)
teach, to **преподавáть (I)**
teacher (*m.*) **учѝтель, преподавáтель ;** (*f.*) **учѝтельница**
telephone **телефóн**
  on the telephone **у телефóна**
television set **телевѝзор**
  to look at television **смотрéть телевѝзор**
tell (once), to **сказáть (I)** *pf.*
ten **дéсять**
tennis **тéннис**
  to play tennis **игрáть в тéннис** (see ¶ 16-2)
than **чем**
thank goodness! **слáва бóгу!**
thank you **спасѝбо**
thanks **спасѝбо**
  many thanks **болшóе спасѝбо**
that (*rel. pron.*) **что** (see ¶ 21-1)
that is **э́то**
theater **теáтр**
  movie theater **кинó** (*not decl.*)
then **потóм, затéм, тогдá** (see ¶ 25-1)
Theodore **Фёдор** (*dim.* **Фéдя**)
there **там**
there is **есть**
therefore **поэ́тому**
these **э́ти**
they **онѝ**
think, to **дýмать (I); подýмать (I)** *pf.*
thirteen **тринáдцать**
this (*pron.*) **э́то;** (*adj. & pron.*) **э́тот, э́та, э́то** (see ¶ 14-1)
three **три**
Thursday **четвéрг**
  on Thursday **в четвéрг**
time **врéмя** (*n.*)

time (occasion) **раз**
    at that time **тогда́**
    for a long time **до́лго** (*adv.*)
    for the first time **в пе́рвый раз**
    for the time being **пока́**
    to spend time **проводи́ть вре́мя**
tired **уста́л, -ла, -ло, -ли**
to **на** (*with acc.*); **в** (*with acc.*); (see **¶ 25-1b**)
to (towards) **к** (*with dat.*) (see **¶ 15-5**)
to (up to, until) **до** (*with gen.*)
today **сего́дня**
together **вме́сте** (*adv.*)
tomorrow **за́втра**
    tomorrow morning **за́втра у́тром**
tonight **сего́дня ве́чером**
too (much) **сли́шком**
tourist **тури́ст** (*m.*), **тури́стка** (*f.*)
towards **к** (*with dat.*)
town **го́род** (*pl.* **города́**)
tragedy **траге́дия**
train **по́езд** (*pl.* **поезда́**)
    to go by train **е́хать по́ездом**
trip **экску́рсия, пое́здка**
true, this is not . . . **э́то не пра́вда**
truth **пра́вда**
Tuesday **вто́рник**
    on Tuesday **во вто́рник**
Tula (*industrial town*) **Ту́ла**
twelve **двена́дцать**
twenty **два́дцать**
two **два** (*m. & n.*), **две** (*f.*)

U

U.S.A. **США** (*pr.* **Сэ Ша А**)
U.S.S.R. **СССР**
ugly **некраси́вый, -ая, -ое**
Ukraine **Украи́на**
unattractive **некраси́вый, -ая -ое**
uncle **дя́дя** (*m.*)
understand, to **понима́ть** (**I**)
unfortunately **к сожале́нию**
united **соединённый, -ая, -ое**
United States **Соединённые Шта́ты**
university **университе́т**
usually **обыкнове́нно**

V

Vanya **Ва́ня** (*m.*)
various **ра́зный, -ая, -ое**

vase **ва́за**
Vera **Ве́ра**
very **о́чень**
village **дере́вня**
voice **го́лос** (*pl.* голоса́)
Volga (*river in the U.S.S.R.*) **Во́лга**
volleyball **волейбо́л**

W

wait, to **ждать (I)** (see ¶ 16-4)
walk, to **идти́ (I)** *act.*; **ходи́ть (II)** *hab.*; (see ¶ 13-2 & 13-3)
walk (for pleasure), to **гуля́ть (I)**
    to take a walk **гуля́ть (I)**; **погуля́ть (I)** *pf.*
wall **стена́**
Wall Street **Уо́лл-стрит**
want, to **хоте́ть** (*irr.*)
war **война́**
warm, it is . . . **тепло́**
was **был, -ла́, -ло, -ли**
wash oneself, to **умыва́ться (I)**
Washington **Вашингто́н**
water **вода́**
we **мы**
weather **пого́да**
Wednesday **среда́**
    on Wednesday **в сре́ду**
week **неде́ля**
weep, to **пла́кать (I)**; **запла́кать (I)** *pf.*
well (*adj.*) **здоро́в**; (*adv.*) **хорошо́**; (*exclamation*) **ну!**
    very well (*adv.*) **прекра́сно**
    well then **ита́к**
went away (once) **ушёл, ушла́, ушло́, ушли́** (*past of pf.* **уйти́**)
what **что**
    what a, what kind of **како́й, -а́я, -о́е**; *pl.* **-и́е**
    what else **что ещё**
    what then **что же**
    with what **чем**
when **когда́**
where **где**
where to **куда́**
wherefore **заче́м**
which **кото́рый, -ая, -ое** (see ¶ 18-2)
white **бе́лый, -ая, -ое**
White (*surname*) **Уа́йт**
whither **куда́**
who **кто; кото́рый, -ая, -ое**
    who is this? **кто э́то ?**
whole **весь, вся, всё; це́лый, -ая, -ое**
why **почему́, заче́м**
wife **жена́**

window **окно́**
winter, in the . . . **зимо́й** (*adv.*)
wish, to **хоте́ть** (*irr.*)
with **с** (*with instr.*)
without **без** (*with gen.*)
woman **же́нщина**
word **сло́во**
work **рабо́та**
work, to **рабо́тать** (**I**); **порабо́тать** (**I**) *pf.*
worse **ху́же** (*adv.*)
    I feel worse **мне ху́же**
write, to **писа́ть** (**I**); **написа́ть** (**I**) *pf.*

Y

year **год**
yes **да**
yesterday **вчера́**
yet, as . . . **пока́ ещё**
you **ты** (*fam. sing.*); **вы** (*pl. & polite sing.*)
young **молодо́й, -а́я, -о́е**
young man **ю́ноша**
younger **мла́дший, -ая, -ее**; *pl.* **-ие**
your, yours (*adj. & pron.*) **твой, твоя́, твоё, твои́; ваш, ва́ша, ва́ше, ва́ши**
youth (*person*) **ю́ноша**

INDEX

NTC RUSSIAN TEXTS AND MATERIAL

Book and Audiocassette
How to Pronounce Russian Correctly

Russian-Language Courses
Russian Face to Face, Level 1
Basic Russian, Level 1
Basic Russian, Level 2

Texts and Graded Readers
Business Russian
Beginner's Russian Reader
Russian Intermediate Reader
Modern Russian Reader for Intermediate Classes
Russian Area Reader
Everyday Conversations in Russian

Literary Adaptations
Trio: Intermediate-Level Adaptations of Pushkin, Lermontov,
  and Gogol
Quartet: Intermediate-Level Adaptations of Turgenyev, Tolstoy,
  Dostoyevsky, and Chekhov

Annotated Russian Literature
Six Soviet One-Act Plays
The Inspector General
The Queen of Spades
Asya

Grammar and Reference
Complete Handbook of Russian Verbs
Simplified Russian Grammar
Reading and Translating Contemporary Russian
Roots of the Russian Language
Essentials of Russian Grammar
Basic Structure Practice in Russian
Russian Composition and Conversation
Just Enough Russian

Language Learning Material
NTC Language Learning Flash Cards
Language Visuals
Songs for the Russian Class

Duplicating Masters
Basic Vocabulary Builder
Practical Vocabulary Builder

For further information or a current catalog, write:
National Textbook Company
a division of NTC Publishing Group
4255 West Touhy Avenue
NTC Lincolnwood, Illinois 60646-1975 U.S.A.